Praise

Accessing our imagination and intuition regularly is crucial to our health on every level, body, mind, and spirit. *Practical Meditation for Busy Souls* will show you exactly how to do this with grace and joy . . . practical and heartfelt guidance to the magic, mystery, and wholeness inside each of us.

—Christiane Northrup, MD,
author of *Women's Bodies, Women's Wisdom*
and *The Wisdom of Menopause*

Everywhere you turn good research affirms great benefits from a meditative practice. *Practical Meditation for Busy Souls* guides and empowers you to live your practice and seamlessly integrate it into your work in the world.

No matter how busy, crowded, or demanding your life, Margo Adair and William Aal have given you a way to source the loving wellsprings of transformation for your own deepening and renewal, for that of your intimate circle and for the transformation of the wider world. You will not only read this book, you will become, like its authors, good medicine for others when they reach out for models of wisdom and integrity.

—James O'Dea, President, Institute of Noetic Sciences

Practical Meditation for Busy Souls is a splendid accomplishment. It is in the tradition of the great wisdom seekers throughout human history, who have known that we can change our destiny by changing our mind. At a time when we seem eager to give our lives over to our genes and DNA, Aal and Adair's message is vital.

—Larry Dossey, MD,
author of *Healing Beyond the Body*,
Reinventing Medicine, and *Healing Words*

A beacon of hope in trying times, *Practical Meditation for Busy Souls* is a trustworthy guide: it doesn't prescribe answers so much as help us discover our own. Full of heart and insight, this marvelous book makes a strong contribution to the creation of a sustainable civilization.

—Joanna Macy, author of *Coming Back to Life*

[T]his new edition makes a vital contribution to the necessary creative interchange between the transformation of our personal lives and our struggle for a radically transformed and humanized society.

—Vincent Harding,
author of *There Is a River: The Black Struggle for Freedom in America* and *Hope and History*

Practical Meditation for Busy Souls provides unique, powerful, and imaginative ways to help change the world by combining the potency of meditation with the strength of standing up to the destructive systems now dominating our world. Mind and heart, imagination and courage—Adair and Aal teach how to bring both inner and outer dimensions to working together for healing ourselves and the earth. Wherever you are on your path, whatever challenges you are up against, this book can accelerate your journey and lighten the load.

—Vicki Robin,
coauthor, *Your Money or Your Life*

Adair and Aal offer powerful guidance in working with direct knowing, setting clear intention and restoring balance in ourselves and our world. This book is full of ways that empower us to honor the sacred in daily life.

—Vicki Noble, healer, teacher, cocreator of *Motherpeace*, and author of *Shakti Woman: Feeling Our Fire* and *Healing Our World: The New Female Shamanism*

After you read this book, you'll never feel totally helpless again! Adair and Aal remind us that there is always something we can do to activate and release our values in the world.

—Christina Baldwin, author of *Calling the Circle: The First and Future Culture* and *Seven Whispers: Listening to the Voice of Spirit*

Practical Meditation for Busy Souls is not about having to go elsewhere to be "spiritual." Instead it shows how to bring spiritual techniques and practices into daily life and into the world. This book reveals a secret our own culture rarely reveals: the spiritual, the psychological, and the political worlds are intertwined. Adair and Aal powerfully bring together all three domains, and, if you use this book, you may be surprised at the changes that you can bring about—in your life and in the world.

—Margot Adler, author of *Drawing Down the Moon* and *Heretic's Heart*

Adair and Aal show a deep appreciation for the contours of consciousness. *Practical Meditation for Busy Souls* offers a journey through the mysteries of mind which enables the reader to tap the great healing powers that flow through each of us. Simple yet profound, this book is a must for anyone wanting to improve their lives.

—Martin L. Rossman, MD, author of *Guided Imagery for Self-Healing*

This book is filled with long experience and wild ideas, it completes the task the feminist movement began some decades ago: weaving together the disparate threads of inner and outer, psychological and political, individual and collective into a vision and means for returning our wounded world to wholeness. As a psychologist, I recommend it to my colleagues—and to everyone who is passionate about healing.

—Chellis Glendinning, PhD,
author of *My Name Is Chellis and I'm in Recovery from Western Civilization* and *Off the Map*

Adair and Aal, both seasoned activists and brilliant thinkers, give us a powerful, fresh framework for understanding and living the connections between personal and global change. It has never been more needed. Please, for the sake of our future, share this book with every activist you know: savor it, talk about it, be it.

—Claudia Horwitz, author of *The Spiritual Activist: Practices to Transform Your Life, Your Work, and Your World*

A great resource for building relationships with mindfulness, connection, and caring at the center, I recommend it to any family, community, or organization which is dedicated to creating equitable, healthy, and loving ways of being together.

—Paul Kivel, author of *Boys Will Be Men: Raising Our Sons for Courage, Caring, and Community* and *Uprooting Racism*

This is an eloquent and practical guide to anyone wanting to expand and grow beyond the usual, mundane levels of daily existence. Margo Adair is a skilled guide who has been there. Highly recommended.

—Barbara Dossey, RN, MS, HNC, FAAN,
author of *Rituals of Healing, Holistic Nursing: A Handbook for Practice,* and *Florence Nightingale: Mystic, Visionary, Healer*

Also by Margo Adair:
Meditations on Everything Under the Sun

Practical
Meditation
for Busy Souls

Margo Adair
and
William Aal

An Imprint of Sourcebooks, Inc.®
Naperville, Illinois

Published by Sourcebooks MediaFusion, an imprint of Sourcebooks, Inc.
P.O. Box 4410, Naperville, Illinois 60567-4410
(630) 961-3900
FAX: (630) 961-2168
www.sourcebooks.com

ISBN-13: 978-1-4022-1020-4
ISBN-10: 1-4022-1020-5

Previously published as *Working Inside Out* by Margo Adair © 2003, ISBN 1-4022-0032-3, Sourcebooks, Inc. Originally published in 1984 by Wingbow Press, Berkeley, California. This is a revised edition.

Adair, Margo
Practical Meditation for Busy Souls / by Margo Adair and William Aal
     p. cm.
Originally published: Berkeley, Calif. : Wingbow Press, 1984.
Includes bibliographical references.
1. Meditation. 2. Spiritual life. 3. Success—Religious aspects. I. Title.
BL627.A3 2003
158.1'2—dc21

2003006718

Printed and bound in the United States of America
VP 10 9 8 7 6 5 4 3 2 1

To the Circles everywhere that honor the ancestors and the future ones.

In memory of Casey Adair, Lynn Johnson, James Boggs, and Helen Lou Gore.

Dedicated to healing the future so coming generations can live in this glorious place we call Earth.

Contents

Using the Audio CD

Five of the meditations from this book can be found on the accompanying audio CD. The meditations are different lengths, ranging from five to twenty minutes, to accommodate the time available in your schedule.

There are frequent pauses during the meditations to allow time for you to perform your own inner work. You may wish to tailor the meditations to suit your preferred rhythm. Simply pause the recording whenever you would like more time to do your inner work before progressing to the next stage of the meditation.

These meditations are designed to inspire spontaneous responses. You will be doing your inner work at the same time as you listen to the instructions. Don't wait for the instructions to finish before beginning to respond. Nor should you wait until the "right" image comes to you—make it up or go with your instantaneous responses. Trust your own experience and give your imagination full permission to play.

To prepare to use these meditations, you will want to turn off your pager or cell phone, unplug the phone, and otherwise take steps to make sure you will not be disturbed. Find a comfortable place where you can lie or sit with your spine straight. (Sitting is best for the third meditation.) Before you start the CD, make yourself comfortable. Focus on your breath for a few moments and let it sink into a full and easy rhythm.

You'll find the text of each audio meditation on the following pages:

Relaxing into Well Being: Working with Symbols (twenty minutes), page 34.

Make a clear path to your inner dimensions. Unwind and tap into healing energy. Focus deep attention to wherever it is needed.

For an explanation of the techniques used in the meditation, also see page 30.

Active Imagination: Aligning Energies with a Positive Vision (fifteen minutes), page 130.

Work with your imagination to discover and align with the best possible outcomes. Set your intention, and your intuition will guide you to your goals.

For an explanation of the techniques used in the meditation, also see pages 97–106.

Running Energy: Centering for the Day (five minutes), page 146.

Access universal energies to maintain clarity, focus, and personal power while at the same time staying open, creative, and intuitive.

For an explanation of the techniques used in the meditation, also see pages 135–139.

Receptive Imagination Offers a Gift of Insight (ten minutes), page 217.

Find vision when you have none; gain clarity when you are confused.

For an explanation of the techniques used in the meditation, also see pages 70–72 and pages 197–198.

Heart Song (ten minutes), page 250.

In the face of what challenges you, allow what makes your heart sing to soften the edges and to guide you.

For an explanation of the techniques used in the meditation, also see pages 197–198 and page 237.

Tools for Change offers many additional meditations on audio cassette, including most of the meditations in this book. For more information, see page 377.

CD Track List

•1•

Reawakening Inner Consciousness

This book is about consciousness—both its mysteries and its great powers. It offers a practice called Applied Meditation*, which weaves together mindfulness, intuition, and intention. Applied Meditation does not take years to master or a peaceful environment in which to practice. There is a calm place that is full of creative healing powers residing inside each of us. It is just below the surface; when we allow ourselves to drop down, we find ourselves filled with a sense of calm. As you work with this practice, you soon will be able to drop into that calm place in a matter of moments, enabling you to maintain your equanimity in the midst of life in the fast lane.

People have used reflection, contemplation, and meditation to deepen understanding and increase well-being for millennia. One of the great paradoxes in life is that looking within offers the experience of being intimately connected to all that is. The act of meditation brings us into communion with the harmonizing forces intrinsic to life itself. With Applied Meditation, we relax and focus our attention, bringing the enormous healing and creative powers that are our birthright to bear in our lives.

---

*Margo has developed Applied Meditation over the last thirty years. Bill has been working with it for some twenty years and joined her in its development over the last decade. Most of the stories are Margo's. For clarity, first person voice belongs to both authors.

Whatever challenge you are facing, this form of meditation will reveal exactly where attention is needed, whether the concern is personal, work related, or in your community. Should you decide to take the journey this book offers, you will come to know that consciousness not only lives inside our psyches, but it also vibrates around us and among us and in the inanimate world. Life itself lights up with magic!

Practical Meditation for Busy Souls teaches you how to make friends with time. A benefit of meditation is that it allows you to feel as though you have expanded time! This alone will make a profound difference in your life; most of us find ourselves in the predicament of having less and less time and more and more to do. Our lives often become so demanding that the joy is squeezed out. With Applied Meditation, you will be able to relax and expand the moment. You will discover that time is generous and can support you. Life changes when you occupy the moment fully, letting go of the belief that the future is better than the present. Time opens and it carries us. The key to expanding time is found in the magical gifts of consciousness itself—the quality of awareness we bring to the moment.

Stress-related illnesses have become some of the most common causes of death in modern life. Applied Meditation enables you to reduce stress and, just as important, empowers you to change the conditions that cause it.[1] Your creative, intuitive, and healing resources will awaken so that you can realize well being, envision new directions, and act on them. You will be more effective in making the needed changes, whether in regard your health, your behavior, your relationships, your work, or the larger world.

This book and CD provide safe paths to explore the vast realms within. They offer a language to communicate with inner consciousness as well as methods for working with it for problem-solving and vision-building. The guided meditations create a clear and simple way to navigate through your inner dimensions so you can use the resources available within to improve the quality of your life and find ways to offer your unique gift to healing the world.

Practical Meditation for Busy Souls begins by addressing the nature of the subjective realm, then progresses through our interpersonal relationships, and finally discusses how we can engage our inner dimensions to help meet the challenges we all face in the world today. Included are some of the latest findings in consciousness studies, mind/body medicine, and quantum physics. I also address how we can begin to recognize and transform many of the commonly held assumptions in American culture that estrange us from the naturally resilient and creative energies within each of us. Liberating ourselves from binding beliefs, we clear a path and release energies to heal our personal lives and to transform our culture into one that sustains life.

When you gain a better understanding of the nature of consciousness and how to tap into the powers of the imagination, intention, intuition, and awareness itself, you will not feel buffeted about by all of the turmoil. Instead you will always be able to find inner calm and tap the powers within to address the particular challenge you face. You will start to participate in shaping your future with clarity and vision rather than reacting to it when it arrives.

Inner consciousness has been dismissed in our materialist technological society. We have been taught to distrust that which connects us to our own truths, to each other, and to the larger whole. It is part of a large-scale dynamic that splits body from soul, people from each other, and humans from the natural world.

Applied Meditation can help us overcome this alienation and the limitations in our lives, allowing us to discard bad habits, heal health problems, enrich relationships, or even grapple with the massive global issues facing humanity. Vast creative, intuitive, and healing powers come through our inner consciousness. When we reclaim our connection to it, we experience wholeness and the feeling of being in communion with all that is, which is at the heart of all spirituality—the merging of the existential "I" into something greater.

This book is dedicated to applying the powers of consciousness to further our individual goals and to secure the future for the generations to come. It is the authors' hope that by working from the inside out, reflection will become a publicly shared activity. Applied Meditation brings a sense of wholeness; with wholeness, we can heal the future.

Development of Applied Meditation

When I was twenty-two, I was catapulted into exploring the realms of consciousness. Until then, I had taken the abilities of my mind for granted, and my attention was focused solely on the external world. My journey began when my friend Gene told me about his experience in a training session consisting of a series of guided meditations. José Silva, a Texas businessperson, developed these methods of "mind control." This approach was a forerunner of the Human Potential Movement.[2] What particularly caught my interest was Gene's description of the last exercise, called "doing case readings." This entailed hearing *only* the name, age, and address of someone you knew nothing about, with the expectation that you would accurately describe this person in full detail. Gene said everyone was actually able to do it! I was intrigued, having had an upbringing in an academic home where reason was paramount. I had always thought that if psychic powers existed at all, only exotic characters born every few hundred years possessed them.

I joined a group that was going to do the Silva exercises together. When it was my turn to do a case reading, although I felt I could not, I went ahead and tried. I relaxed, and then Jane, another participant in the group, gave me the name and address of her friend Martha. When I heard Martha's name, nothing happened. No voice surfaced to tell me about her, yet people were waiting for me to say something.

Left to my own devices, I had to use my imagination. I proceeded to talk about Martha for forty-five minutes, feeling all the time as though I were simply making up a story. The thoughts felt as ordinary as anything that had ever gone on in my mind. When I was finished, I opened my eyes and Jane told me that everything I had said about Martha was true.

I had accurately described her character and physical appearance, including a gray print dress that buttoned up the back and a pair of black "old lady" shoes with brown laces. I imagined black spots on her stomach and a chalky substance at the base of her spine. It turned out that she had an ulcer, cancer of the spine and that she wore the dress I described all the time. Jane said that everything was correct except she couldn't understand my description of the shoes, because Martha had always loved to wear the latest style. Two weeks later, I ran into Jane and she told me that the last time she'd seen Martha she was wearing "old lady" shoes—black with brown laces!

I was awed by this experience: my mind had abilities that I had never dreamed of! What was so astounding was how ordinary it felt while I was describing the case. A thunderbolt had not come out of the sky illuminating the truth. To this day I view this as the most profound experience of my life. I knew I wasn't one of those extraordinary people born every two hundred years; and everyone else in the group had also been successful at doing these readings.

Having accurately done a case reading, I then felt obligated to pay attention to what went on in my mind, for all I had done that day was make up a story—I had simply used my imagination, yet everything I had said matched reality. I realized that my imagination was as real as the ground we stand on. The Silva Method teaches that if you imagine something, you can create it; so I started to direct my imagination toward changes I wanted to make, and that worked too! For the first time I began to pay attention to my mental processes and to direct my imagination. I discovered that I had capabilities that, when applied, changed every aspect of my life. I have been enthralled and humbled ever since this initial experience by the awesome capacities of consciousness.

I have guided hundreds of people through the process of case readings. Everyone can do it. Somehow, our minds have access to information beyond our physical senses. The implication of this is awesome. You may view these phenomena as accessing the collective unconscious, or the presence of God, spirit, or the ancestors. In whatever way you make sense of the mystery, it is vital to realize that we all have access to *direct* knowledge and that we can participate in the co-creation of reality.

In some mysterious way, imagination itself is the medium of psychic awareness and is entwined with probability. It is as though we are each held by the universe, and that the whole of the universe can be experienced by looking within. In the receptive state of contemplation, you can hear the whispers of spirit. Some believe that God offers guidance as a result of prayer. To me it is as though there is a mysterious, self-organizing force that runs through all that exists. Physicist David Bohm's theory of implicate order posits that reality is like a hologram.[3] We are all part of the whole, and the whole lives in each of us. There is no real separateness in the universe. (A characteristic of holograms is that cutting something in half results not in two different halves but in two smaller wholes.) The ancient Hindu and Buddhist concept of Indra's Net is parallel to Bohm's contemporary theory. Indra's Net depicts the universe as a net of jewels. Each being forms a jewel on the net and every jewel is reflected in each one. Many mystics of great religious traditions hold this perspective of nonduality.

The objective and subjective worlds reflect one another. The act of asking when in a state of contemplation always brings knowledge. The question acts as a flashlight, angling a beam of light on the specific spot where the answer resides. The trick is to have a *clear* question. You will find yourself intuiting an insight that illuminates what is true and reveals a path toward greater states of well-being.

We all have ways of using our intelligence that have gone virtually untapped. It is when we relax, yet continue to remain alert that the part of our consciousness surfaces that experiences our connectedness. Creative and intuitive powers arise, as well as healing energy.[4] As you journey inside, a whole world opens up before you.

The Dance of Imagination and Mindfulness

With Applied Meditation, you will experience calm spacious awareness that grounds you in the present moment and allows you to recognize what is taking place. In this spaciousness, your creativity and intuition come alive and can be directed toward transformation.

The practice of Applied Meditation works with inner consciousness in three intertwined ways. The first is to be mindful of what is taking place in your subjective landscape working with what I call the Inner Witness. This can be likened to the mindfulness of Buddhist meditation practices. It grounds you in the present moment and watches what is transpiring in your subjective landscape, revealing what patterns of energy are present. The Inner Witness recognizes what the beam of light illuminates when asking a question. I do not mean to imply that the Inner Witness is a noun—it is awareness that has no form. It is as though the Inner Witness's knowing has neither end nor beginning and is in a perpetual state of relaxed attention, revealing imbalance and what is needed to regain it. As meditation practice deepens, one becomes increasingly mindful in the midst of daily activities. This mindfulness offers the key to freedom, because choice lies in the space *between* stimulus and response.

The second is using the Active Imagination, which can be likened to creative visualization and the setting of intention. You work with the Active Imagination when you know what you want, that is when you have a specific vision you are striving to realize. This may be the cultivation of a new health habit, the completion of a project or the passage of legislation—whatever your desire. You use the Active Imagination to set it in motion. You do this by pretending your vision is *already* true. This creates a north star, helping you navigate into new experiences. Working with the Active Imagination brings new patterns of energy into play, catalyzing transformation inside and out.

The third way of working is useful if you are unhappy with a situation but lack a vision toward which to strive—which means that the Active Imagination has no raw materials to play with and cannot create a positive vision. If you are stuck, then you need an insight to illuminate a way out of your bind. This is when you use the Receptive Imagination, engaging your story-making capacities to discover insight through imaginative inquiry. Whenever you are unhappy with your experience and lack a vision of positive alternatives, your Receptive Imagination can call on creative and intuitive powers so you can see the situation with fresh eyes. The insight is just what is needed to enable you to create a positive vision and "power it up" with your Active Imagination.

The Inner Witness reveals if you have a vision and whether it is plausible. This, in turn, tells you whether to ask a question of your Receptive Imagination or to set intention with your Active Imagination. In the spacious awareness of the Inner Witness, what is needed is self-evident. As you embark on your journey, you will find yourself working with all of these aspects of consciousness simultaneously. They will always inspire healing, well-being, and creativity. You will come to know your own inner landscape intimately and be able to trust your deepest experience. The practice of Applied Meditation reconnects you with the ground of being.

Theory of Consciousness

The transformation in my life came about in the opposite way from what usually happens to people. Originally, I had no understanding of how consciousness worked, yet my life changed profoundly when I began to direct my own imagination. Normally, we're taught something and then learn to apply it—theory precedes practice. For me, it worked the other way around. I always experience directed consciousness working, and then later begin to piece together why it works. In other words, my rational understanding follows my experience. This is true, I suspect, for anyone who follows intuition.

I use electroencephalographic (EEG) measures as a framework to understand consciousness. Our brains continuously give off electromagnetic pulsations, which can be measured by an electroencephalograph. EEG levels refer to the different rhythms of these emanations. There seems to be a correlation between what we subjectively experience and the objective brainwave emanations. The different levels, called beta, alpha, theta, and delta are each part of a complete spectrum.[5] The brainwave emanations originate in different parts of the brain and correspond to different kinds of activities.[6] At any moment, all the levels of EEG waves are active, but there is a predominant rhythm.

In Western culture, we are familiar with beta consciousness, the state most associated with rational thinking. In the majority of schools, this is the aspect of our consciousness most emphasized. Reading, writing, and arithmetic are all beta functions, as are cause-and-effect thinking, goal orientation, and the experience of clock time. The linear thinking of beta is categorical, critical, and computes large amounts of data in sequence. Beta consciousness often originates in the left hemisphere of the brain, which specializes in linear processing. It is where we are when we multi-task. In beta, we deal with lots of particulars in a logical, goal-oriented manner; it is a necessary state of consciousness for coping with contemporary, urban living. Beta consciousness both promotes and maintains competitive life in the fast lane.

I think of beta consciousness as if it resides on the surface, and of the inner consciousness—alpha, theta, and delta—as residing deeper; alpha right below beta, moving down to theta, and below to delta in the depths. At these deeper levels of consciousness, we experience reality holistically. We do not separate things; we make connections. We do not categorize; we synthesize. In these states, we are not critical, nor do we order things in a linear manner. Instead, we make things whole. We experience reality in images, patterns, sensations, and a quiet knowing that has no form.

The insights that emerge out of these levels of awareness hold the key to healing, both personally and in the larger world. It is in these states that the imagination lives and through which intuition comes. In deeper states, awareness becomes spacious, and the Inner Witness is present. Most forms of meditation, prayer, contemplation, hypnosis, imagery work, and trance states take place in alpha and theta.

To understand the term holistic, imagine that you can't figure out how to solve a mathematical formula. You give up and go for a walk. In a relaxing activity such as this, you will be predominantly at the alpha level because you don't have to think about what to do next. As you walk, the solution suddenly appears like the proverbial light bulb flashing on— not the specific answer, but an unquestionable sense of the whole pattern. You have just had the "aha!" experience. Everything becomes clear; you can go home to your work, and your beta mind can then easily ascertain the missing parts of the equation. (When you know how to work with the Receptive Imagination, you can simply go into a meditative state, ask, and receive an answer.)

While dancing, you've probably had the experience of losing the beat if you begin to think about what your feet should do next; in that case, you have slipped into beta. When you are in the groove, you are in alpha. Peak performance in athletes is closely associated with bursts of alpha. Alpha is a familiar state; rhythmic activities such as running, dishwashing, or any repetitive work induce it. This is because you don't need to decide what to do next. Linear thinking is unnecessary. Most people spend a good part of their time in alpha. The alpha level is fluid. You find yourself thinking about something, and you have no idea what led you there. You are in alpha when you are daydreaming.

Theta and delta, unlike beta and alpha, are not as familiar. These levels of consciousness are active when your focus is in one place. You may have heard the term "one-pointedness of consciousness." This refers to the Samadhi experience strived for in many Eastern religious traditions. A complete focus of awareness occurs at these deep levels.

If your survival becomes under immediate threat, all of your attention will be called to focus on the situation at hand; anything else is simply not in your awareness. For instance, an automobile accident lasts only a few seconds. Yet in memory, it feels as if it had lasted half an hour, like a slow-motion movie. All of your energy was focused on surviving, and rather than being spread out on lots of issues as it is in the beta state, all attention was funneled into exclusive awareness of the threatening situation. This has the subjective effect of expanding time. People who have near-death experiences often report that their entire life paraded before their eyes— this is complete focus of energy and expansion of time.

When you are in the beta level of consciousness, the other brainwave patterns are present as well, but they are scattered. However, the deeper the level of consciousness, the more synchronized all the brainwaves become. The degree to which brainwave patterns are synchronized corresponds to the degree to which we feel in sync with what is going on around us. Inner calm corresponds with brainwave harmonization. In a state of inner calm, the left and right sides of the brain work together, and the different parts of the brain operate in synchrony.[7] Thus the difference in spectrum from beta to theta is simply the difference between the focus and concentration of awareness—at beta it is spread out; at theta it is completely concentrated. At beta it is particular; at theta it is holistic.

Alpha, situated right between beta and theta has characteristics of both. Say you are relaxing on the couch and daydreaming. At a time like this, you are aware of your objective circumstances. For example, you know that you are lying on the couch and that you need to get up at a certain time for an appointment or to take a cake out of your oven. All of this is in your awareness while you are still daydreaming.

On the other hand, if you suddenly realize that you have been dreaming without being aware of where you are—or that you have already missed your appointment or you have burnt the cake—you were at the theta level (and no longer goal-oriented). This is the "hypnogogic state," wherein the contents of the dream become reality and have a three-dimensional quality. The dream itself is extremely vivid, and your objective circumstances have faded from awareness. In alpha, your daydreaming consciousness is more spread out, and in theta, more concentrated. In alpha, you are daydreaming in an offhand manner; in theta, your dream is as real as life.

Someone at theta level is in a very suggestible state of consciousness. They are only aware of what is happening in the moment and have no concept of anything else. Theta level is uncritical. It does not divide or categorize things;

it simply experiences. Because theta exclusively focuses on the moment, it is not linear or goal-oriented; whatever may happen next is irrelevant. Considering alternatives is not possible while at the theta level.

Some developmental psychologists say that an individual's personality has essentially been formed by the age of three. Although I do not think that our personalities are static, one explanation for this is that up until this age, children function predominantly at the theta level. This explains why infants are totally engrossed in whatever is occurring in the moment, and why toddlers cannot grasp the concept of what's happening next. Theta consciousness does not possess the critical capacities of beta or the ability of beta to understand time. As a result anything occurring during these years becomes a person's definition of reality.

Research in neurophysiology has revealed a new, more dynamic picture of human development.[8] Our brains remain flexible far into our adulthood. We can reset our neural pathways with biofeedback and meditation practices. The good news is that the act of meditation itself expands and strengthens the "happy-thoughts" parts of the brain. Richard Davidson[9] and others studied Tibetan monks who are long-time practitioners of a style of meditation focusing on compassion. These monks, as well as novices, show long-term activity in a part of the brain associated with happiness. In a similar way, Applied Meditation offers a powerful set of tools to help you reset your neural pathways to promote happiness, compassion, and create more flexible responses to the conditions in your life.

Inner Consciousness

Inner consciousness is the ground from which all behavior springs. Creativity, intuition, and healing power all come through the imagination, which lives in our inner consciousness. More than that, our imagination is the carrier of all our interpretations of what has happened and of all our anticipations of what will. Our belief systems shape how we respond to all that occurs. They are the glasses through which we view the world and anticipate what is likely to unfold. Our behavior is always loyal to our beliefs. Everyone has had the experience of learning something rationally, but acting to the contrary. In this case, the cliché, "I just don't have it down yet," is literally true. This type of learning is intellectual and rational, and it does not yet reside in your inner levels where beliefs are stored.

Belief systems are the way we organize memories into our personal definitions of how the world works; they are the assumptions from which we operate. They stem either from early childhood experiences, continual repetition of social messages, or from traumatic incidents. For example, you may find yourself tense every time you get in a car because you once had an automobile accident (belief: cars equal danger), so you may try to reassure yourself by reasoning, "It is okay. The brakes are fixed." Yet this doesn't relieve your tension. A beta thought has little energy; anything that happened while you were in theta is another matter. For another example, if you are a woman who has learned that being assertive helps you get your needs met, but to your dismay, you still often defer to others (belief: Nice girls aren't aggressive). In each case, you continue to act out of deep-seated beliefs, despite what you tell yourself rationally.

If you want to change these patterns, you need not wait years before you can embody a new behavior. You can use your Active Imagination to reset your thinking. Because you behave out of your inner belief system messages, you need to insert the desired message at an inner level. Give yourself an alternative from which to act. You will find yourself able to act in accordance with your choices—no longer thinking one thing, yet doing another.

Whether it is the result of a traumatic incident in the past (e.g., the car accident) or from the programming by the propaganda of our society (e.g., the message that women should be passive), we will continue unwanted patterns until we repossess our inner consciousness. We need to be mindful of what we hold in our subjective landscapes and clear unwanted debris out of our minds.

Beliefs shape our experience. For example, if you lived next to a freeway with the constant noise of traffic during the first three years of your life, the chances are you wouldn't be fully comfortable in the quiet of the country. Something would be missing, because your belief system defines the world as noisy. This discomfort may be something of which you are not fully conscious and only experience in a vague and ill-defined way. When you are not sure of the source of your malaise, you can utilize your Receptive Imagination. In this case, you would conjure up an image of your uneasy self. This gives your consciousness a focal point with which to work. Next, make up a story with your uneasy self in the lead role. Ask what she is feeling. In your story, you will find a part of yourself remembering that life "should" be noisy. Once you discover this, you can speak to this aspect of yourself, reassuring it that some great places are quiet. This reframing releases energy and allows a different point of reference to become a source from which your experience springs. You have just broadened your capacities to be at ease in the country. It works when you engage your Receptive Imagination and then set intention with your Active Imagination.

Our belief systems—our memories—are stored deep in our consciousness at the theta level. We remember things holistically: if you smell the scent of a flower, you are not going to remember what you learned about that flower in biology class; instead, a whole scene in which that scent was present will flood your awareness. Our memories function associatively, not logically. If a radio was playing a song at the moment that you had a car accident, it is likely that every time you hear the song again, tension will grip you. This is why people with post-traumatic stress disorder (PTSD) have triggers that bring on flashbacks.

When children are of elementary school age, they are predominantly at the alpha level (actively getting programmed). It is not until adolescence that we have full access to our critical capacities and begin to function predominantly at the beta level. Alpha, residing between beta and theta, is powerful because in that state, you can be both active and receptive, simultaneously. It is the threshold between inner and outer consciousness.

When you use Applied Meditation, you will be predominantly in alpha. In alpha, you can choose what you want to work on (active) and then be effective in doing so (receptive). With the Active Imagination you can reprogram yourself—i.e., give yourself the messages *you* choose—by changing the beliefs from which you act. Your deeper levels do not argue by pointing out alternatives. They are suggestible and will absorb the new information, and you will have a new resource out of which to act.

Alternatively, you can call up insight from deep within by employing the story-making capacities of the Receptive Imagination. The story provides a stage, inviting insight to appear—a clear question and playful imagination is all that is needed. You will find yourself discovering new ways to approach your concerns.

The Active and Receptive Imagination re-create beliefs together. When you allow yourself to relax, your Inner Witness surfaces and offers spacious awareness in which to play.

Putting Theory into Practice

When you know how you want to change your life, you simply use the Active Imagination to insert the information at the appropriate level. Imagine that the desired experience is taking place or it already has. Imagine it in full detail. If the information that you want to introduce doesn't have anything contradicting it deeper down—in other words, if there are no counter-messages at the theta level—then putting in a new message is a simple, straightforward process. One application is usually enough for it to sink in.

For example, if you need to awaken at 7:15, all you need to do is enter the alpha level and tell yourself, "I will awaken at exactly 7:15 in the morning" and imagine yourself doing so, as well as expecting yourself to. If there is nothing contradicting the suggestion at the theta level, such as a childhood message from your mother who always said, "You never get up on time," it will simply sink in. Your inner consciousness will have a new message from which you will find yourself responding by awakening at exactly 7:15. This works on the first try because you do not have a lot of energy focused on the issue.

Now if you want to change your response in an area that has some charge to it, such as a phobia or a deeply implanted message ("I can't get up on time"), you do it the same way. Working in the alpha level takes longer because you need to accumulate more energy around the new message than around the old.

If you want to work more quickly by working at the theta level, it is best done in partnership with someone experienced with these states. Because theta is not goal-oriented, by the time you have relaxed that deeply, you've forgotten what you were going to do—you "space out." Even if you manage to remember the pattern you wanted to transform, it is more likely that you will simply reinforce it, because a person in theta awareness is caught up with the experience of the moment and doesn't have the capability to reframe it.

When I work with people individually, I ask them how they think about themselves, how they see *their* issues, what their inner resources are, and what their vision for positive outcomes might be. When I lead them into a deep meditative state, I speak to their inner consciousness in their language, helping them bring their strengths to bear on the challenge they are facing. This enables them to reframe how they perceive the problem and establishes an alternative way of being. Hypnotherapy and interactive imagery also work with many of these same principles.[10]

If you are working on your own to improve a problem like feeling nervous every time you travel in a car because of a previous automobile accident, you can change this with the Active Imagination by replacing your old picture with a new one. Enter the alpha state and imagine feeling relaxed riding in a car. This may be rather difficult, given your past experience, so you should think of something that does feel relaxing— maybe it's listening to music. Imagine yourself listening to music until you are feeling wonderful, and then imagine yourself in a car listening to music on the radio. If you lose your good feelings at that point, return to the image of listening to music without the car, and keep doing this. Eventually you will be able to imagine yourself maintaining good feelings while in the car. With more practice, you'll be able to imagine being comfortable in the car without music. Now you'll have a positive message to focus on ("it is pleasant to ride in a car") and you will find yourself able to do so comfortably.

It's a simple process—just a matter of taking the time to replace the old messages and accumulate new energy around fresh ones. The important distinction is that beta works with logical thoughts, while our inner levels work with feelings, sounds, sensations, and images. The difference we are looking for is not in thinking the car is safe, but in *feeling* that it is. Working with how one carries memories, reframing them with imagery, has been used with great success for PTSD.[11]

Repossessing our Inner Lives to Reclaim our World

Einstein tells us that the imagination and intuition are the most important aspects of intelligence.[12] We are taught how to use rational consciousness, but receive virtually no training for tapping the creative, intuitive, and healing powers of inner consciousness.

Inner consciousness has been fully mystified by modern culture; our inner levels are contemptuously dismissed. We have been taught to believe that everything must be rational and logical, that whatever resides in the "subconscious" is "out of control" and that if psychic powers exist at all, they are paranormal. We've been led to believe that the contents of the imagination are, by definition, unreal, that daydreaming is a waste of time, and that if you can't explain *why* you know something, you don't really know it.

For all intents and purposes, the very ground of our being has been pulled out from under us in modern society. We have been taught to distrust our own awareness, and instead to look to authorities for the answers to our problems. In order to succeed in education, the business world, or politics, we learn to be "objective" and "reasonable," preventing us from accessing inner consciousness. We have lost our autonomy and creativity.

Making matters worse, since World War II the entertainment industry has had unprecedented access to and influence over our imaginations. When we relax we are in a suggestible state of awareness, since the critical capacities of our rational minds have vacated.

> For the first time in human history, most of the stories about people, life, and values are told ... by a group of distant conglomerates that have something to sell.[13]

We have become a captive audience for the entertainment industry, whose programming clogs the passageway to our deeper experience. We are discouraged from daydreaming—instead we go to the movies, watch television, or listen to downloads from the Internet. This is a dangerous situation.

Our inner processes have an immense impact on our lives, whether we pay attention to them or not. Both our bodies and our behavior are completely loyal to the images we retain in our minds, not to what we tell ourselves rationally. We relax when we are being entertained. We get negative messages coming and going: we distrust our own awareness, and we have become captive to the mass media's programming, which fills the places out of which our behavior springs.

> The spread of television unified a whole people within a system of conceptions and living patterns. Because of it, our whole culture and the physical shape of the environment, no more or less than our minds and feelings, have been computerized, linearized, suburbanized, freewayized, and packaged for sale.[14]

Programmed for consumption, we uncritically accept the messages conveyed through the media. We find ourselves wanting and buying the latest computer or media player, the newest "improved" remedies, the latest diet, and impractical automobiles. Worse, we threaten our own bodies with eating disorders and one another with violence. Collectively, we have been reduced to being an audience, and our culture has turned into a consumer society where enjoyment comes from things rather than from each other. All this propaganda has been shoveled into our depths, blocking access to our inner processes, suffocating both our creativity and our intuition.

Until we repossess those parts of ourselves, we will be increasingly relegated to leading alienated, uncreative lives.

However, it is when we look within that we feel connected. Our deepest selves experience our heartfelt connections with one another. When we are alienated from each other, it's because we are also alienated from our deepest selves. When inner consciousness is given its rightful place in the schema of our lives, we access a sense of wholeness and reclaim both our creative and intuitive capacities—the very ones we need the most given the circumstances we face.

Reclaiming our inner world is best done with others. The meditative experience itself is more potent in group settings. People meditating together create a field of energy that supports everyone. When we meditate together, a deep resonance is created which in turn strengthens the fiber of relations. It makes for both stronger meditations and stronger relationships. Families, communities, and organizations who reflect together reclaim a sense of wholeness. There is a richness that comes from sharing experiences as we journey through our inner landscapes. As we share, we develop creative community resources for solving problems, envisioning the world we want to create and entering into it.

·2·

Bringing Meditation into Your Life

Using the Meditations: Creating a Context

We expect spiritual work to be surrounded with lights, colors, and whispering voices. In short, we expect to sit back and be entertained by the awesome. It is important to understand that the alpha state is nothing extraordinary—you frequently function in that level of awareness. It is just under the surface and easy to enter at will. Actually you will find that it is the *ordinary* that is extraordinary. What you thought you had "made up" turns out to be real and coincidences occur that are consistent with an intention you set.

Western culture views meditation and hypnosis as exotic; this is part of the mystification. Calm spacious awareness, creativity, and intuition each reside within each of us. You don't have to go far to discover answers to daily problems that arise in your life. Simply pay attention to—and take seriously—a very familiar part of yourself that you've probably never realized could be of use.

Previously, you might have felt a little guilty if you caught yourself daydreaming or staring into space, because you thought you were wasting your time and not accomplishing anything. Our society tells us we must always be productive and that it is not okay to be in the clouds, to relax, and to let your mind wander. With Applied Meditation, you get to bring the clouds down to earth, moistening the ground of your life to allow for new growth. In meditation, time expands and, becoming present to your self, you can view your life with compassion. You get to be productive in your daydreams. You will be amazed at how wise inner awareness is. The journeys through your inner dimension are always enjoyable, full of humor, and a celebration of life.

The last portion of this and each of the rest of the chapters consists of guided meditation scripts, offering guidance for you to voyage through your inner landscape. The meditations speak directly to inner consciousness using metaphor, repetition, rhythm, and rhyme—the kind of language to which inner consciousness responds particularly well. Simply reading the meditations slowly will induce a meditative state. The lines in the meditations will angle the light of your awareness. Your job is to concentrate on what is illuminated. Do not focus on the words, but instead notice what they evoke and work with what images and feelings arise. Fill in the outlines of your first impressions with colors, sounds, and sensations. Have fun and use your childlike abilities to make believe....

To gain the most benefit, I recommend that you set aside a regular time and go through the book at your own pace from start to finish. Work through the meditations at whatever rate is comfortable for you. Feel free to skip any that cover issues with which you are not concerned. You are likely to find some that you will want to use repeatedly.

I recommend that you start with the meditation at the end of this chapter (also the first track on the CD). This establishes the groundwork for the rest of the book. The first meditation gives you a way to easily access your inner dimensions and guides you in a process of creating symbols to evoke relaxed states at will. You will continue to use these symbols for the other meditations or when you want to meditate on your own. The chapter's meditation sections open with an induction that invites you to use your relaxation symbols. Then, after all the meditations in the chapter, you will find a "count out" to return to an outer focus of attention. Both of these are to be used with all the meditations in the chapter.

Though you can work with the meditations on your own, they are best experienced with others. The nature of the energy you will be working with is such that its potency expands with the number of people meditating together. When I meditate with others I find that my experience is much richer and my inner work more effective. I suggest that you set aside a regular time and, instead of watching television, bring family and friends together, make some popcorn, and discover the movies of your minds. Develop your own programming. Meditating together is a powerful way to deepen bonds.*

Maintaining a relaxed and receptive state of awareness is easier if you do not have to concern yourself with what to do next—a linear process that will only activate your beta consciousness. If you do the exercises by yourself, I recommend that you read them aloud and record each meditation for later listening.** Using a recording will solve this problem. If you prefer, you can highlight particular passages, keep the book in front of you, and open your eyes for each step (this won't disturb your meditation). Some find themselves meditating while reading the passages; if you choose this approach, to get each passage's full effect, I suggest that you subvocalize so you "hear" the words in your mind. Regularly close your eyes to absorb the meaning of the passage you just read and work with what it evokes.

---

* If you would like help contacting people in your area who are also interested in creating an Applied Meditation Practice Circle, please contact us at circle@toolsforchange.org.
** For information about recordings of other meditations besides those in this book, visit www.toolsforchange.org.

All the meditations are written poetically, so you'll find yourself naturally reading in a trance-inducing tone. However, do not rush, because it is important to remember to give time for inner work. Some sections of the meditations are simply written to create an atmosphere that invites the inner consciousness; these sections can be read in one continuous flow. Other sections invite inner work (for example, inner conversations, re-shaping of memories, etcetera). When this is the case, it is important to take time and, therefore, some silence is necessary. I have inserted periods to signal pauses: " ... " indicates a short pause or the time it would take for a few deep breaths; " ... ... " indicates a longer pause—thirty seconds is usually enough time. When there are lists of questions or affirmations, you will want to give a short pause between each of these. Do not give too much time; the inner consciousness is fluid and will use the opening as an opportunity to slip away. One trick to give time while also keeping the focus is to repeat a sentence or two. This will both reinforce what is happening and provide the needed time to do inner work.

You probably have the impression that total peace and quiet is needed in order to meditate, so if you are trying to relax and find yourself aware of noisy neighbors or the ticking clock, you may conclude that you are not relaxing properly and can not meditate because of all the distractions. To the contrary, the more you are relaxed, the more you will be aware of the surroundings and your inner state. For example, when you are relaxing, you notice how tense your neck is—that is okay. Normally you are so tense you are unaware of your stiff neck; it is only when you relax that it becomes apparent. Hearing the neighbors outside does not mean that you need to listen to them; it just means they are noisy neighbors. Meditating is simply settling down a bit; the mind/body does not need to be totally relaxed.

Whenever you meditate, breathe from your belly in a relaxed manner and keep your spine straight. This promotes an easy flow of energy, which will help you maintain a relaxed yet alert state. There are many types of cushions and benches on which to sit while meditating. Each one aims to help you maintain a good sitting posture. Feel free to use a chair if your knees or back require it. Some prefer to meditate while lying down, in which case it is still important to have your spine straight. You may change positions while meditating. It is common to fall asleep while meditating, because you are learning to maintain that edge between sleep and wake awareness. Do not worry, I have been meditating for more than thirty years, and I still fall asleep occasionally. In fact, when I originally went through the Silva processes, I slept through half of it! One trick you might try is holding an arm up—when it drops it will wake you.

There are a few requirements, however, for your meditation practice. Arrange not to be disturbed. Noisy neighbors don't interrupt you—they are not asking you for anything—but the phone does, so unplug it and put a note on your door. Also be sure that your clothing is loose enough to allow for easy breathing. Finally, keep a shawl or blanket nearby, because when you meditate, like napping, your metabolism slows down and you can chill easily.

If you can't remember all that happened in a meditation, it may help to read the meditation passage again. In doing so, you will find yourself remembering more easily. If there are still large blanks in your memory, you may want to work with the meditation again. On the other hand, the inner work has often taken place even if you cannot recall the details; new pathways have been laid in your psyche.

Breathing is your anchor in meditation. In meditation you access a part of intelligence which organizes experience in patterns—rather than the logical sequences of rational, beta awareness. Often you may find yourself thinking about all kinds of things or feeling "spacey." Do not be concerned. That is the nature of the deeper states of awareness. They are very fluid. When you get sidetracked, just bring your attention back to your breath. You can regain your concentration by focusing on the sensations of breath for a few moments; then proceed with what you had been doing. With practice, you will be better able to maintain focus where you choose.

Creating Your Own Practice

The meditations in this book offer enriching experiences, but the real power of the work comes from developing an independent practice. It is important to meditate on your own without the outside stimulus of a recording or a group setting. Practice applying the techniques you learn in the meditations to make them your own. Take five to fifteen minutes, once or twice a day, to reinforce what you have discovered, created, or committed to while working with the book's meditations. Your independent practice holds the key to a rich inner life. When you reclaim your inner world, you'll find well-being in the midst of the demands of daily life.

When you practice alone, it will feel different—maybe not as "deep"—because it is easier to follow someone else's instructions than to tell yourself what to do and then do it. This is particularly true if you have been doing these meditations in a group setting. In your independent practice, if you do not feel as if you are in a meditative state, *pretend* that you are and go through the motions anyway. You will discover that it becomes more and more effective each time you practice.

A regular practice is important because then Applied Meditation becomes a part of your daily routine. If you do not practice regularly, it is not likely to occur to you to meditate when you really need to. The fact that inner consciousness is especially responsive to repetition and ritual means you will be creating well-worn paths into your psyche. It is in the discipline of regularity that creativity and intuition appear. Some like to create a sacred space to meditate.

You might want to make an altar on which you can put items that represent what you hold in your heart: a picture of a loved one to whom you might want to channel healing energy, symbols, or notes with affirmations and intentions. (As you progress through the chapters ahead you will learn how to work with all of this.)

You will become deeply intimate with your inner landscape and adept and agile at navigating within. Familiar with the quality of consciousness that surfaces when you are relaxed, you will be able to access deep intelligence in the midst of your activity with a little practice.

A sense of wholeness and connectedness will begin to be present all the time, not just when you are meditating. You will find yourself more relaxed, grounded in the moment and able to maintain alignment with your higher intention. The channels to deep knowledge will be clear, so you will find that intuitive insights arise and bring the exact understanding you need. You will get to enjoy life rather than chase it.

Applied Meditation works best when you use it regularly. The more you meditate the more adept you will be at tapping into deeper levels of awareness.

After meditating, it is good to take time to write or draw what you have experienced. This will enhance your ability to remember what occurred in your meditations. It will also begin to bring the harmonizing energy and insights that you experienced into your daily life. Keeping a journal allows you to review what you experienced at a later time. This clarifies the difference your practice has made, which in turn increases the benefits manifold. The more you experience meditation working for you, the more you expect it to, creating a self-perpetuating effect.

As your practice evolves, you are likely to have more issues on which you want to work. You might find it helpful to make a list so you do not need to remember all the different things you want to do while meditating. You need only open your eyes for a moment and glance at your list. This technique is particularly helpful for affirmations. Remember, alpha consciousness is not linear. As you learn more techniques, you can integrate them into your daily practice, using as many in each meditation as you find helpful. When you focus on multiple areas, it is good to do so in the same order each time. Well-worn paths allow easy movement in consciousness. Your practice carves out new neural pathways, and your thoughts easily move in new ways.

Relaxation: Working With It

The body does not distinguish between what your brain tells it and what is actually happening. Professional athletes routinely perform mental rehearsals as part of their training. Amazingly, simply imagining yourself in an activity sets off many of the same biochemical responses in the body that actually engaging in the activity does. Brain research on skiers shows that the electrical activity associated with thinking about a particular movement caused the same brain activity as the movement itself. EEG patterns in the brains of weight lifters that simulate lifting are the same as when they actually lift weights. Other research shows that mental rehearsal of exercise is one half as effective as actually doing the exercise.[1]

At each moment, your body is responding to whatever you are imagining. If you have a fear of heights, just imagine yourself near a cliff's edge and your adrenaline will start pumping. Conversely, if you imagine yourself on a sunny beach, your metabolism will slow down.

It is impossible to feel stress and relaxation at the same time. Relaxation invites the alpha state. Applied Meditation uses the body/mind connection, suggestion, and breath to help you release physical, mental, and emotional tension. The first meditation is a relaxation exercise in which you will learn a technique that enables you, with a little practice, to relax in a matter of moments whenever you wish. Soon you will learn to recognize the particular quality of inner awareness so that you can tune in to it at will, whether or not you're relaxed. You will be able to meditate on a rush-hour bus.

The first meditation at the end of this chapter (and on the CD) leads you through a process of working with breath and body awareness to relax at several levels; first you will be guided to physically relax and then you will create something that symbolizes that relaxation for you. You can invent whatever you want—a gesture, a picture, a sound, anything—but be sure it is specific and easy to recall (butter melting on a stack of pancakes). The next time you want to relax, all you'll need to do is bring your physical relaxation symbol to awareness, and your body will respond accordingly.

The meditation will then guide you to relax your mind. This does not mean that thoughts stop; only that your mind calms down and opens. Your awareness becomes spacious, and you can watch your thoughts go by, rather than being caught by them. They will no longer feel rushed; instead, they will take on a daydream-like, meandering quality. When your mind is relaxed the Inner Witness and imagination surface. You will then create a symbol for mental relaxation.

Next, you will be guided through a process for emotional relaxation, so that the entire meditation will be experienced without any strong feelings that may have been present at the start. Just as the mind naturally relaxes into a quality of spaciousness, when you relax emotionally, your heart opens. Relaxation is as normal to the mind and heart as it is to the body. If you let your breath be full and easy, you will find that you remain relaxed throughout your meditation and that time takes on a spacious quality. Again, you will form a symbol, this time for emotional relaxation.

After your body, mind, and feelings are relaxed, you will focus on what you are grateful for and what you hold as sacred. Then you will create a symbol for the creative, self-restoring center from which you will do your Applied Meditation work. Your inner self will know that after focusing on this last symbol, you are ready to begin your interior work. Henceforth, whenever you want to meditate, you simply bring each of your symbols to awareness and you find yourself in your creative self-restoring center in a matter of moments.

Many people feel that they have to wait until their symbols come to them from somewhere—only if it "comes" will it be correct. This is a subtle way we often discount ourselves: believing that what is right must come from another source. When creating symbols, give yourself permission to make up whatever you like. There is no correct symbol; you are working with your own associative process. Therefore, whatever you choose is the right one for you. If a number of symbols come to mind, arbitrarily choose one, or let them coalesce. If you keep changing, your inner consciousness becomes confused. If we used a different word to represent the color green each time we referred to that color, the word would become useless. This does not mean you can never change your symbols. If you discover one you like better, use it—just be consistent. You are creating paths through your psyche; as they become well worn they easily bring you into deep dimensions of awareness. Practice using your relaxation symbols; and you will be amazed at how soon you will be able to quickly and fully relax and gain access your deeper intelligence.

The inner world is as expansive as the outer. Whenever a meditation invites you to enhance your inner awareness, you can use one of the following techniques: Concentrate on the sensations of your breath, imagine yourself as a leaf gently fluttering down from a tree or floating down a stream, or imagine being a bird soaring through the sky. Another method is to use the power of suggestion by telling yourself you will count downward from ten to one and that each descending count will take you into a deeper state of awareness, and then count yourself down. Or you may find your own way to enhance your inner awareness. What works for me is focusing on my bones; this always takes me deeper. Follow your inclination.

Breath is as important in meditation as it is in life. When you are tense, you are not breathing fully. You are cutting off energy flow, which only perpetuates further tension. Simply stopping and concentrating on breathing alleviates stress and clears the mind. We always take a deep breath before embarking on a difficult task. *Breath is your home in meditation.* If ever tension arises, use your breath to release it. You don't need to do anything—just experience the sensations of breath.

During the count out of the meditation, it is suggested that you "feel revitalized." The meditations do revitalize you, but it also takes time to adjust to an outer focus of attention, so do not worry if you do not feel chipper right away. Some choose to use a bell in addition, or as an alternative, to a count out; do what feels right to you. As soon as you finish meditating, I suggest you take a moment to write the highlights of your reflections.

Relaxing into Well-Being: Working with Symbols

Make yourself comfortable, close your eyes ... Relax ... Focus on your breath ... Let your breath be full and easy ... as relaxed as the breathing of a sleeping baby ... As you exhale, feel yourself relax ... Feel your body relaxing into the support of whatever you're sitting or lying on ... Appreciate that the earth has always supported you ... Let yourself relax into this support ... Each breath renews you ... Each breath caresses you. Feel your body breathing ... Feel the sensations of breath as breath comes in through your nose or mouth ... You can feel it moving in ... Sense it moving through your whole body ... Every cell of which you are composed breathes ... Sense your body breathing ... renewed with each breath ... and releasing all the energy that is no longer needed with each exhalation ... Breathing ... It is good to simply be quiet and rest your attention on breath ... Breath relaxes ... Breath renews ... Waves of breath rolling through ...

Take a moment and scan your body. Notice if there are any particular areas that are calling your attention ... Notice areas of tension ... Move your awareness to one of them ... Send your breath to this place ... Feel it breathing ... almost as though your breath were drawn in and released right from this place ... As breath releases, it dislodges any tensions and carries them away ... Feel yourself loosening up with each exhalation of breath ... more relaxed ... more relaxed with each breath ... Breathe right through the area ... As you exhale, sense your breath carrying out the tensions ... Just breathe them out. You may want to envision a color or sound moving out with your breath, as this part of your body releases and relaxes ... With each breath feel yourself letting go and settling more into the support of the chair or whatever you're sitting or lying on ... into the support of the earth itself ... each breath more relaxed ...

Tell your body it can relax ... Feel it relaxing more and more ... ... Send your breath wherever it's needed ... from the tips of your toes ... through your legs ... your torso ... your arms and hands ... ... Breathe ... Let your whole body relax ... Breathe ... Send your breath wherever it's needed ... It feels good to relax ... Waves of breath relaxing you ... caressing you ... renewing you ... ... Breath heals ... It feels good to relax ... Whenever you focus on your breath and your breath is full and easy, your whole being relaxes ... Send your breath wherever you like and your relaxation deepens ... ...

This is your physical relaxation level. Create a symbol that represents this relaxation for you (or if you have one, bring it to awareness now) ... ... Know that whenever you bring to awareness your symbol for physical relaxation, your whole body relaxes as it's now relaxed in a matter of moments ... Tell your body this now ... Expect it to be true ... Know that every time you bring to awareness your symbol for physical relaxation, your body responds by relaxing as it is now relaxed in a matter of moments ... Tell yourself this ... Your symbol for physical relaxation tells your body to relax ... it gives it that message ... Know that every time you practice using your symbol for physical relaxation you'll enter deeper and deeper states of relaxation with greater ease ... Expect this to be the case ... ...

Now, to relax your mind, imagine being in a very peaceful, serene, and quiet place ... a place that is magical to you ... It could be anywhere you like ... It could be a place you've been or a place you create in your imagination ... a place that is especially peaceful and serene ... Let your imagination transport you into this place now ... Imagine what would be below your feet ... What would be in front of you? ... What would be on either side of you? ... Feel the quality of this place ... the quality of the air ... the smells ... the sounds ... the colors ... the textures ... It is a wonderful place ... It is a sanctuary ... your sanctuary ... peaceful ... serene ... special ... ...

Whenever you come here, your mind opens into its natural state of spaciousness, where you are fully relaxed and fully alert at the same time ... Here, your breath is like the breeze that clears the air ... Your breath clears your mind ... and your mind opens into spaciousness ... As you breathe in, you draw in the peaceful qualities of this special place ... Feel peacefulness

moving through you ... through your whole being and your
mind relaxes ...

Create, bring to awareness, a symbol for mental relaxation ... ... This
is your mental relaxation level ... Know that every time you bring
your symbol for mental relaxation to awareness, your mind will
relax as it is now relaxed in a matter of moments ... Tell yourself
this now ... and know that every time you bring this symbol to
awareness, your mind will relax more deeply ... more quickly ...
Expect this to be the case ... Tell your mind this is true ... that
when you bring your symbol for mental relaxation to awareness,
it will relax ... as it's now relaxed ... in a matter of moments ...
Relaxing into its natural state of spaciousness ... as spacious as the
skies ... lots of room for whatever crosses the sky of your mind.

Become aware of the emotional climate present in you ...
Notice feelings that may be causing you to pull back from life a
little ... feelings that may be tugging at you, and telling you how
you should be or how others should be ... All the pushing and
pulling ... any anxiety, frustration ... any feelings causing you to
shut down a little ... Imagine as though you could breathe right
through them all ... and your breath carries them out ... Imagine
that they drop down into the ground by the sheer weight of
themselves and the soil transforms them, for all that drops into
the earth is transformed into nutrients for new life ... Give
yourself permission to emotionally relax ... Breathe out and
release all the difficulties ... ... Feel your heart getting lighter ...
more open ... ...

Appreciate yourself for all the efforts you have made ... Appreciate your good heart ... Tell yourself about it ... Offer yourself loving kindness ... Absorb it into your heart ... Feel as though your heart smiles. Feel your heart getting lighter ... warmer ... Feel your heart relax into its natural state of generosity and compassion ... This is your emotional relaxation level. Create, bring to awareness, your symbol for emotional relaxation ... ...

Know that every time you bring this symbol to awareness, your feelings relax ... your heart relaxes, as you are now relaxed, in a matter of moments ... Each time you practice working with your symbol for emotional relaxation, you relax emotionally more easily and more quickly. Expect this to be the case. Tell your feelings that next time you bring this symbol to awareness, they'll respond by relaxing as they're now relaxed ... ...

Now take time to remember to bring to awareness what you feel grateful about ... what you cherish ... what you love ... Let these aspects of life pass through your awareness now ... ... Life is sacred ... Feel yourself relaxing into your gratitude ... ... In this place, you feel your connectedness to all that is ... to all of life ... This is your creative, self-restoring center, where you can tap healing energies. Create, bring to awareness, your symbol for your creative, self-restoring center ... ... Know that whenever you bring this symbol to awareness, you will quickly enter this state of consciousness. Tell yourself this now ... Expect it to be true.

This is your creative, self-restoring center ... Here, you experience spacious awareness ... calm ... vast ... quiet ... alert ... Here, the Inner Witness emerges ... Awareness is vast ... This is where insight is found ... This is where intuition is awakened ... This is where creativity is released ... This is your creative, self-restoring center. You can work with this state of awareness with greater ease every time you practice ... Here, you are increasingly able to focus wherever you choose for as long as you choose ... Your imagination ... creativity ... and concentration are all enhanced ... Your intuition is keen ... Trust spacious awareness ... ...

Here, you reside in spacious awareness ... The Inner Witness is present ... revealing what is true ... Wherever you focus your awareness, you discover what is true ... Here you activate your imagination ... Your imagination is fluid and free ... Wherever you focus your creativity, you shape probabilities ... Your creative imagination shapes reality ... Your Receptive Imagination brings intuitive insight ... Wherever you focus your imagination, intuition speaks to you ... You discover insight ... powerful ... Your inner world is as vast as the outer ...

If ever you find yourself distracted or off balance in any way, all you need do is return to your breath ... Focus on your breath ... it brings you to your center ... Breath is your home in meditation ... Trust your experience ... ...

Take time now to enhance and explore your inner awareness by any method of your choosing ... ...

Consciousness opens ... Here, you can listen deeply ... Here, the Inner Witness grounds you in the present moment ... Your intuition brings you insight and deep knowing ... Your Active Imagination aligns you with the best possible realities ...

Now, do any work that you would like ... You may simply want to reside in this calm by focusing on breath ... Or you may want to take a few moments to focus on affirmations, creating an alignment with the realities you choose ... Or you may want to share presence with a concern, letting your intuition offer you insight ... You may want to focus on a particular upcoming event that is important ... Imagine it unfolding in the best possible way for everyone ... Remember times of peak experiences and bring that energy into the event ... Let it glow ... Take time to do whatever work you would like now. This is your creative, self-restoring center ... Healing happens here ... Creativity arises here ... Intuition becomes apparent here ... ...

You may want to channel positive healing energy to anyone who may be in need now ... or any situation that could use some positive energy ... Do this by simply focusing intention and imagining the situation or the person surrounded by positive healing energy ... In this dimension we are all connected ... ...

Know that every time you enter these dimensions of awareness, you receive beneficial effects ... Healing happens ... Intuition becomes more and more keen and available to you ... The

Inner Witness is fully present ... Creativity is fluid ... Expect this to be the case ...

You can return to these dimensions of awareness any time you choose on your own by simply working with your symbols for physical, mental, emotional relaxation, and your creative, self-restoring center. These symbols will bring you right into this state of awareness ... And you can do whatever inner work you would like ... You can return to outer levels of awareness any time by counting yourself out, just as I am about to do ...

In a moment, I'm going to count from one to five. At the count of five, your eyes will open, and you'll feel revitalized, refreshed, relaxed, remembering all that you've experienced and bringing with you the energies you've tapped ... ready and able to act on them in your life ... feeling a sense of wholeness that will be with you throughout this day, throughout all of your activities.

Making yourself ready to come out to outer conscious levels now ...

ONE—becoming more aware of the room around you ...

TWO—coming up slowly now ...

THREE—coming up ...

FOUR—bringing with you the energies you have tapped, remembering everything you have experienced ...

FIVE!—eyes open, revitalized, refreshed, relaxed, bringing with you all the energies you tapped, ready and able to act on them in your life, remembering all that you've experienced and knowing you can return to these dimensions whenever you choose.

Now take a moment to jot down your experience.

•3•

Creating a Language to Speak to Your Deeper Self

When you meditate, you are predominantly at the suggestible alpha level, so take advantage of this receptivity and develop your own programming—thereby, with an act of will, choosing to program your own development. If a TV advertisement can con you into buying a kitchen gadget, why not choose to do something you really want and set your own intentions? As described earlier our bodies continually respond to our inner messages; remember that simply imagining what you're afraid of activates your adrenal glands. If you give yourself a suggestion that you are healthy, your body will respond accordingly; this is simply done by *pretending* that it is so.

Affirmations for Aligning Intention

An affirmation is simply a positively stated sentence of how you would like to be, such as: "The whole of my body is healthy." That may sound simplistic because you know the whole of your body is not fully healthy; all of us have something that ails us. However, your inner consciousness continually communicates with your body; and inner consciousness is noncritical—it believes anything. Cultivating a belief that your body is healthy will enable your body to be more effective in fighting potential sickness, and it will give you additional strength to heal the ailments existing within.

Working with affirmations is simple—so simple that one might slough it off as silly. When I began using affirmations, my beta mind thought it was foolish. It's okay to think that—remember the beta mind is critical, but each beta thought has very little energy. Feeling like it's dumb to use affirmations doesn't stop it from working—inner consciousness is noncritical (i.e., suggestible), and each alpha thought has more energy. The only thing that will stop it from working is not using it; so go ahead, perhaps thinking all the while that it is an absurd activity.

A while back, I had an experience that reinforced my appreciation for the power of affirmations. I had a major disagreement with one of my closest friends. For many months we talked about it, but were never able to reach a resolution, making it really difficult for us to enjoy our friendship. We decided to go to a mediator who tried to help us work through the disagreement. That, too, was unsuccessful. We each sincerely wanted to resolve the issue—but to no avail. Several weeks after that attempt, an idea came to me in a meditation to use an affirmation: "I reside in the care we have for each other." I used the affirmation regularly, and sent a note to my friend inviting him to do the same. About a month later, we saw each other again and somehow, inexplicably, the year-old tension had dissolved. The affirmation must have drawn on the intuitive knowledge available at deeper levels, for we found ourselves moving along a new course. The use of that affirmation was the only new element in our relationship—nothing else had changed. If I hadn't known how to use these energies, I might have lost a friendship close to my heart.

It is experiences like this that humble me. What initially felt simplistic and trite in fact had a profound impact. I have discovered that when working with inner consciousness solutions come about without the usual accompanying understanding of why or how. It is never linear or reasonable—it just happens. Sometimes the solution is very subtle; in this case, I could not point to a solution, but I could not point to the problem either—which is solution enough for me.

To make your own affirmations, think of aspects of your life that you would like to change and imagine how you would like them to be instead. For each issue, create a sentence that captures the essence of the experience you would like to cultivate. Compose a sentence that describes what you would like to happen as though it were already true. Make it simple, positive, and in the present tense. Your inner consciousness is not linear, but instead very childlike. You do not have to have an analysis of why something is needed or how it will happen—justification is unnecessary. You simply need a statement of the desired condition. Always state it in the present tense because inner consciousness takes things quite literally. You do not want to become healthy because that is perpetually in the future; you want to *be* healthy. Inner consciousness resides in the perpetual present; the future is not part of its experience. Don't say, "I will be healthy because I eat well," but, "I eat well, and I am fully healthy."

Because of the noncritical nature of your inner consciousness, affirmations should always be stated positively. Notice what happens when I say, "Do not imagine a lemon." You immediately and unavoidably think of a lemon. If you use the affirmation, "I am not sick," inner consciousness just hears "sick." It's easy to understand this if you think of young children who are much more responsive when you state things in a positive way. Rather than saying "Stop making all that noise," it is much more effective to say, "Be a little quieter." We should begin to watch the negative suggestions we are constantly giving ourselves (a friend of mine calls them "neffirmations"). For example, "Whenever I talk in groups, I sound stupid." Notice how this statement is positively expressing something you do not want. Similarly, if you want to feel secure speaking in public, saying, "I am not stupid," is ineffectual, whereas saying, "I am intelligent and articulate when expressing myself in groups," helps enormously.

In addition, you do not want your beta mind to give your inner self a number of alternatives by stating the affirmations differently on different days. Your inner consciousness, just like a child, will only become confused. You want to impress it with a clear message, using the same statement repeatedly (like a symbol).

Affirmations work because you are in a suggestible state of awareness when you are meditating. They reset your "auto pilot," so to speak. Your intuition goes to work beneath the surface and you will find yourself perceiving aspects of your daily experience in a fresh way. Often you will find that you have an impulse to do something in a novel way. These insights and impulses may feel awkward, but if you look deeper you will notice that they are coherent with the affirmation. It is crucial that you act on them, for they are the birthing of a new way of being—one that ushers in the experience you choose.

A truism with affirmation work is that what you focus on is what you get. When working with affirmations, it is important to feel as much as possible that they are true. At the moment that you repeat the affirmation, as much as you can muster, pretend that it is already true; generate the feelings that would be present if it were a true description of your experience. Be sure not to focus on the inaccuracy of the affirmation, for that will only perpetuate the reality you want to change. If the affirmation were already completely true, you wouldn't need to use it. It is a given that there is a contradiction. Avoid looking at the gap between your experience and the affirmation. This is likely to defeat your purpose because you will conclude that the affirmations are not working. Instead, move through your daily activities with the assumption that the affirmation is working under the surface. For example, if you say to yourself, "I am healthy," do not proceed to focus on your ailing knee, but concentrate on the vitality your body does have. Whenever your knee starts to hurt, do not decide that the affirmation has been ineffective, but remember your intention and assume the affirmation is gradually taking hold.

Overall, be mindful of the underlying expectation you bring to working with affirmations. As with all inner consciousness work, *the results are determined by what you anticipate*. Like wearing a miner's light, what you see is determined by the turn of your head. Since each of us is constantly looking to have our point of view validated, it is good to look for what is working, rather than what is not. If you use an affirmation while expecting that it probably will not work, it will not. Try to suspend judgment and instead cultivate a curiosity to discover the possibilities. Watch for results instead of trying to prove to yourself that it is not working. If you do this, the contradiction between your daily experience and the affirmation will slowly dissolve.

Some people prefer to speak the affirmations aloud, because hearing the words gives them an added power. You may want to create a jingle. Or you might want to use just one word that connotes a quality you want to bring into your life, such as trust, cooperation, love, joy, or generosity. I suggest that you write down your affirmations and post them in places that you regularly see, like the door of your refrigerator or your bathroom mirror; simply catching sight of them out of the corner of your eye will reinforce them.

You can also repeat affirmations while doing rhythmic activities such as exercising or cleaning, because you are in the alpha state and it will be just as effective as it is when you are meditating. You can also combine breath awareness with affirmations. For instance, you can say, "As I breathe in I am grateful to be alive. As I breathe out, I offer compassion to all life." You can use a number of affirmations, one right after the other, or you may want to use just one repeatedly. In either case, use the same wording. You can refine them as you experiment with the use of affirmations, and you will discover the format that is most comfortable for you.

It is important to use the affirmations repeatedly—inner consciousness is responsive to repetition. Every religious tradition uses rituals, such as the repetition of certain words—as in chanting—or the regular use of certain gestures. The purpose of the traditions is to establish a clear intention, to invite particular energy to be present, and to access deeper experience. Similarly, repetition of affirmations is a powerful way to create a channel through which deeper knowledge surfaces. In time, you will come to a fuller realization of the power that you draw by speaking each affirmation, moving beyond intellectual understanding and creating conditions in the whole of your being for the affirmation to manifest. None of this occurs logically. You will find yourself unconsciously behaving differently and your perceptions subtly altered. The affirmation has moved you into alignment with your intention. In the induction for each meditation section, there are new affirmations that address the particular issues dealt with in that chapter. It is good to use affirmations every time you meditate.

Setting Intent in the Instant with Symbols

Symbols are ancient ways to access healing power.[1] A symbol, by definition, represents more than itself. For instance, anything you feel sentimental about is a symbol. There may be a kind of flower that has particular significance to you because it represents the person who gave it to you and the love you shared, which means more than simply the look and smell of that variety of flower. Our lives are full of symbols; some are very personal while others are culturally shared, like the wedding ring.

A symbol, being more than itself, is a focal point of meaning. It does not need logical or sequential thought processes in order for it to evoke meaning. Because inner consciousness is holistic, non-sequential, and more focused, its principle language is symbols. By definition, a symbol elicits a particular set of associations and responses when you bring it to awareness. Therefore, if you want to behave in a particular way, you can create a symbol to represent that behavior, bring it into your awareness at the opportune moment, and you will find yourself acting in accordance with it. You have already experienced how effective this method is, if you have been using your relaxation symbols.

Your behavior and your inner messages move into alignment by use of a symbol. You will not need to go meditate about your intention; simply bring to awareness the personal symbol you previously created for the quality you desire to embody. This is very useful because when you are in the midst of a situation, you do not have the time or inclination to stop and meditate. For example, I am a very goal-oriented person, which is a useful trait because it enables me to accomplish a lot, but there are times when I get very impatient. I have a symbol of an elephant's ear. Whenever I bring it to awareness, I slow down and listen. If I hadn't already created a symbol in a meditation to use whenever I might need it, my impatience would overwhelm me.

A woman in one of my classes had an image of herself as a klutz. She played left field on a softball team and her body kept responding to this self-image, sabotaging her ability to play well. In meditation, she imagined feeling graceful and coordinated; then she created a symbol for it. After that, when she was in the field and a fly ball was hit, she brought her symbol to mind and caught the ball. It worked because when the ball was in the air, she didn't have enough time to give herself a pep talk, but she could remember her symbol instantaneously. To her amazement, she became the team's star!

Whenever the symbol is in your mind, your body responds instantaneously. The symbol also acts as a north star; you intuitively orient in the direction that is coherent with your desire. It helps you navigate so that the choices you make align with your intent. The trick is to first get in touch with the desired attribute—not to think it, but to feel it. In meditation, strive to conjure up the experience of the attribute as much as you can muster, and then create a symbol for it. Then tell yourself that next time you bring your symbol to mind you will respond accordingly. Condition yourself by focusing on your symbol the next few times you meditate. You can also create an affirmation that says you will remember to bring the symbol to awareness whenever you need it. We act out from our inner messages; the symbol is more than a beta thought. It becomes a source of behavior.

You can have specific symbols for many kinds of energy: creativity, trust, cooperation, clear communication, deep listening, or anything you choose. For example, if you are about to go through a round of job interviews, it is a good idea to have an appropriate symbol to use while being interviewed. It will greatly increase the chances of getting the job you want.

In the symbol-making meditation, you can create a symbol representing any particular energy you choose. To help you connect with that energy, the meditation will guide you through experiences of your past when you felt it most strongly. If there are no such times, *pretend* that there were, or do whatever occurs to you to help you *feel* the energy. Maybe imagining yourself embodying the qualities of a role model will work best. Remember inner consciousness is non-critical. The point is to feel the quality you want to cultivate; it makes no difference if you do this by recalling memories of yourself or another. After focusing on the energy, create a symbol that represents it. Whatever symbol you create is the right one, for it is what you associate with the energy that makes it effective. Symbols do not necessarily have to be pictures, but it is important that they be specific and easy to recall. You may wish to use a physical gesture or a particular tone—whatever your inclination. I also suggest that you create an affirmation that says you will remember to bring your symbol into your awareness whenever a situation arises in which it will be of assistance. You will want to create a separate affirmation for each symbol.

The first symbol-making meditation, "Internalizing a Quality," is for general use; be sure to choose in advance the quality for which you want to create a symbol. I also recommend that you begin with one or two and then increase your vocabulary of symbols gradually so your deeper self comes to know each one, rather than confusing it with too many at the beginning. Like affirmations, it is good to post your symbols in places where you will see them.

If you do this, you will find the effectiveness of the symbols and affirmations growing more rapidly, for each reminder strengthens the energy, and you will be better able to act on its power. It is also good to focus for a few moments on the power and quality of the symbol every time you meditate.

MEDITATIONS

Induction

Close your eyes and focus your awareness on your breathing, breathing with your belly. Feel the rise and fall of your breath ... Let your breathing find its own most comfortable rhythm ... breathing that is as relaxed as the breathing of a sleeping baby ... Feel the rise and fall of your breath ... Let the rhythm of your breath soothe the whole of your body ... Bring to awareness your symbol for physical relaxation ... Give your body permission to relax ... relaxing into the support of the earth. It can relax now ... Breathe, breath caresses your body ... Let the awareness of this symbol soothe your body into relaxation ... It is good to give your body space and time to relax. Feel tensions dropping away ... Know that every time you bring this symbol into awareness, you will enter deeper and deeper states of physical relaxation with greater and greater ease ... Tell yourself this now ... ...

When you are ready, bring to awareness your symbol for mental relaxation ... Feel your mind relax into its natural state of spaciousness ... ... Watch the chatter of your mind calming down ... thoughts move in and out of awareness as easily as you breathe ... lots of room for whatever thoughts cross the sky of your mind. Let the rhythm of your breath calm your mind ... Let your mental relaxation symbol calm your mind ... Here, sounds do not distract you; instead they enhance your inner focus. Here, it is as though all your thoughts were the puffy clouds drifting through a sunny afternoon sky, the sky of your mind ... It is good to give your mind space and time to relax ... Tell yourself that whenever you bring your mental relaxation symbol to awareness, the whole of your mind will enter deeper and deeper states of mental relaxation with greater ease every time you practice ... Expect this to be the case ... ...

When you are ready, bring in your symbol for emotional relaxation, notice the feelings that are present now ... If you discover any feelings that are clamoring for your attention, take care of them in whatever manner occurs to you ... Let yourself emotionally relax. Imagine letting all the "shoulds" soak into the ground and nurture yourself. Give yourself permission to relax emotionally ... Feel your heart relaxing into its natural state of compassion and generosity ... ...

When you are ready, bring to your awareness your symbol for your creative, self-restoring center. Remember your gratitude ... ... Acknowledge the sanctity of life ... Feel yourself at a stable level of inner consciousness ... Feel the quality of awareness as you reside in your creative self-restoring center ... Know that you are learning to work from your creative, self-restoring center with greater ease every time you practice. Here, your imagination expands, intuition surfaces, and creativity opens; your powers of concentration are also enhanced and permit you to focus wherever you choose ... This is your creative, self-restoring center ... Here, you have complete control and you may accept, reject, or put aside for later consideration anything that I say ... Here, you will discover a rich and beautiful landscape of your receptivity and creativity unfold before you. You will experience vivid and meaningful sensations and imagery ... new realities ... As these realities appear, they will guide you to new dimensions of being ... Here, you can make use of the wisdom of your inner self, discovering the expansive power of your inner being. Your inner being is a part of the universal energy which permeates all life ... This is the energy which dissolves limitations, enabling you to discover deep knowing, tap the harmonizing energies of the universe and create change ... Know that all of this is so ...

Now take time to explore and enhance your inner awareness by any method of your choosing ... You can concentrate on the sensations of your breath, feeling yourself go deeper with each exhalation, feeling as though your awareness actually rests on your breath ... Or if you like, you can imagine yourself as a falling leaf or a soaring bird—whatever you choose ... ...

Finishing what you are doing ... Your consciousness is receptive, creative, relaxed and alert ... You will easily follow these words and remember the whole of your meditative experience.

Affirmations

You can cultivate wellbeing by working with affirmations. I am going to suggest several affirmations. Upon hearing one, if you wish to affirm it, repeat it to yourself after me. Feel the power of the words. Breath life into them ... For the moment, strive to feel as though the affirmation is already true ... In so doing, you align your energies and you will find yourself living in ways that conform to them. You will intuitively act in accordance with each affirmation and they materialize in your experience ...

I believe in myself ...

I trust my awareness ...

I am alert when I meditate ...

I am enriched by my deepest dimensions ...

I am fully present and mindful in each moment ...

I am curious and always learning ...

I am increasingly attuned and responsive to my intuition ...

A spring of creativity continually flows through me ...

My fears transform into challenges; they are my teachers ...

I always find positive approaches ...

I am glad to offer my whole being good care ...

The whole of my body/mind is resilient ...

I have all the energy I need to do as I choose ...

Time is generous, I relax into the moment and it carries me ...

I make wise choices ...

I cultivate a joyous heart ...

All my relationships are mutually supportive and loving ...

All my needs are always met—there is enough for everyone ...

I celebrate belonging to the community of life ...

I offer my gifts to heal the world ...

I am resilient; I maintain balance amidst change ...

I trust the future ...

Know that in focusing on affirmations, you have evoked patterns of energy ... These energies have already begun to move into your experience. You will find yourself intuitively acting in alignment with the affirmations. These affirmations get stronger every time you focus on them ...

Now create one affirmation of your own choosing. Pick one particular area in your life you would like to improve ... ... Imagine how you would like it to be ... Feel it as a present reality ... Experience its reality through all of your senses ... ... Create a statement describing this reality. Make it simple, positive, and present tense ... Take time to do this now ... ...

Bring your awareness back to these words knowing that you will remember this affirmation for future use, knowing that the energies have been awakened. Know you will find yourself intuitively acting in alignment with the affirmation. The more you use it, the more it will manifest. Tell yourself this now.

Now we are going to work with breath and an affirmation of gratitude and compassion. Take a moment and focus on your breath. Feel the sensations of breath rolling in and out of your body ... Breath carries life ... ... Now as you inhale, repeat to yourself: "I draw in gratitude." ... Repeat this a few times with each in breath and feel your gratitude as you do. "I draw in gratitude." ... Experience your gratitude more and more deeply with each inhalation of breath ... ...

Then when you are ready as you exhale add: "I offer compassion." .... . Breathe in gratitude, breathe out compassion ... With each out breath, repeat: "I offer compassion." ... Feel gratitude to be alive and compassion for all life as naturally as breathing in and out ... ... Know that as you work with this practice your gratitude and compassion continue to deepen ... ...

Internalizing a Quality

Imagine soothing energy, whatever that means to you—it may be sounds, feelings, vibrations, textures, a knowingness ... Imagine soothing energy ... calming energy ... imagine yourself surrounded by soothing energy ... Let it soak into your body, breathe in its softness ... Imagine soothing energy settling into you ... Imagine settling into this soothing energy ... Feel it nurturing you ... soothingness soaking deeper and deeper into you ... comforting you, healing you ... soothingness gently moving through you ... imagine that if you listen, the soothing energy carries a soothing music ... you can almost hear the quiet hum of beingness itself—the music, the tones of life itself ... Let the cells of your body sway with it ... surrounded by soothing energy, gentle energy, almost as though you're floating in it ... ...

As you are receptive, quietly residing in yourself, bring to awareness another quality you would like to work with, a quality that you would like to cultivate. Love or joy or grace or humor or another quality ... whatever quality you like ... Knowing you can work on others another time, choose a specific one now ...

Repeat the word to yourself several times ... ... Witness its energy ... Repeat the word over and over and over again ... Feel its meaning ... Reach out to it intuitively ... Does it have texture? ... color? ... sound? ... taste? ... Let it touch you ... ...

Let the quality share the space you occupy ... Breathe in the quality ... Sense it bathe all the cells of your body ... Your breathe carries it, you thoughts are shaped by it ... ... Your heart smiles at the touch of it ... ... Your whole being is endowed with it. Feel it pulsing through you ... ... Create a symbol or gesture for it ... Tell yourself that whenever you bring it to awareness you invite its full presence into the scene ... ...

Sense what it inspires you to do in your life ... Like the sun shining, sense the quality pouring into your life ... Feel your life shifting and making room for it ... Imagine embodying the energy in all that you do ... Feel it in detail ... ... What can be done in your life to nurture it? ... ... Feel gratitude for the ways it enriches life ... Imagine what you might do as a gesture of thanks ....

Symbol-Making for Evoking Instant Alignment

Symbols are the language that speaks to your inner self. With symbols, you can tap the power of universal knowingness, bringing forth whatever power you would like. Now you are going to create a symbol for an ability you would like to cultivate. You are going to use the vast receptive and creative powers available to you. Know that here, time is fluid. You can remember and relive experiences vividly, bringing their powers to bear and retaining their powers by containing them in a symbol ... You can use the symbol time and time again to call upon this power. When you do, your energy aligns with it and you will find yourself feeling and acting in ways that embody the capacity you are cultivating. Know that this is so.

Bring to awareness a specific capacity you would like to cultivate ... Remember a time in your life when this capacity was present, or you can create an imaginary time ... If you like, think of someone who embodies this capacity and imagine what it is like to be like this person ... However you like, imagine a scene charged with the energy that accompanies this ability ... Give details to the scene ... Feel the atmosphere of the scene ... Notice how your body feels ... Exaggerate the quality ... Breathe life into it ... ...

Now, either remember another scene where this capacity was fully present or become even more deeply aware of the scene you have been experiencing ... Discover the personality of the ability ... Now, experience a time in the future when you are expressing this ability, when it moves through you ... Imagine it in detail ... How does it feel? ... Feel the quality's energy in your body. Feel its power ... ...

Now create a symbol that represents this experience ... If a couple come to mind, either choose one or let them coalesce into one. Make it up ... What you create is right for you.

This is your symbol. Know that whenever you bring this symbol to awareness, you will find yourself moving into alignment it ... Tell yourself that whenever you bring this symbol into your awareness, you will find yourself acting in accordance with it, intuitively knowing whatever you need to, to fully express this capacity. Tell yourself you will remember to use your symbol whenever you need it ... Know that every time you use it, it becomes increasingly powerful ... Feel your power; you are fully capable. Know that this capacity deepens over time as you work with your symbol; expect this.

Breathing Out Tension and Opening Time

Breathe ... In meditation your breath is your home. Arrive here in this meditation. Breathe ... Send your breath wherever it may be needed ... breathe through tension ... Settle in ... Breathe out and let go of all anticipation ... Breathe out the hurry and settle into your breath here ... Breathe out and let go of any re-runs ... Your breath clears you ... Just feel the sensations of your breath ... Rest your attention on your breath ... You can always return to your breath; take refuge in your breath ...

Your breath centers you. You can breathe in calm and breathe out any energy you wish to release ... Your breath is your home ... Breathe ...

Let your attention rest on your breath ... ... Let the rhythm of your breath gently rock you ... soothe you ... calm and quiet you ... Breathe, feel the sensations of your breath moving in and out of your body ... Let the past go ... arrive in the present ... Breathe ... Be with quiet awareness ... Breathe ... Be aware, listen to the quiet of awareness ... ... Experience awareness ... Breathe ... Be in awareness ... held by awareness ... Breathe. You need not do anything; just be in awareness ... Witness ...

Each time you exhale, you settle into the present even more than before. Simply be with your breath. With each breath you settle more and more into the present ... more of you settles ... All of you present ... Whole.

Be aware of your exhalations. Follow your exhalations. Imagine following your exhalations moving out from your body ... Breath moves out into the expanses of space. Breathe. Follow your breath ... Imagine that your exhalations carry you into the expanses of space. Imagine it ... As though each time you exhale your horizons extend further and further ... ...

Follow your exhalations ... Horizons expand—lots of space, infinite space ... Breathe. Follow your breath ... quiet ... expansive ... There is room for anything, room for everything ... Follow your breath into the infinity of space. Quiet ... Expansive ... (Repeat this paragraph.)

Just as there is lots of space, know that there is lots of time—all the time you need ... As you follow your breath, experience the broadening of time ... Sense how this is. You have all the time in the world—you always do ... As you rest in breath, feel time open ... ... With each exhalation you settle into the present ... Openness happens ... ...

Breath opens. Space opens ... Time opens ... With each exhalation time and space expand out as you settle in. Sense this ... Witness, breath opens, space opens; time opens ... Relax into time ... Time carries you. Relax into it ... lots and lots of time—it carries you ... You always have all the time you need. It is true. In the present, time is infinite ... Inhabit time. Do not chase it. Relax into it ... ... It carries you. Time brings the gift of the future. Time holds the past. Time is a gift. Be friendly to it ... ... Time carries you; relax into it. You need not chase after it or try to get ahead of it. Relax into it and it supports you ...

Time is generous. You always have all you need. It is true. In the present, time is infinite ... In the present there is room for life. The present is where life lives ... As you exhale, send your breath to those places in your life that feel cramped ... ...

Imagine that your breath opens space there ... lots of space. Expansive. Breathe ... Create a symbol for what you are experiencing now ... Whatever you like ... Tell yourself whenever you bring it to mind you will relax into the moment and feel the generosity of time ... Expect this to be the case ... As you practice working with your symbol you'll find yourself relaxing into time more and more easily, more and more fully.

Count Out

Now go over the details of your meditation experience ... Acknowledge the healing and creative energy that revealed itself ... Review any insights you have gained ... any choices you may have made ... Imagine further opening to and acting on this energy ... Embody it ... Breathe it ... Project it into the future ... ...

Make yourself ready to come out to outer-conscious levels ... Know that you can return to these dimensions of awareness whenever you choose ... Know that whenever you enter these levels of consciousness, you receive beneficial effects and become a more centered being. Each time you meditate, you are increasingly able to maintain your focus of attention wherever you choose for as long as you choose. Every time you work in your creative self-restoring center, your abilities are enhanced ... and you tap the harmonizing energies of the universe; they heal you. Tell yourself you'll remember to work with the energies you have tapped ... Note when you want to meditate again ... Appreciate the gifts you have received in this meditation.

In a moment I am going to count from one to five ... At the count of five, you will open your eyes feeling refreshed, relaxed, and revitalized, remembering all that you've experienced ... bringing with you the energies you have attuned yourself to ... being fully ready and able to act on these energies in your life, and knowing you can return to these dimensions whenever you choose.

ONE—coming up slowly now ...

TWO—becoming aware of the room around you ...

THREE—at the count of five, you will open your eyes feeling revitalized, refreshed, and relaxed ... bringing with you all the energies you have connected with, having full memory of all that you have experienced ...

FOUR—coming up now ...

FIVE!—eyes open, feeling refreshed, relaxed, and revitalized, ready and able to act on the energies you have experienced, feeling a sense of wholeness with open heart and spirit ...

It is a good idea to write down or draw any affirmation or symbol you created.

•4•

The Nature of the Inner Dimension

There is a paradox in working with inner consciousness that is best described by trying to drink water without a glass—it goes right through your fingers. Inner consciousness is fluid and nebulous. Sensations are gone as fast as they come. However, you know that if you concentrate and focus your attention, you can get a drink of water without a glass. Because the nature of our inner dimension is qualitatively different from the material world around us, we have no framework for understanding what we experience when working with the inner dimension.

There is a vulnerability—an insecurity—that you feel when working with the inner consciousness, because there is no objective world to brush against and obtain your bearings. Inside, you find yourself in a shifting, amorphous reality that has no evident signposts. Trying to apply everyday definitions, you may find yourself doubting your ability to navigate the inner realms, but this is not the case. When you understand the dynamics of inner consciousness, you will find yourself more able to trust and work with inner dimensions.

Conflict between Inner and Outer Consciousness

Meditation is about maintaining a state of relaxed attention, the stage between sleeping and waking awareness—the alpha level is equally active and receptive. However, your beta (rational) consciousness does not go away. Instead, as you have probably discovered by now, it continually judges everything you experience. In our society, beta consciousness is what we have been taught to use and value most—it has been given full control. Your beta consciousness is likely to feel threatened by your beginning to work with other parts of yourself; so it reacts by injecting judgments: "I'm not relaxed," "I just made that up," "That's dumb," or "I'm going to be late."

People usually mistakenly see this as a reflection of not meditating properly and attempt to silence these thoughts by arguing, "I am, too, relaxed." But argument is not a very relaxing activity. It is a full-time job to try to quiet the beta mind because it has an infinite store of such distractions. As long as you are trying to deal with them, you are not focusing your attention on your inner work. The beta mind succeeds in diverting you from your task, thus maintaining its power. You can choose not to respond to all that the beta mind says— just let it run its critique; let your beta-voice critics take a box seat in the theater of your mind as you go about your inner work. They can watch, and comment, but they are not on stage.

Awareness and attention are not the same thing. When you find yourself entangled in an inner argument, simply bring your attention back to your breath. Doing so invites the spacious awareness of the Inner Witness, and you will find that there is ample room for your entire process. You can then choose what takes center stage.

While your beta mind attempts to divert you, your inner consciousness is likely to be rebelling as well. Once your beta voices take a box seat, you will find that you have to contend with the spotlight of your attention bouncing at random all over the theater of your mind; your inner consciousness does not want to focus. You have probably spent most of your life ignoring inner consciousness, so be patient with it; it needs time to get used to the idea of working. It is carefree and would rather play than be disciplined. Since it has been free to do what it pleases when you are not focusing your attention on it, it now tries to evade you. One of its diversionary tactics is to bring in random images. Sometimes it gets even more rambunctious and tries to frighten you with scary imagery. When you find any of this happening, do not worry about it. Just move your attention to your breath. *Focusing on breath will stabilize your meditation.* Then place whatever you had been working on back on center stage.

Always use your breath as your anchor. Putting attention on the sensations of breathing develops mindfulness. You will be able to notice when your attention strays, so you can bring it back. Strive to be mindful and notice what you are choosing to focus your attention on. You are at the controls behind the spotlight of awareness, and you can choose to focus wherever you wish. Inner consciousness is not linear. You may space out or find your attention wandering. That does not mean you have to go back to the beginning of the scene; it just means you allowed center stage to be in darkness, but you can choose to re-illuminate it by going back to where you left off. Just breathe and refocus. Do not be too quick to judge your process. Again, be mindful when a dreamlike story or image that seems random appears. Before bringing your attention back to center stage, examine the image, look for meaning. You will often find a metaphor offering insight into the issue you are working on.

You can be aware of noises while at the same time attending to your inner work. Remember, just because you have noisy neighbors does not mean you have to listen to them. If you become too distracted by sounds or discomfort, turn them around and make them work for you. You are in a suggestible state, so tell yourself, "All the sounds will cause me to be even more focused on my inner processes." Or be more creative. Recently, I was leading a meditation on the Fourth of July; we were meditating on what our different ancestors were doing in 1776. Soon after I began, firecrackers started going off in the street just outside. I incorporated the noise by saying that each bang was taking us back another generation. As a result, the meditation was even more effective.

There are two other common ways inner consciousness succeeds in avoiding disciplined work. It might make your body feel restless or itchy, or your throat congested—again distracting your attention. In as detailed a manner as possible, imagine drinking warm syrup and pretend that it is soothing your scratchy throat. Note that this is the opposite of wishing you had some cough syrup. Instead, you want to pretend that you are drinking cough syrup. To your amazement, you will find your cough receding. The other way inner consciousness evades you is that sometimes you will find yourself feeling as if you had been asleep, and you will come out of the meditation with large blank spots in your memory. It is akin to the metaphor that the play goes on, but the stage is dark. There are several things you can do to avoid this. You can give yourself an affirmation such as, "When meditating, I remain aware and alert to all that occurs." Sitting with your back straight will also help. However, if you continue to have blank spots in memory, there are some procedures you can use to fill them. Logic will not work because inner consciousness does not have a story line with a beginning, middle, and end; it is more like a patchwork quilt. Memory works associatively, not sequentially. Musing over an image, word, or sensation that you know was a part of the meditation often allows you to recall the rest. Glancing over the meditation script will also be helpful. Occasionally you might find that you have blank spots in your memory, yet the changes you wanted to work on manifest themselves anyway. (The play does go on.) This happens when your inner consciousness finds it easier to work below the surface, because your conscious awareness encumbers it.

The Character of Inner Consciousness

Inner consciousness is holistic; its language is symbolic and metaphoric. It often expresses itself in rhyme, puns, and sensations in the body. One person's symbol for mental relaxation was a train entering a very peaceful countryside (train of thought). One of the pleasures of working with your inner self is that it invariably has a good sense of humor.

When some people meditate, they experience various physical sensations and responses. For instance, their body may feel as if it has grown bigger or heavier, or maybe they feel tingling or heat sensations. Others find that they start to nod or feel as if they are whirling, or their eyelids flutter, or their bodies twitch. Whatever the sensations, they are no cause for worry. These are simply natural responses to energies being released and moving in unfamiliar ways. Your body responds to whatever image you hold in your awareness. If you find yourself uncomfortable, imagine the antidote (e.g., if you have a whirling sensation, stabilize yourself by imagining that you are growing roots through the floor and into the ground).

Everyone is endowed with an imagination; how the imagination works, however, differs from person to person. In English, it is much easier to describe what something looks like than how it feels. I happen to be a visualizer, so the meditations I write are likely to be slanted toward the visual. But consciousness works in different modes—some of us predominantly feel things in our bodies, some hear things, some know things, and for others seeing is predominant.

Honor what is most natural for you. You can make your experience richer by employing each of your inner senses and imaging how whatever you are focusing on looks, feels, smells, and sounds.

In the material world things take time to happen. Time and space create limits and maintain linear and logical progressions. The inner world is altogether different; as it is holistic and sequence is not something within its experience—it operates in simultaneous patterns—time is meaningless. If I say, "red balloon" you do not have to go looking for it to imagine it; it is there the instant you hear the words.

We are accustomed to everything taking time, when you work in a meditation, whatever you are working on, the chances are you will feel as if you did not do it well because it did not seem to take any time or follow any logical progression. When you focus on a healing image, for example, the image is fleeting. It has no duration, so you feel you must recapture it to ensure its effectiveness—but then it seems redundant. Do not worry; that is just part of the process.

Always be mindful of how your imagination depicts the subject on which you have chosen to work. Pay careful attention to the way you imagine the issue. This will provide insight into the current conditions. The representation itself metaphorically reflects what is true at the moment.

To gain insight with your Receptive Imagination, the meditations often direct you to imagine talking to and asking questions of your inner self. *The process of making up a story provides a context in which the operative energies reveal themselves.* You want to personify what is taking place, as though whatever you are focusing your attention on has intelligence and you can converse with it. This gives you a focal point with which to work. Use the story-making capacities of your imagination. Just make it up as I did when I did the case reading. Activate your childlike capacities of make believe.

The imagination is the medium of psychic information. When you make a story you discover insight.

In meditation it is as though everything exists in the perpetual here and now. It is not as if you ask a question and then get an answer; both usually occur at the same time. When you move the spotlight of your attention, it does not take time to illuminate the new area. You find that as you formulate a question you already know the answer. This may make you may feel as though you knew it all along, and, therefore, it is not the answer you are looking for. It is a common mistake to expect an answer after asking and therefore dismiss what is instantaneously apparent. The act of bringing the question into focus is the act that simultaneously reveals the answer. Always be mindful of what you are experiencing while you are formulating a question. Your Inner Witness will notice the instantaneous impressions that break into the light of awareness as you clarify your question. These impressions reveal what is currently true.

If you do not seem to be experiencing anything, make something up. Do not wait for it to come to you; if it were going to come to you it would be there already. I have done psychic case work for many years, and I have guided hundreds of people through the same exercise. Some people feel as if the information just comes—seemingly out of the blue. Others feel as if they had made up the whole thing. In either case, the readings are equally accurate. It just takes longer and feels more laborious when one "makes it up." If you do not sense an answer to your inner question, give yourself permission to invent one. The act of creating a story provides a stage upon which intuitive information can appear. Contrary to what we have been taught, with inner dimensions, the imagination is the purveyor of direct knowing.

Often, the answers you find will seem simplistic. They may be obvious, cliché, corny, or trite. We've all been conditioned to discount these qualities and taught that only complicated or unique solutions can be worthwhile. What we need to remember is that ideas are seen as cliché because they have been so widely experienced. Inner consciousness resides in the realm of universality and interconnection. When questioned, it dips into collective knowledge. If we discount an answer because it is cliché, we divorce ourselves from the lessons others have learned. The answers we come to may not be original, but they are wise, and wisdom is never complicated.

When meditating about the difficulty with my friend, the affirmation that came to me certainly was corny: "I reside in the care we have for one another." Had I not taken it seriously, it's likely I would no longer have the friendship. The assumption that answers to problems must be unique or complicated and that simple solutions will not help keeps us powerless. When we allow ourselves to act on the obvious, we free ourselves from limitations. The purpose of Applied Meditation is to bring knowledge from the universal realm into the particular issues of daily life; this requires acting on our own insights.

Intuitions, Thoughts, and Feelings

Intuitions, thoughts, and feelings are all different aspects of our experience, and it is good to be able to distinguish them. Beta thinking is intellectual, categorical, sequential, logical, and it judges in an either/or manner. Its messages are easy to recognize for they are never subtle, but always straightforward. Emotions are pushy; they always carry a charge— attachments, desires, aversions, "shoulds." When you find yourself with a message, and you want to be clear where it is coming from—whether intellectual, emotional, or intuitive—ask yourself questions like these: Is it critical? Does it establish an either/or category? Is it complicating? Does the answer have a lot of force? Is it pushy? Is it difficult to ignore (emotional)?

Intuition is never pushy. The messages it offers are always holistic—not logical or sequential. They are without conflict, subtle but clear, with no "shoulds"—they simply exist. Sometimes there is a felt sense that accompanies them, sometimes there is a knowing with no form. You will find that there is always a quality of knowing that accompanies an intuitive message. You can ignore them, but you can not argue with them. You can easily take them or as easily leave them. They are background awarenesses that create a sense of the whole. They are often the first impressions that come to mind, but in this society, the first to be discounted, for their knowing does not have reason attached to it. When you do not know why you know something, it is an intuition. With intuitions, you will have an unquestionable sense of knowing—it just feels right. Ask yourself how or why you know what you know; if you can not answer, then it is an intuition. With time, you will discover the particular way that your intuitive sense works. It is as though your intuitions whisper. In the spacious awareness of the Inner Witness, you can hear them. Unlike your intellect or your feelings, your intuition will rarely get you into trouble; instead it will almost always keep you out of trouble.

Meditation develops mindfulness by focusing on breath and bringing one into spacious awareness. There is a quality of detachment present. As mindfulness develops, you will find yourself easily seeing the origins of different inner messages, as well as recognizing insight as it arises. You will find that the Inner Witness becomes more and more present the more you meditate—not only accompanying you on your inner journeys, but in your life.

We have been conditioned to look for drama in our lives, so we expect it in our meditations. But inner consciousness is subtle, never forceful, and rarely dramatic, so people often conclude that they must not be meditating properly. Look for meditation's power not in how it feels when you are doing it, but instead, in the changes that begin to occur in your life. If you do not feel as though you are meditating correctly, pretend you are and go through the motions anyway. If you do, you will find that the changes begin to manifest themselves.

The more you meditate, the less distinct the different levels of awareness become. Going deep does not feel so deep any longer, and you also find yourself with more profound insights in regular waking awareness. This is because the inner passages have opened, and the movement of awareness from one level to another has become so smooth that it all feels like the same level. Another paradox about working with inner consciousness is that the more you meditate, the less you need to do so.

Induction

Focus on your breathing, breathing with your belly ... bring to your awareness your symbol for physical relaxation and allow the whole of your body to relax ... Let your body relax ... Relaxing more and more with each exhalation of breath ... Send your breath wherever it is needed ... Feel tension dissolving ... Feel yourself letting go into the support of the earth ... .

When you are ready, bring to your awareness your symbol for mental relaxation ... feel your mind relaxing ... becoming calm and quiet ... spacious, as spacious as the sky, ... Your thoughts, like puffy clouds, drift in and out of the sky of your mind, as easily as breath moving in and out ... .

When you are ready, bring in your symbol for emotional relaxation. Give yourself permission to emotionally relax ... Let go of any "shoulds," any feelings pushing or pulling at you. Breathe them out ... . Take a moment and offer yourself some loving kindness ... Feel your heart relax into its natural state of generosity and compassion ... Feel your heart open ... ...

Bring to awareness your symbol for your creative, self-restoring center ... Feel your gratitude to be alive ... Sense your whole being open ... You are

MEDITATIONS

in healing space, sacred space ... receptive ... creative ... mindful ... alert ... relaxed ... You are now centered at a stable level of inner consciousness where you find faculties and senses opening out far beyond those that you usually use in your waking awareness.

You are now consciously developing intuitive skills you have always had ... You are at your creative self-restoring center—the threshold between your inner and outer realities ... Here, you discover a rich, beautiful landscape of your receptivity and creativity ... you discover new dimensions of being, as you open, more and more of these energies flow through you ... Just as using your muscles keeps your body strong and resilient, working in your creative self-restoring center keeps your creative and intuitive powers clear and accessible ... Here, you experience the pure awareness of the Inner Witness ... you realize the calm expansive power of spacious awareness. Breathe, and rest in the quiet ... The Inner Witness rests in universal beingness ... Here, you experience yourself as part of the energy that permeates all life ... Here, you gain the wisdom to make this world a more harmonious place ... As you work with the Inner Witness, you find yourself with deep understanding of whatever it is you are focusing on ... Rest in the quiet of breath and knowing becomes apparent.

In a moment, I am going to count on a descending scale from ten to one; at each descending count, you will feel your awareness move deeper and deeper into your inner dimensions ...

TEN—moving down now ...

NINE—deeper and deeper ...

EIGHT—relaxing into yourself ...

SEVEN—returning to yourself ...

SIX—deeper and deeper ...

FIVE—moving deeper ...

FOUR—very aware and very alert ...

THREE—moving down ...

TWO—into your deeper dimensions ...

ONE!—deep in yourself ...

Here your imagination is extremely fluid and you can direct it where you choose ...

I'm going to suggest several affirmations ... If you wish to affirm them to yourself, repeat them to yourself after me and feel as though each affirmation is already fully true. As you speak the words to yourself, feel the power of the words. Let them evoke sensations and visions ... In doing so you will find yourself living in ways that conform to the affirmations.

I believe in myself ...

I trust my awareness ...

I am alert when I meditate ...

I can focus my attention wherever I choose, for as long as I choose ...

I am enriched by my deepest dimensions ...

I am fully present and mindful in each moment ...

I am curious and always learning ...

I am increasingly in attuned and responsive to my intuition ...

A spring of creativity continually flows through me and out into the world ...

My imagination is fluid and free ...

I remember my symbols when I need them and call them to awareness ...

Time is generous, I relax into the moment and it carries me ...

I am glad to offer my whole being good care ...

I cultivate a joyous heart ...

I celebrate belonging to the community of life ...

My increasing personal power is for making this world a more harmonious place to live for all beings ...

I am resilient; I maintain balance amidst change ...

I trust the future ...

Know that in focusing on affirmations, you align yourself with the affirmations on all levels and you will discover yourself acting in accord with them. Take a moment and breathe in gratitude as you inhale ... and breathe out compassion as you exhale ... Gratitude to be alive; compassion for all life ... ...

Now take time to focus on any of your own affirmations or symbols.

Stretching the Imagination

Imagine a piece of fruit. What kind is it? How ripe is it? What color is it? ... Imagine holding this piece of fruit in your hand ... Sense the texture of the skin, imagine the feel of it in your hand ... the size, the weight ... You may literally want to move your hand around as you imagine these things. It is as though you were literally holding that piece of fruit ... Feel its size ... its texture ... its temperature ... Imagine its weight, its consistency ... Imagine taking your fingernail and breaking the peel ... bring it up to your nose and imagine what it would smell like. Imagine if you were to squeeze the juice out of the fruit, what sound would that make? ... Imagine drinking the juice, what would it taste like? ... How would it make your mouth feel? ...

Know that your imagination is facile. To further explore the fluidity of inner consciousness we are going to experiment with body sensations ... Feel your body ... aware of the position your body is in ... Now imagine your body to be the

consistency of a stone ... a smooth stone that is at the bottom
of a stream bed ... Imagine water rushing over ... Feel your
body as though it were a stone on the bottom of a stream
bed ... How does it feel? ... Listen carefully, detect the
sound of the stream flowing ... Make it up ... imagine the
sensations, the sounds ... ...

Now let your body become the water rushing over the
stone ... fluid, moving, clear running water washing through ...
bringing out all the subtle colors of the stones below you ...
Imagine your body is the stream of water ... feel it, sense
it ... ...

A breeze caresses the stream above ... Sense it. Imagine
becoming the breeze dancing over the stream, over the
land ... The breeze, it goes everywhere ... Be the breeze, feel
yourself get bigger ... be the wind, you are the wind. It goes
everywhere caressing the land ... Feel the shape of the
landscape ... Listen to the sounds as you pass by ... You might
even find that you catch scents and carry them in your travels ...
...

Now notice the rays of the sun ... Let your body become the
rays of the sun. Feel it in your body, be it in your body ...
warmth, radiant light, brilliant fire ... Let your body be it ... ...

Now bring your usual body sensations back into your body ...
feeling your usual physical self ... Now, listen, listen to the
crackling of the fire ... listen to the blowing of the wind ... listen
to the gurgling of the stream ... listen to the crackling rocks as

they roll over one another where the stream moves very rapidly
... ...

Know that your imagination is extremely fluid, that your psychic
senses are very keen—the more you work with them, the
sharper they become ... Your inner awareness perceives the
deepest subtleties of reality ... As you work with your inner
senses they become more and more agile ... You are
increasingly able to direct your inner awareness as you choose
each time you meditate ... Know that all of this is so ...

Now, with your deep awareness you can witness the different
aspects of consciousness and discover their character. Your
intellect ... notice its ability to figure things out, notice its
ability to make distinctions ... Your emotions ... they are
always moving, full of color, full of desire or aversion ...
Your intuition ... it simply knows, it experiences patterns of
energy ... Your Inner Witness is the light of awareness ...
Spacious, present whenever you bring your attention to your
breath, your Inner Witness arises. Trust that in the quiet of
awareness, clarity is always evident.

Bring different issues in your life to awareness and witness what
you know about these issues ... Notice what you think and
what you feel with each issue as you bring it to awareness ...
Witness when different aspects of yourself are active, when you
respond to which ... ...

Engage your Active Imagination by envisioning positive
outcomes as though they are already memories; engage your

Receptive Imagination by conversing with any concern— personify it and talk to it. It gifts you with insight ... ...

Know that every time you meditate, you receive beneficial effects on all levels of your being ... That every time you meditate, your imagination becomes increasingly agile and your intuitive powers become more and more finely tuned. Know that each time you meditate, you increase your ability to navigate through the inner dimensions; you become increasingly able to maintain whatever level of awareness you choose, for as long as you choose. You are increasingly able to keep the Inner Witness present in all your meditation work ... Know that this is so.

Count Out

Finish what you are doing and make yourself ready to come out to outer conscious levels ... ...

Know you can return to these dimensions whenever you wish. You may want to project when you will again meditate ... In a moment, I'm going to count from one to five; at the count of five, you will open your eyes remembering all that you have experienced ... feeling refreshed, revitalized and relaxed ...

ONE—becoming more aware of the room around you ...

TWO—coming up slowly now ...

THREE—at the count of five, you will open your eyes feeling relaxed, revitalized, and refreshed, remembering all that you have experienced ...

FOUR—coming up now, bringing with you your sense of well-being ...

FIVE!—eyes open, feeling refreshed, revitalized, and relaxed, remembering all you have experienced ... having brought with you your sense of wholeness—open heart and spirit ...

•5•

It Is All Energy

When I did the psychic case reading described in Chapter 1, it was an awe-inspiring experience. It meant that I was no longer a separate entity moving through the world, but that in a mysterious way, I was somehow intimately connected to everything. I have never been a religious person. I was raised in an academic home, but for me this was a religious experience. It revealed that we are all a part of a cosmic whole. Consciousness suddenly lit up with magic!

My consciousness was infinitely more than I had ever imagined. Until then, I had always taken my own awareness for granted and paid attention only to the external world. It all turned around. Suddenly, my imagination was as real as the ground I stood on. If I could know details about someone by simply directing my imagination, there was much more to the intricacies of the universe than I had ever been taught. Though impossible to adequately express in words, the experience taught me that somehow each of us is held by the web of life—as though there is an invisible energy that connects all that exists. And consciousness itself is mysteriously entwined with this energy.

The scientific era has taught us to clearly separate the subjective and objective, the mind/body, the personal and political, spirit and matter, heaven and earth, and God and everything else. Western rationalism has taken the life, the soul, out of everything. Before the onslaught of dualism, most inhabitants of the world experienced it as charged with spirit—everything possessed consciousness and was part of a living whole. The scientific revolution ushered in a new viewpoint: the world is made up of separate inanimate parts that together make a vast machine of matter and motion obeying mathematical laws. Science has succeeded in separating us from the whole and convincing us to view the objective as inert—in other words, dead. Not only have we lost our place in the world, the world itself has died and has therefore become exploitable. This is the beginning of alienation. As Fritjof Capra describes:

> To Descartes the material universe was a machine and nothing but a machine. There was no purpose, life, or spirituality in matter. Nature worked according to mechanical laws, and everything in the material world could be explained in terms of the arrangement and movement of its parts. This mechanical picture of nature became the dominant paradigm of science in the period following Descartes. It guided all scientific observation and the formulation of all theories of natural phenomena.
>
> The drastic change in the image of nature from organism to machine had a strong effect on people's attitudes toward the natural environment. Implicit in the organic world view of the Middle Ages was a value system conducive to ecological behavior. In the words of Carolyn Merchant: "The image of the earth as a living organism and nurturing mother served as a cultural constraint restricting the actions of human beings. One does not readily slay a mother, dig into her entrails for gold, or mutilate her body .... As long as the earth was considered to be alive and sensitive; it could be considered a breach of human ethical behavior to carry out destructive acts against it."[1]

All That Exists Is Alive

Western culture views women as being closer to nature. Women are "naturally" emotional and intuitive; men (Western "white" men) are more rational. (In racist consciousness, the darker one's skin color, the closer to nature one is assumed to be.) The primacy of human over nature, male over female, and white over color have been images that have allowed the exploitation of nature, as well as exploitation of women and people of color.[2]

The scientific method studies nature and teaches us not to trust our own nature. To know is, by definition, not to feel and not to be involved, for feelings cloud issues and make them immeasurable. Scientific methodology has primarily dealt with that which is quantifiable or measurable. The degree to which the human element enters into the experiment is the same degree to which it is invalidated. Science holds a monopoly on knowledge. Therefore, by definition, knowledge resides outside of us. If knowledge is exclusively attained externally, that effectively restricts us from the vast knowledge to which consciousness has direct access.

Distrusting our own knowledge, we find ourselves dependent on the "authorities." Only experiments reveal the "facts," not direct experience. How often do we discount ourselves for not being "objective"? Our experience is suspect until it is scientifically substantiated.

Western rationalism teaches us to believe only that which has been proven—never trust the obvious. Consequently, we are taught to be suspicious of our own experience. After five hundred years of Western rationalism, most of us in the modern world have fully internalized this. When people do psychic readings in my Applied Meditation training, they often discount the most accurate pieces of information. Remember, they are given only the name, age, and location of the person to which they are to tune. They have no basis upon which to judge what is accurate and what is not. On one occasion, I was giving one of the participants named Joe a case of a man who was paraplegic. Joe kept saying he was not getting anything. I told him to make it up. Eventually he said that he saw a man sitting in a wheelchair, who he did not think could walk. When Joe was done, he opened his eyes, and I informed him that the individual he had read was paralyzed from the waist down as a result of a fall from a roof. Joe's jaw dropped. He said that the moment he heard the name of the person he saw a fleeting image of a person falling in midair. He had dismissed the image immediately.

These spontaneous impressions, the ones that appear instantaneously, are always the clearest and the most frequently dismissed. There are profound implications if the moments in which we are most tuned to the truth are the very times when we discount our awareness. There is nothing more fundamental to giving up one's personal power than not to trust one's own awareness.

It's not that we should discount what science has discovered over the centuries. Rather we should be very clear that it is not the sole purveyor of truth or that rational thinking covers the whole of human knowledge. There have always been holistic currents in science; over the last few decades they have re-emerged as physicists, biologists, neuroscientists and philosophers are bringing science back into the cosmic whole. As Fritjof Capra relays:

> Physics has gone through several conceptual revolutions that clearly reveal the limitations of the mechanistic world view and lead to an organic, ecological view of the world which shows great similarities to the views of mystics of all ages and traditions. The universe is no longer seen as a machine ... but appears as a harmonious indivisible whole; a network of dynamic relationships that include the human observer and his or her consciousness in an essential way.[3]

It is not only inner consciousness that functions in simultaneous patterns, but the very building blocks of the material world also seem to do so. Gary Zukav describes:

> The distinction between organic and inorganic is a conceptual prejudice. It becomes even harder to maintain as we advance into quantum mechanics. Something is organic, according to our definition, if it can respond to processed information. The astounding discovery awaiting newcomers to physics is that the evidence gathered in the development of quantum mechanics indicates that subatomic "particles" constantly appear to be making decisions! More than that, the decisions they seem to make are based on decisions made elsewhere. Subatomic particles seem to know instantaneously what decisions are made elsewhere, and elsewhere can be as far away as another galaxy![4]

Not only does matter (i.e., atomic particles) appear to have consciousness, but in addition, our consciousness seems to be connected to theirs. Objectivity itself is discovered to be fluid and contextual, in agreement with what many mystics have said for millennia: there is no separateness in reality. Capra explains:

> The crucial feature of quantum theory is that the observer is not only necessary to observe the properties of an atomic phenomenon, but is necessary even to bring about these properties. My conscious decision about how to observe, say, an electron will determine the electron's properties to some extent. If I ask it a particle question, it will give me a particle answer; if I ask it a wave question, it will give me a wave answer. The electron does not have objective properties independent of my mind. In atomic physics the sharp Cartesian division between mind and matter, between the

observer and the observed, can no longer be maintained. We can never speak about nature without, at the same time, speaking about ourselves.[5]

This dualistic objective worldview has trained us to ignore aspects of reality that have seeped into the scientific laboratory where there are experiments with results that fully defy the classic materialist explanation. We are now told that the very building blocks of matter—the atoms—have no separate objective reality. It can no longer be an issue of linear cause and effect when separate subatomic, atomic, and molecular particles respond to one another instantaneously.[6] Quantum physicists refer to these connections as "nonlocal." They are unmediated, unmitigated, and immediate. In these circumstances, there is no medium carrying a message; that distance does not diminish the effect and effects are simultaneous. There are several approaches to investigating the impact of nonlocality in human experience. All point to an underlying web of connection that binds us together.

Here is a case in point: Edgar Mitchell, the sixth astronaut to land on the moon, conducted an ESP experiment in space with his friend Joseph Rhine, a pioneer researcher in parapsychology. Mitchell attempted to telepathically transmit a particular sequence of symbols (a circle, a cross, a star, or a pair of parallel squiggly lines) to six colleagues. The correlation between what he focused on and what his colleagues "got" calculated out to a one in 3000 chance![7]

Larry Dossey, a medical doctor who has investigated the power of consciousness and prayer for many years, coined the term "nonlocal mind." He describes many double-blind studies that have been conducted to assess if prayer or mental intentionality from a distance makes a difference in healing. In a wide variety of investigations, ranging from healing wounds to impacts on plant growth and from improving heart conditions to AIDS, numerous studies have now shown beyond a doubt that prayer and intention can have a positive impact on health and healing.

He further reports that even nonhuman consciousness affects the material world, as an extensive series of experiments conducted in France with baby chicks demonstrate. Chicks imprint on their mother and follow her around wherever she goes. They can also imprint on anything that moves near them after they hatch. For this study, chicks were imprinted on a robot that had been programmed to move randomly in an enclosed space. The chicks loyally followed the robot wherever it went. Then the investigator separated the robot from the chicks with a glass wall. The chicks could see the robot but could no longer follow it throughout the whole space. Now that they were separated, the robot, though still programmed to move randomly, spent two and a half times longer in the area by the wall, as close to the chicks as it could get. When chicks that had not been imprinted were placed behind the glass instead, both they and the robot exhibited fully random behavior. Eighty groups of fifteen chicks each were tested; in each case, researchers duplicated the original results.[8]

Psychokinesis is the term used for the direct influence of mind on matter. Research by Gellor, Mikhailova, and Kulagina has shown that objects can be moved simply with the power of mental concentration.[9] Princeton Engineering Anomalies Research (PEAR) studied psychokinesis for more than twenty years using random events generators (REGs). PEAR has established, through literally millions of tests, that the REG responds to mental intentions of operators and that it does not matter how close the person applying intent is to the generator.[10] What is particularly fascinating is that people or whole groups who have emotional bonds have even more of an effect than an individual does.

PEAR also placed thirty-seven REGs around the world—think of it as an EEG monitor for the world. These machines registered more variance away from randomness than any other time in their history when the planes struck into the World Trade Center. It is also interesting to note that New Yorkers seem to make their own REG. A year later, on September 11, 2002, the winning lottery number in New York State was 9-1-1! More than five thousand New Yorkers won.[11]

There have been numerous experiments investigating Extra Sensory Perception (ESP) in which the subjects were asked in advance whether it existed. Those who said they believed in ESP scored better than chance; those who were not sure scored statistically equal to chance. Most interesting is that those who said there was no such thing as ESP scored *below* chance! Not only are our behavior and our bodies loyal to our beliefs, our intuition is too![12]

One of the most active areas of research in the past twenty-five years has been what has come to be called "remote viewing," which is acquiring information about a person, place, or event distant in time or space when the viewer has no prior knowledge of the subject under investigation—similar to doing the "case readings" I have spoken about. There is extensive documentation of individual remote viewers finding lost people or things and also of their making accurate maps of locations they had never seen.[13] The CIA pursued both research and intelligence activities using remote viewing for more than two decades. The most famous program, called Stargate, yielded spectacular results, ranging from locating aircraft that had crashed to finding kidnapped hostages.[14]

All of these occurrences necessitate rearranging the secular materialist way we view the universe. It is only because of our narrow frame of reference that we define such occurrences as paranormal.[15] The impacts affect what one perceives and what happens in the external world. We are all part of a whole, and consciousness itself is a participant in what occurs—not simply reflective and responsive—a participant in the creation of the phenomenon.

Inner and Outer Realms Dance Together

The Silva Method teaches the power of positive thinking—if you want something, all you need to do is imagine it, and it will manifest, whether it is a parking place, an apartment, a partner, or a job. After I discovered the powers of my imagination—its ability to receive information—I was inspired to experiment and see what other powers it might have. "Coincidences" suddenly became a daily experience. All kinds of things started manifesting themselves in my life after I had projected them with my imagination. I did not understand how or why it was working, but my experience showed me that it did, indeed, work. It was as if the world, up until that point, was out of sync—everything was random. When I began taking responsibility for the contents of my imagination and deliberately setting intention, everything moved in synchrony. Random events ceased to occur and coincidence was suddenly filled with significance. I like Carl Jung's term "synchronicity," a causal, meaningful coincidence. His illustration:

> A young woman I was treating had, at a critical moment, a dream in which she was given a golden scarab. While she was telling me this dream, I sat with my back to the closed window. Suddenly, I heard a noise behind me, like a gentle tapping. I turned round and saw a flying insect knocking against the windowpane from outside. I opened the window and caught the creature in the air as it flew in. It was the nearest analogy to a golden scarab that one finds in our latitudes, which, contrary to its usual habits, had evidently felt an urge to get into a dark room at this particular moment.[16]

These "coincidences" and events are a part of our everyday experience, yet have been pushed aside or ignored by mainstream society. When we stop dismissing these phenomena, life takes on a glow with magic.[17] Objectively, consciousness permeates the material world, affecting which ones of the myriad possibilities transpire. Subjectively, the material world permeates our consciousness in multiple ways. The vocabulary of the imagination is composed of past memories. This limits the possibilities one can imagine— what is conceivable. Anticipation prefigures the future; that is, what you anticipate paves the path for your actions and what you meet on the path. Also, intuition is perpetually present. It shapes how we imagine what we imagine. Matter affects mind; mind affects matter. The whole lives both subjectively and objectively.

We are all part of a great and mysterious co-arising. Joanna Macy explains this Buddhist concept:

> Things do not produce each other or make each other happen, as in linear causality; they help each other happen by providing occasion or locus or context, and in so doing, they in turn are affected. There is mutuality here, a reciprocal dynamic.[18]

We can consciously participate in this process.

Most indigenous cultures view people inside the whole— working with the connections. Rationalism patronizingly views their rituals as "primitive." Yet these rituals express a different way of knowing and being in the world. Often events seen as paranormal or fake by academics in the scientific traditions are well known in the oral cultures. When I was a child, I went to many Pueblo rain dances in New Mexico where, by the end of the day, rain usually came down upon us all—often the first rain for many weeks.[19]

There are many stories that parallel my experience.

> "In 1992, the Hopi elders visited the United Nations, and there was a lunar eclipse the night after their presentation. Torrential rain and flooding occurred in New York City. The

storm abated after the Hopi elders created a circle of prayer."[20]

Our imagination affects what happens to us, whether we choose to participate in the process or not. Consciousness is always interacting with the environment. I think of it as magnetic energy being attracted to particular probabilities while repelling others. The law of this phenomenon is the attraction of opposites within the unity of opposites—energies that resonate with each other attract one another. Kammerer tells us, "We thus arrive at the image of a world mosaic or cosmic kaleidoscope, which, in spite of constant shufflings and rearrangements also takes care of bringing like and like together."[21] When I refer to thoughts and attitudes, I mean a material force affecting the environment.

This can often be seen if you look into your past; you will notice how events happen in clustered sequences. Seemingly unrelated positive events congregate together, and so too the opposite, difficult incidents happen together. You could call them streaks of good or bad luck. It is true except that luck is by definition something operating by chance, randomly disconnected from ourselves. The energy you exude is an ingredient in causing these "random" circumstances to occur.

I no longer believe that there is such a thing as chance. Instead there is a coherence in all that exists. Things occur out of the coalescence of energies. We always hear, "What goes around, comes around," "As within, so without," "As you sow, so shall you reap." The day you are in a bad mood is the day your car gets sideswiped while parked and the plumbing gets clogged, and likewise, the day you are feeling good you get offered a promotion and a dear friend you have not seen in years unexpectedly arrives in town. I am not saying your moods created these events, but that it is part of the whole— it is likely that part of you was aware of these probabilities, and therefore you were in a good mood. What you expect is not only determined by your past experience, but is also shaped by the fact that consciousness is perpetually attuned to—and entwined with—what is taking place objectively. *In an elegant dance, the subjective and objective continually mirror one another.*

Synchronous events frequently occur as puns. A friend of mine recently expressed how tired he felt using the term "deflated"; he got two flat tires that week. Any residual skepticism I had on this subject evaporated as I was read *The Seth Material,* the first book in a series by Jane Roberts. This book was the first material I had read that enabled me to understand rationally why I could imagine something and then it would occur. While reading it, I said to several friends, "This book has been turning my idea of reality upside down!" After reading the first book, I was anxious to get the second, *Seth Speaks.* Many people apparently were going through the same process as I was, because I went to numerous bookstores only to discover they had all just sold out. Returning home, I called a number of other stores and finally found one that had one copy left. I asked that they hold it for me. When I picked it up, I discovered that this copy's cover had been bound upside down!

A woman in one of my classes said that when she was younger, her life was full of what she had always thought were coincidences, but they all stopped when she took the advice, "Do not expect anything, you will not be disappointed." For the first time, she understood why the coincidences had disappeared. Now she was delighted to cultivate positive expectations again. Yet we allow ourselves to worry, having no idea that our fretting is adding to the likelihood that the very things we fear most will occur. It is time we turn it around.

Religious traditions conclude that prayers work. If you have faith, your prayers will be answered. *I think this means that you do not always get what you want, but you do get what you expect*. Wherever your attention is focusing, wherever your imagination goes, and whatever you anticipate is all a feeding power of probabilities. *It is as though affinity is the way of the universe; there is a marvelous coherence in all that is.* Consciousness en masse creates a sea of probabilities in a great cosmic arising. It seems to me that the largest concentrations of energy dictate what probabilities materialize. If we know that this is true, we can participate by taking responsibility for energies we exude. We can set intention, thereby decreasing the likelihood of discordant events occurring and increasing the likelihood of positive events occurring. Participating in the world of probabilities is sacred work and a gift the universe offers.

Cultivating Faith

People say getting what we expect is a self-fulfilling prophecy. That statement is true, but it is time we stop being victims and realize that we can be prophets. Great amounts of energy lie in deeper levels of awareness where more focused and concentrated consciousness resides. When we direct our imagination while meditating, it has much more potency than in our usual waking consciousness. We can choose where to focus it, thereby increasing our influence on what happens in the world around us.

Your primary focus should be on what your desired outcome would be like. You should not deny negative circumstances that you may find yourself in; at the same time you should expect change to occur in spite of them. When any dissatisfaction comes to mind, open to the lesson embedded in your experience, and then always have your last image be one of movement toward a positive reality.

Do not try to prove that your projections are working by watching to see if the problem has begun to dissolve. This puts focus on the problem and perpetuates it. Assume energy is working under the surface whether you experience it yet or not. Set clear intention, focus on the projection, and then let it go to do its work. A couple of years after I had begun working with inner consciousness, I had an experience that taught me how to hold a positive intention while in the midst of challenging circumstances. As it often does for many of us, my problem boiled down to economics. At the time, I was making a living doing odd jobs. I spent many of my waking hours worried about how I was going to pay the rent; I spent many of my meditative minutes imagining money manifesting. The fact that I did not know how I was going to pay the rent was entirely more real and had a lot more energy connected to it than all my imaginings of money did. Whenever I finished meditating, I still had to face the reality of my bills.

Then one day in meditation it came to me: I was focusing more on the problem—the bills—than on the solution—income. Having more money simply was not believable in the face of all those bills. I had to make it believable, so I changed my tactics. I decided that I needed three things: to get out of debt, to have a functional car, and to be able to focus on developing Applied Meditation. I then projected for this to occur within six months. This way what I was currently experiencing did not contradict the possibility of change. I was building faith in the solution emerging.

I created three images symbolizing this: I imagined taking my friend out to dinner in celebration of paying her all that I owed, I also imagined myself happily driving my fixed car, and finally, I saw myself saying "no" to a job prospect because it interfered with my focus on Applied Meditation. Given my lifestyle, it was fully plausible that in six months all of this could be true. I did not know how it would come about, but I just assumed it would. This released me from the trap of seeing my current situation as a reflection of my failed projection. I did not need to compare my projection with my current situation. In the ensuing months, while meditating I would momentarily picture each of these images. It was not hard; after a while I meditated on these images less often as other concerns became more prominent. After about four months, I had stopped focusing on them altogether.

Exactly six months later—not a week early, not a week late—it all came to pass. (Had I not been keeping a journal of my meditation practice, I would have lost the connection between my projection and what unfolded, losing the opportunity to qualitatively deepen my faith.) I was in the process of rebuilding my car's engine. I had visualized finding a newer Volkswagen bus with a blown-up engine for sale for $200 into which I could install my rebuilt engine. Time had run out and my mechanic was going to put it back into my old car. The day before this was supposed to happen, I found just what I was looking for—a Volkswagen bus with a blown-up engine for sale for $200!

If that was not magical enough, the engine in the newer bus turned out to be perfectly functional. Coincidentally, the oil light malfunctioned and lit up at the same time that the bus ran out of gas. The previous owner assumed that the engine had blown up. I happily put that bus's engine into my old car and the new motor into the newer bus. At this point I had two running automobiles. Now, another coincidence: the friend to whom I owed money happened to be in the market for a car. I gave her my old car, which was worth more than the original debt, so she gave an additional $300 to the previous owner of the bus. In the end, everybody was happy. All that I had asked for had come to pass: I had a functional car, I was out of debt, and that was the first week that I began teaching Applied Meditation.

As is usually the case when projecting what you want, events occurred in surprising ways. I did not spend hours in meditation. Whenever frustrations arose, I would bring to mind the three images of the resolved issue. I would assume that underneath, positive energy was at work. Each of the symbols was meaningful, plausible, and easy to imagine. The projections of the Active Imagination are part, but not all, of the process. You also have to act on the energy. It does not just come to you; you have got to meet it halfway. If I hadn't been actively looking for a bus, I would never have been told about the one I found.

It seems to me that energizing realities with the Active Imagination does two things: it creates or empowers the probability, and it also sensitizes you to knowing intuitively what directions to follow to bring it about. Your projection becomes a North Star. Do not get caught in the details of your imaginings. Work with them in order to generate energy. The details are just a way for you to engage your imagination and get a *feel* for your desired experience. Release the particular details that you conjure; it is your intentions and expectations that matter. The universe is much more creative than we are. I could not have put together such an unfolding of circumstances in my wildest dreams!

Imagination is a two-way street—it is not only the stuff of which probabilities are made, but is also the medium through which you receive information. With the Active Imagination, you not only breathe life into probabilities, but you also familiarize yourself with those that already exist, psychically attuning yourself to them. Not only is the environment responding to you, you are responding to it, moving into sync with each other.

For example, if you are projecting to find a parking place, you will intuitively make the correct turns while driving to discover it. Your imagination is also a receiver of information. You did not create the parking place; you became attuned to it. It is as though setting clear intention creates magnetic headlights. You both attract and are attracted to that which has affinity with your projection.

Finding a Positive Orientation

We get what we expect; the trick is to expect what we want. *Wishful thinking and expectations bring opposite results.* The difference is that a wish rests on the assumption that it is beyond possibility, like the cow looking over the fence at the greener pastures, whereas an expectation assumes a desire will unfold—no fences are present. The catch-22 is that the very issues with which you would like to have a more positive experience are the same ones in which your experience shows you otherwise. It is tricky; you do not want to go into denial. That will only compound your problems, because denial blocks energy flow. It is essential to cultivate a positive vision.

Inner messages are the source of our behavior. *If negative images are all that you have about a concern then you will find yourself replicating the very experience from which you want to free yourself.* Without a vision, you have no alternative resources from which to draw, and your intuition has nothing to align with or orient you toward.

When you notice you are feeling unhappy with your situation, ask yourself what you want. On any important issue, if you have no plausible and positive vision, then you need to find new possibilities that open your imagination.

You can use several different strategies to find positive points of reference. One strategy is to ask yourself what would be the opposite state of affairs. For instance, if you are trying to overcome shyness, then feeling relaxed and communicative with strangers is likely to be desirable. Then stretch your imagination and pretend this is your experience. Adjust your projection until you find one that is desirable and plausible. At this point, you have a new vision to affirm and energize.

Another way to find a positive reference point is to think of something at which you excel and imagine bringing that sense of confidence into the area you are working on transforming.

For example, if you are a talented sculptor, imagine yourself feeling inspired, satisfied by your work, and confident that you accomplished what you set out to complete. Take this quality of confidence and imagine embodying it when you are meeting new people. This will take some practice, but you will find that eventually you will be able to imagine the new way of being. Imagining a role model is also helpful. Witness the qualities that this person portrays, and then pretend that you embody these same qualities. As your subjective experience changes, so too will your objective experience.

It is also good to do some research to find positive reference points with which you can work. For example, if you want a relaxed relationship with your children ask your friends to tell you about an outstanding moment when they felt especially close with their child or a time they overcame a difficult situation together. You can also hear a story about an exemplary parent that they know. When you are inquiring about the outstanding moment they or someone else had with their child, be careful that you do not commiserate with each other about things that are not working; this only reinforces your sense of lack. And you do not want philosophy either, you want descriptions of what works. You want to hear only shining examples. Be inquiring and gather the details of what happened. How did it feel? What made the situation so positive for them? It is these details that open the imagination and give a feel for what could be your reality. This process expands the repertoire of your imagination, and you will find yourself inspired with possibility. Your Active Imagination will then have a rich store of resources from which to create new experience. Envision a desirable scenario with your children; then step into the vision and feel what life is like from that position.

There are a variety of ways you can apply a positive reference point. A student of mine once got into a tiff with her boss. As a consequence, her job was on the line, and she was very distraught. She found herself staring at a picture of a holy man with flowers in his hair. This picture always made her happy. She began to imagine the holy man superimposed over her boss's face, and her boss became holy to her. She meditated on this for a week. The next time she saw her boss, she felt love toward her and acted accordingly. With her hostility gone, their relationship was comfortable, and my student retained her job.

Your beta consciousness is likely to think all of these exercises foolish. However, inner consciousness is suggestible and it, not beta, is the source of behavior. What you are searching for are positive points of reference. When you find a positive orientation, you will no longer be stuck with an unsatisfactory experience and instead be able to orient in a positive direction. A shift will take place both subjectively and objectively.

Nothing new comes about without having imagined it first. (If none of the above methods provide a plausible vision, then you will need to use your Receptive Imagination to discover a way through the situation. See Chapter Eight.)

When you work with the Active Imagination, be simple and specific in your projection. This will enable you to experience the sensations and feelings associated with what you want. Well-being does not happen in a void, it happens in a context. It is a result of specific conditions. To feel good, you need to imagine what would bring about the feelings. Perhaps living in a new space will make you happy; imagine what it feels like to already be living there. Use the story-making capacities of your imagination. Conjure the vision and step into it—see it, feel it, and even smell it. Be in the vision as though it is your experience. Breathe life into the vision. Imagine looking back on living in the new space as though it were full of memories. How has your life transformed since you moved in? Create all of this in full living detail.

It works energetically; it is not logical. When you work with the Active Imagination, you do not need to worry about how, why, where, or when something is going to occur. All you need to do is feel as if it has already occurred. Endeavor to take it for granted, just as you do with your memories. As a result you will both project the quality of energy that attracts what you want, and you will intuitively move in the right direction. It is as though you have created both an internal compass and a magnet. Your intention is set.

Always be specific, simple, and positive in your projections. Be clear about what your goal is and how it feels to have attained it. Strive to imagine how it would feel, look, sound and even smell. The more detail you offer your projection, the more energy it carries. If you have confusion associated with it, the power of the projection is diminished proportionately. Likewise, the more you expect your goal to manifest, the more likely it will. The process works proportionately to your faith. It is good to begin with small issues; they are easier to characterize and not clouded by disbelief. If you start in an area you consider trivial, you will not be as likely to have feelings that obscure the issue. You still want something that is possible (it is okay if it is unlikely, but it needs to be possible). The clearer you are, the more it will work. The more it works, the more you believe it is going to work the next time. *Faith comes from experience.* As you cultivate faith with small successes, you can take on bigger issues. Start with parking places and bus connections, and then slowly work up to the issues that really make a difference. It is the faith in its working that makes it work.

The Inner Witness Sheds Light on Your Projections

The irony is that, although the imagination is seen as unreal, we are supposed to be able to imagine anything. You can think anything you want, but to imagine it clearly is another matter. To illustrate, imagine grasping the doorknob on your front door, imagine turning it, and then pulling the door open. You probably never bothered to imagine this but the point is, if you did, it would be no trouble. Now try imagining what it is like to be free of an allergy you have had your whole life. Clearly imagining yourself liberated from a life-long issue is not so simple.

There are both external and internal limitations that prevent you from being able to imagine whatever you want. On one hand, your imagination is psychically attuned to what is possible—the environment may not yet contain the possibility of your desire. On the other hand, your past experiences are the raw materials your imagination uses to cook new meals. If there is no flour in the pantry, it will place severe limitations on the bread you bake. Someone who has lived in poverty all her life is unlikely to imagine what it would feel like to be economically secure. She knows only what it is like to wish for it, which is quite a different matter.*

Working with your Active Imagination in the presence of the Inner Witness will enable you to inspect your projections closely. Doing so illuminates what is needed. Being mindful will enable you to notice just what you can and what you currently cannot imagine. You will discover the specific ways your projections may fall short of what you desire or if what you desire is somehow just not plausible. At this point, you can employ your Receptive Imagination to discover what will bridge the gap. This is where deep transformation occurs.

---

*In this chapter we are addressing the dynamics of individual energy projection and do not mean to imply that the solution to our economic malaise resides in the way we each project our imaginations. This is a social issue and will be addressed in Chapter Ten.

Be mindful that striving to be positive does not mean denying any of the challenges life presents. When you engage the Inner Witness, you will notice the quality of energy present in your subjective landscape. That is, you will notice when you are open or if you are constricting and withdrawing from life's offerings; and you will also notice when you can imagine something and when you cannot. *With Applied Meditation what you cannot imagine points to where you most need to focus your attention.*

Because the inner consciousness is quite literal, it is crucial that you inspect your projections to ensure that you are ready for them to occur. Make your projections detailed enough that you can experience the whole of their implications. Step into the vision. Use your childlike faculties of make believe and discover what the projection would actually be like. The Inner Witness will reveal if these projections will really increase well-being or if there are aspects that need to be adjusted.

In the presence of the Inner Witness, it is important that you extend your awareness to include others. How do they feel about the projection? This will give you invaluable information, revealing if adjustments are needed not only for you, but for others too.

The Ethics of Applied Meditation

This is sacred work and not to be applied lightly. There are great powers in these dimensions; power, of whatever kind, always needs to be approached with humility and applied ethically. When making a projection that involves others, do so with the intention that it will only occur if it is desirable for all concerned, and further, that it benefits the planet itself. Listen deeply. Doing so will serve to bring us into deep intimacy with those we share our lives with. When we all do this, we create community that holds us all as sacred.

Be humble, and be aware that you do not necessarily know what is best. Projections are always loyal to the intention in which they were created. Intention establishes the groove through which the energy moves. Be mindful; notice your motivation. *Think of your projections as offerings to the universe, not demands—suggestions not requirements.* Never put forward anything with an investment in the outcome, or feeling that your way is the only way.

With the Inner Witness present, you will be able to make projections with an open attitude. In openness, projections move us toward wholeness. If you are mindful, attachment recedes and generosity emerges.

The work of the Active Imagination is to establish clear intention, make specific projections, focus on them regularly, and release them. If you are too invested in a particular outcome, you will not be able to avail yourself of intuitive information, which only causes trouble. Avoid feeling that your way is the only way; you do not want to approach a situation with the motive of controlling it. You want to take the attitude that the best outcome will manifest.

You want to target your projection with humility. This means that you will need to be specific enough that you generate feelings in the process of conjuring. However, you do not want to impose your agenda on others. A very interesting study sheds light on this conundrum.

Biologist Glen Rein wanted to test for the most effective strategy of inhibiting the growth of cancer cells when using directed intention. He recruited a healer named Leonard Laskow. Rein prepared petri dishes with the same number of cancer cells in each. Laskow used a number of specific strategies in focusing intention as he held each dish. His first intention was that the natural order be reinstated and the cell's growth rate return to normal. With the next, he used a Taoist visualization that calls for imagining only three cancer cells surviving. For the third, he offered unconditional love and compassion to the cancer cells, then he also visualized the cells "dematerializing and going into the light." He also combined some of these with one another. The most powerful (nearly twice as effective) was asking the cells to return to the natural order in combination with the vision of only three cancer cells remaining. This one inhibited the growth by 40 percent. It seems that being specific and open to the universe's version of natural order simultaneously is the best way to go.[22]

You do not want your ego to employ these powers. Its view is too narrow, and it will only cause problems for both you and others. This work is about coming to live in reverence with one another and the earth, not about getting what you want. In a culture of generosity, we will not turn to the greedy aspect of ourselves. Working with these energies with a loving heart secures not only our personal futures, but also the world's future.

It is important to remember that our individual imagination is a material force affecting the environment, but we live with others who, needless to say, also have imaginations. Your individual imagination does not create reality; it simply interacts with it. When you work with your Active Imagination, you strengthen the probabilities on which you focus. If there are more people imagining otherwise, it will not occur.

The world of probabilities is not private, but shared. Channeling energy by focusing on positive outcomes for those in challenging situations will offer added support where it is needed and will enable us all to reclaim the experience of being embedded in a larger reality in which we are interdependent participants in the co-arising realities we share.

Conscientious Consciousness

We get what we expect, not necessarily what we want. For example, as women we have been taught to experience ourselves as vulnerable and weak, expecting to be overpowered and needing protection. I know that this is the last feeling I should have when I walk in the streets. I do not blame myself for feeling vulnerable. There are good reasons for my feelings, but I know that vulnerability is the energy that will draw an assailant. (Remember the unity of opposites: energies that resonate with each other attract one another.) Therefore, whenever I feel vulnerable, I notice the feeling, and do whatever I need to do to feel powerful—whether that be exploring and transforming my worries, learning self-defense, or being with friends—but I never allow myself to go into the street alone if I feel insecure.

When you care about something, it is only natural to have some worries. Worries are a double jeopardy—you are already troubled, and now you realize that the concerns themselves are adding to the likelihood that what you fear most will actually happen. Most people want to know whether their worries come from their own emotional limitations or from their intuitive awareness. The boundaries between objective and subjective dissolve when working with Applied Meditation. That is not the issue; the worry does not live either inside or outside. The very fact that you are imagining it means it is a probability. Denial further compounds the situation.

With inner consciousness, worries can be transformed into messengers who carry the specific information you need to heed. Worries become a gift if you let your imagination give shape to your anxieties and witness their unfolding. With the Inner Witness, you can look closely at the scene you are afraid might come to pass. It might take you a while to be able to do this, because tension is likely to arise and squeeze out the presence of the Inner Witness. If this happens, remember to focus on your breath and breathe through the tension. Eventually you will be able to maintain spacious awareness and be able to closely inspect your projection. You want to get to know the details of the scene: the atmosphere, the place, the weather, the people involved, and what everyone is doing. The Inner Witness does not get tangled in worries, so it can see the nuances of your imaginings. You will want to use your Receptive Imagination to gain further insights and your Active Imagination to change the scenes into more positive scenarios. This will both shift the operative energy and point to strategies on which you can act in your life. Here it is crucial to witness what seems plausible, as well as to notice if the images keep reverting back to your initial worry. Keep working with both your Active and Receptive Imagination until you find a scene that feels good to you. This process will reveal exactly what can be done or what needs to be avoided so that your worry cannot manifest.

If your imaginary scene continues to revert to the worrisome one, take it as a warning, and be cautious about the situation. On the objective level, you want to ensure that the particular ingredients of your worries never have a chance to assemble themselves. As opposed to what some may believe, working with the Inner Witness and the imagination takes you into reality, not away from it. With mindfulness and intuition, you have a choice. Do not dwell on your worries, but take them as messages and attend to them. If you have changed the problem, but still have a little residual negativity hanging around, you will want to transform it.

Mental Housecleaning

The most powerful method I have discovered for transforming negativity is what I call Mental Housecleaning. It resolves the dilemma of needing to have a positive orientation, but at the same time not wanting to get caught in denial of negative experience. Years ago, I was teaching a class with a friend, and we were not getting along, making it difficult to do a good job. I could not rationally decide what to do. I tried a problem-solving method which I had learned from the Silva Training called "The Glass of Water Technique." After using it the next time I meditated, a fountain appeared. It was not an off-the-wall image that often appears while meditating; I knew exactly what it meant. I proceeded to place an image of my friend in the fountain to be cleansed by the water springing up through the base. As I imagined all this, I was not struck by anything specific; it just felt like a story I had made up. It was not like a lighting bolt struck and everything changed dramatically. But in the aftermath, every time I was with my friend, our interactions were relaxed and easy. Using the Mental Housecleaning device had cleared a space in my consciousness and made new perspectives possible. It was a symbolic gesture inviting my deeper levels to transform, loosening my entrenched position and providing space for new experience.

Inner consciousness takes things quite literally. When you create a Mental Housecleaning device, imagine a process that transforms energy and does not simply store it—for example, use burning with a fire, composting, or feeding your concern to a fly-eating plant. You might simply drop the energy into the ground to be transformed in soil. Always use the same imaginary process, and your inner consciousness will come to recognize your intent. The beta mind is likely to spew multiple discounts to your efforts. Use your device anyway—the discounts of beta will not have power. Your alpha level is suggestible and will respond to symbolic messages, and it is your deeper consciousness from which your behavior springs.

Mental Housecleaning is useful in working out problems in all kinds of relationships. You may have been in situations where, even when you and your friend have made agreements to change, irritation still arises all too easily. We are creatures of habit, your inner consciousness is still in the habit of being irritated, and you continue your old patterns. Mental Housecleaning will easily help you shift away from them.

Mental Housecleaning clears your mind of bad habits, but will not necessarily solve the problem itself; rather, it provides space for a resolution to emerge, a resolution that, otherwise, you probably would not have noticed. Always project the last thought to be positive; this acts as the direction that your consciousness continues to move. Intention and expectation set the path upon which your consciousness travels. Mental Housecleaning creates an opening through which you can discover new perspectives.

Sometimes a problem that you have tried to Mental House Clean will persist. In this case, the chances are that your inner consciousness is giving clues that the problem is not exclusively a negative habit on your part, but that it has something positive to offer you—some lesson is still to be learned and requires closer attention. In this case, you can employ your Receptive Imagination to discover the insights you need in order to move on. Once you have acted on the insights, your Mental Housecleaning will succeed.

Mental Housecleaning is helpful to cleanse yourself of any negative habits of the mind. If you are mindful, you can notice when you habitually see yourself or your circumstances in a negative light. That is if you are cynical, reactive, envious, or stuck in circular thinking. I call these states "cul-de-sacs of the mind." They are traps keeping us from being present in the moment and experiencing life from an open and fresh perspective.

Mental Housecleaning is also useful to counter the images that you may have inadvertently absorbed from the mass media.

Mass Media Mesmerizes Us into Mindlessness

If we take seriously the idea that consciousness influences reality, then we cannot ignore the impact of the media on our subjective landscapes. When we watch TV, we are in the alpha level. Much to the gratification of the advertisers, it is a highly programmable state of awareness. For too many of us, television has become a companion who is always there, does not argue, and is full of entertainment—the problem is that we are not in the habit of arguing with it either.

Remember, we do not distinguish between the real and the unreal—we simply act in accordance with the images present in our consciousness. Whether we are actually confronted by a mad dog or simply imagine that we are, as far as our adrenal glands are concerned, it is the same. There is no difference when we watch TV. We are constantly awash in a sea of images and no matter how much we may use rational discrimination, our bodies and psyches respond to them. Notice the bodily sensations you get when watching a horror movie. Eric Peper, an expert in biofeedback, tells us that:

> The horror of television is that the information goes in, but we do not react to it. It goes right into our memory pool and perhaps we react to it later but we do not know what we're reacting to. When you watch television you are training yourself not to react and so later on, you are doing things without knowing why you are doing them or where they came from.[23]

For many of us, television has replaced life. The image in the box has become more vivid and "real" than our everyday experience. It claims the center of our attention. Jerry Mander tells us:

The people who control television become the choreogra-
phers of our internal awareness ... By (television's) expro-
priation of inner experience; advertising makes the human
into a spectator of his or her own life. It is alienation to the
tenth power.[24]

When listening to the radio or reading, we create our own
images; the insidious aspect of television is that it provides
the images for us. They go directly into inner consciousness.
We become passive receptacles for the images it bestows on
us. Now we do not live life, we watch it; then the most excit-
ing moments in our actual lives get compared to what we
saw on TV.

Television is now being recognized as an addiction in our
society—two out of five adults and seven out of ten
teenagers acknowledge that they have a problem.[25] How bad
is the problem, really? Ninety-nine percent of American
households have a television set.[26] The average person in
the United States spends over four hours a day in front of
the television, though it is likely to be turned on for seven
hours a day. This adds up to an estimated nine to eleven years
devoted to television viewing in an average life span.[27]

American children average four hours a day watching TV,
which is nearly 18,000 hours by the time they graduate from
high school. This is 5000 hours more then what is spent in a
classroom.[28] Now classrooms have been invaded by TV with
Channel One:

A marketing program that gives video equipment to desper-
ate schools in exchange for the right to broadcast a "news"
program studded with commercials to all students every
morning .... Channel One boasts, "Our relationship with 8.1
million teenagers lasts for six years." ... According to Mike
Searles, President of Kids R Us, "If you get this child at an
early age, you can own this child for years to come.

Companies are saying, 'Hey I want to own the kid younger and younger.'"[29]

We've become mindless consumers, but there is an even scarier aspect:

If commercials are the appetizer and dessert of each TV time slot, violence is its main course, the meat and potatoes that make the sponsor's message stick to your ribs. To the advertiser, violence equals excitement equals ratings.[30]

An hour of prime-time television includes about five violent acts. An hour of children's Saturday morning programming includes twenty to twenty-six violent acts. The average American child will witness 12,000 violent acts on television each year, amounting to about 200,000 violent acts by the time he turns eighteen years old .... In a University of Illinois study, people who had watched the most violent TV between birth and age eight committed the most serious crimes by age thirty.[31]

An appalling number of juvenile crimes—torture, kidnapping, rapes, and murders—have been traced to events portrayed on televisions .... A boy's television habits at age eight are more likely to be a predictor of his aggressiveness at age eighteen or nineteen than his family's socio-economic status, his relationship with his parents, his IQ, or any other single factor in his environment.[32]

Boys are conditioned to be violent towards others, while girls turn the violence inwards: along with all the images of the ideal put forth in TV programming and commercials comes the inevitable inability to measure up and ensuing low self-esteem and self-destructive behaviors. For girls in particular, the ideal borders on emaciation; anorexia and bulimia are now epidemic. Eighty percent of fourth-grade girls are on diets, and one in five women in the United States has an eating disorder.[33]

If we do not want to be homogenized, the best thing to do is turn off the set or talk back to it for your own self-protection, so your deeper levels of consciousness do not absorb it all noncritically in the name of reality. The people responsible for the programs will not hear your arguments, but your deeper awareness will. Talk back and take back your consciousness! Every time you compare yourself to a movie star, bring in the affirmation, "I believe in myself."

You can protect yourself from the destructive messages by imagining yourself surrounded by an invisible mirror that bounces away the messages that you do not want to absorb. Studies on distant mental influence show that one can block being influenced by simply imagining oneself surrounded by a protective bubble.[34] Setting intention not only impacts how energy moves out but also what enters into us.[35]

Our creativity arises from deeper levels; if it is not buried under the sludge we will have better ways of spending our time than in front of the television. Get out the popcorn, invite your friends over, and do an Energy Circle together (see Chapter six). You will be entertained with images that fuel desirable futures.

Induction

Focus on your breathing ... Let your breath be full and easy ... each breath rolling through your body like waves ... breathing ... Bring to awareness your symbol for physical relaxation ... Give your body permission to relax ... Feel your body relax more and more with each exhalation of breath ... Breathe through any areas of tension and feel your body relaxing into the support of the earth ... relaxing more and more as you move through this meditation.

When you are ready, bring to awareness your symbol for mental relaxation ... Let your breath be like the breeze that clears the air ... Let your breath clear your mind ... and your mind relaxes into its natural state of spaciousness ... as spacious as the skies ... relaxed ... open ... clear ... alert throughout this meditation ...

As your mind continues relaxing, become aware of the feelings present in you now ... Give your feelings permission to relax ... Bring to awareness your symbol for emotional relaxation ... Let go of all the feelings that push at you or pull at you ... any anxieties or distractions or frustrations ... any feelings that somehow cause you to constrict yourself ... Give yourself permission to let them all

MEDITATIONS

go ... down into the ground, transformed in the earth ...
breathe them out ...

And take a moment to appreciate yourself ... to offer yourself
loving kindness ... To appreciate your goodness ... Feel your
heart lighten ... as though it smiles ... Sense your heart relaxing
into its natural state of generosity and compassion ... ...

When you are ready, bring to awareness your symbol for
your creative, self-restoring center ... Remember the
goodness of life ... Remember what you hold sacred ... what
you feel grateful about ... what you cherish ... Feel yourself
relaxing into the sanctity of life itself ... Here, awareness is
spacious ... You are held by awareness ... The Inner Witness
is present ... The receptive imagination brings forth intuitive
knowing ... The creative imagination awakens your inner
visionary ... Here, you can align yourself with energies ...
discover energies ... create probabilities ... Here, you shape
energy ... This is your creative, self-restoring center, where
you feel yourself a part of all that
is ... Take a few moments and appreciate this space ...
Know that each time you exhale you move deeper into this
quiet space ... potent place ... alert ... aware ... open ...

You will remain alert throughout this meditation—tell yourself
this now ...

I am going to suggest several affirmations. If you wish to affirm
them, repeat them to yourself after me knowing that in doing
so you create patterns of energy both within and around you,

causing your life to align itself with the power of the words. Expect the affirmations to manifest themselves within and around you.

I believe in myself, I believe in my experience ...

I trust my nature, I trust nature ...

I live up to my fullest potential ...

I always discover and align with positive possibilities ...

I expect the best to manifest ...

I am fully present and mindful in each moment ...

I listen to my intuition. It guides me in the right direction ...

My fears are transformed into teachers, empowering me to move forward with courage and insight ...

I always successfully protect myself ...

My life is in harmony with the life around me ...

I make wise choices ...

I cultivate a joyous and generous heart ...

My life is full of love and laughter in all my relations ...

My life is whole, my life is embraced by the whole of life ...

All my needs are always met, there is enough for everyone ...

I offer my gifts to healing the world ...

What I offer is needed; what I need is offered ...

I am resilient; I maintain balance amidst change ...

I trust the future ...

Now take time to focus on any of your own affirmations, knowing that as you focus on affirmations you create patterns of energy to which your life will conform ... ...

Take a moment and breathe in gratitude as you inhale ... and breathe out compassion as you exhale ... Gratitude to be alive; compassion for all life ... ...

You may also want to focus on any quality symbols you have been working with ... ...

Finishing what you are doing ... alert and ready to follow what I have to say to you ... Now take a few moments to enhance your inner awareness ... Feel yourself sinking deeper with each exhalation of breath ... ...

This is your magnetic center of deep knowing, potent energy resides here. Here you can adjust energy, align energy, create probabilities. This is your center of receptivity, of creativity.

This is a very powerful place to do your interior work. Here you reside outside the usual boundaries of space and time. From this place you have access to all knowingness. Awareness is spacious, the Inner Witness present. Here you can experience all that is known. Here you can look at any aspect of life and know its true nature ... Know your own true nature. Here wisdom resides. You can look at any fears, any anxieties, any particular feelings, anything, and you can discover what to do. Here, all your knowingness resides. Breathe, and knowing is present ...

Here your inquiring mind can acquire whatever knowledge you ... All you need to do is focus your attention where you choose and witness what takes place in the light of awareness ... Honor knowing ... In this deep place of inner awareness you can discover realities, you can shape realities ... Here you discover and create reality ... It is in this dimension that magic is born ...

Mental Housecleaning

Know that your consciousness is your dominion ... Your consciousness is loyal to your choices ... You choose the qualities of energy that reside here. Your inner consciousness is responsive to your suggestion.

Now create a ritual of transformation in your consciousness. Create a Mental Housecleaning ritual—use the transmuting powers of nature. Create something like fire, a compost pit, whatever you like—be sure it transforms energy ... recycling the old making space for the new ... ...

This is your Mental Housecleaning device. Know that you can use your Mental Housecleaning device to convert, to transform any negativity, making space for new creative perspectives to reveal themselves. Tell your deeper consciousness this now, tell your deeper consciousness that whenever you symbolically put anything through your Mental Housecleaning device, your consciousness will then transform the constricting energy, making space for new energy to emerge ... Know that this is so, trust it ...

You can use your device whenever you are stuck in negative patterns; simply symbolize the habituated pattern and put the symbol into your Mental Housecleaning device ... When you do this keep your intentions clear and positive. After using your device always move your attention in a positive direction or focus on an entirely different concern trusting that deeper within a conversion is taking place ... Know that when you use your Mental Housecleaning device you speak to the deepest levels of being which respond; the energy shifts and a metamorphosis occurs. Know that this is so.

Whenever you do Mental Housecleaning, always be specific ... Recreate the concern in your awareness, be aware of the atmosphere in which it lives, symbolize it, and put the symbol through your device, then move your consciousness into a new direction expecting the transformation to take place deeper within you. Take time to work with your Mental Housecleaning device now ... ... Know that you have released yourself from patterns of the past ... transformation is taking place. New experience is emergent. Expect it ...

Tell yourself that you will remember to use your Mental

Housecleaning device whenever you need to clear the debris in your mind enabling you to be fully present, clear, and creative ...

Self-Protection

Think of times when you have felt especially safe and secure, Remember times of safety, protection, security. The times in the past where you have felt these qualities present. Let them be present now. Imagine breathing them in ... ...

Breathe in the sense of safety ... Exhale and feel yourself settle into security ... Feel it in your body ... Bring these energies into the present ... As you breathe in, sense your body filling up with the sense of safety ... Breathe safety ... Imagine it ... As you exhale, breathe the energy out and create a bubble of protection surrounding you ... ... You may want to imagine yourself in a bubble of light, energy, music, however you wish to imagine yourself surrounded by, and immersed in, protection ... ...

Create a symbol for this experience. It may be the bubble itself or it may be something different ... Know that whenever you bring this symbol into your awareness, you will protect yourself from any influences that might threaten you. You will find yourself intuitively knowing what you need to do to protect yourself ... Whenever you use your symbol of protection, you fully claim your space ... you embody your full power ... Feel how powerful this is ... You inspire others to respect you ...

Whenever you use this symbol, you create boundaries allowing only positive influences in ... negativity bounces off ... Sense how this is the case ... Suggest to your inner self that whenever you bring this symbol to awareness it will tune you to the information needed to remain safe ...

Wherever you are, you can protect yourself from other people's energy, from germs, from attack, from advertising ... whatever it may be, by simply bringing this symbol into awareness ... Know that this is so, tell yourself this. Whenever you need protection, you just bring your symbol to awareness and your space will be honored... You'll inspire respect. Sense how your symbol awakens courage and you successfully stand your ground. Your symbol not only protects you from the outside, but also evokes deep power inside ... power that rises to the occasion ... Imagine it ... Breathe power ... Feel it ... Expect that your symbol always secures the scene ... ...

Tell yourself you will remember your symbol and use it whenever you need it.

Stretching Your Confidence into a New Area

Experience the warmth you feel for the beauty of life, the wonder of the world, spectacular landscapes ... delicate flowers ... a child fumbling as she learns to make her own way through the world ... Feel your compassion, feel the compassion you have for all of life, your love of life itself ... ...

Draw this quality you are now experiencing into yourself ...
Breathe in compassion ... compassion, for who it is that you
are. Breathe it into the whole of your being ... Breathe in
tenderness for your own nature ... Immerse yourself in
compassion, let yourself be affectionate towards who you
are ... ...

Remember yourself in the past, all the years that have gone into
making you who you are ... Unique experiences, a combination
of experiences that only you have had ... Believe in the lessons
of your experience ... Recognize your intelligence ...
Acknowledge your true nature ... Tell yourself what you
appreciate about yourself ... ...

Witness how you receive this acknowledgement, sense if there
are any places that this love bounces off, where it does not go
in ... or any place that needs the love to go in deeper ... With
breath, send loving right into those areas ... Feel them open to
caring energy ... Breathe, feel them softening ... becoming
receptive ... Massage yourself with loving
energy ... ...

Now remember an area in life in which you are fully competent,
an area you have fully mastered. It may be something you think
of as insignificant and simple—no matter, choose an area in
your life where you believe in your experience; do not worry if
the area seems trivial or unimportant—what is important is that
you are fully proficient ... Acknowledge your proficiency ... Feel
your know-how ... Breathe in your competence ... Feel your

confidence ... Exaggerate it ... ...

Create a symbol for self-confidence ... Now choose an area in your life that you would like to enhance ... Choose one particular ability that you would like to develop in yourself ...

Know that in these dimensions of awareness, you have the ability to tap universal consciousness. You have the ability to tap knowledge directly; you can go past ordinary ways of learning and directly tap the source of all knowing. Pretend that you can ...

Your symbol acts as a magnet drawing to you exactly what you need ... Imagine shining your symbol into the arena you have chosen to embrace ... as though your symbol were to infuse the scene with power ... Imagine your symbol flooding the area with the powerful energy of competence ... Imagine it glowing, pulsating, charged with power ... Breathe it, let it sing inside you ... Feel the energy ... ...

Now shine this energy into the future. Imagine your future self immersed in all this energy ... Witness transformation ... Powerful ... Step into the vision and feel your future self fully able in this new way ... Dynamic ... Be your future self ... Feel your confidence symbol make your steps steady in this new area of your life ... Notice how your confidence gives you courage ... your steps steady and strong. Breathe this way of being ... ...

Talk to your future self and your symbol for self-confidence to

discover what you can do to cultivate this way of being ...
Sense if there is anything you need to give up in your life or in
your self-image to make room for this new way of being ... ...

Imagine doing what is needed ... Know that if you can imagine
it, you can create it ... You are now aligned with this energy ...
Give yourself permission to believe in yourself ... Let any
residual skepticism soak down into the ground to be
transformed by the soil, or put through your Mental
Housecleaning device, making room for this new energy to
come through ... ...

Appreciate yourself for this transformation ... Tell yourself what
you will do to cultivate your mastery ... Tell yourself that you will
remember to bring your symbol to mind whenever you need it.

Fear As Challenge

Now imagine a place of power ... It could be one that you
create or one you have been to before ... Imagine a place
that's charged with potent energy. Create your place of
power ... feel the power of this place ... Breathe in the energy
of this place ... Sense power, strength, vital forces in this place
... Breathe power ... in and out.

Imagine yourself standing in this place and drawing up all the
power it has to offer, through the arches of your feet, the
palms of your hands, or anywhere it's inclined to come in.
Breathe it in ... infusing the whole of yourself with the energy

here ... empowering your whole being, every cell, every thought, every feeling—the whole of your experience charged with power ... Feel how centered you are with this energy moving through you ...

Now bring to awareness your symbols for protection and confidence. Or if you have none, remember the experience of safety ... then acknowledge and feel your self-confidence ... You are courageous; it is from these wellsprings of energy that your courage emerges. Experience courage, experience your courage. Breathe it in from your symbols, draw it up from the earth. Courage, it moves through you ... ...

Now choose one particular fear or anxiety to work on ... Bring it to awareness. As you do, know that you can breathe out any tension that might arise. You can always breathe out tension; as you do, the Inner Witness reveals what is true for you ... Here in the light of spacious awareness there is room to witness. Breathe out the charge and witness what is so ... Recreate the times you have felt this particular fear, do not bring the fear too close, just bring it close enough so that you can keep your energy moving smoothly ... continuing to feel courageous and safe ... Witness this fear ... Separate yourself from it and witness ... Breathe any tension that comes up ... Let it drain away. Give the fear form and color and personify it ... Give it a personality ... The fear is no longer within you at all; it is personified before you ... Imagine it ... Talk to it ... Get to know it ... It has a character all of its own ... Find out where it is coming from ... Notice its quirks ... Endeavor to make friends with it ... See what it has to offer you ... What it is protecting you from ... Bring your symbols into the conversation and hold council ... ...

Be receptive, listen to what you need to know from your place of power, from your symbols, from this character before you ... Ask the character for a gift. Know that fear is a great teacher. When you open to it, it transforms into a highly sensitive friend offering crucial information ... What gifts does it have for you now? ... Let it give you power, it offers a key to new ways of being ... ...

Imagine that your newfound friend has a beam of light with which it can illuminate possible futures and you can see what it illuminates and explore potentialities ... Witness the opportunities for learning ... Witness where caution may be useful ... Witness what awakens the old familiar fear ... Notice what the fear is protecting you from ... ...

With your newfound friend and your symbols find the places receptive to a shift in energy ... Notice where a rearrangement of the scenes reconfigures the outcomes ... Shape positive potentialities. From this place of power you are the creator ... You might find these places receptive to change inside you as well ...

This light can be used to finely attune yourself to potential situations. It can give you the knowledge that you need to move through situations in a very courageous and protected way ... It can give you the information you need to rearrange probabilities, making the potential scenes positive for all ... ...

If you wish, you can decide to walk down the path created
by the beam of light and embrace the challenges, make them
your own, let that beam of light empower you to move
forward ... See where you can go with it. Step into your
liberated self ... ...

Appreciate the fear that has become your friend, your
challenge, bringing you the gift of learning. Imagine that as you
move down your path fears always transform into friends gifting
you with new perspectives ... making life interesting. Imagine
that whenever you come across fear you can talk to it and
receive the gift hidden inside ... learning from it, becoming a
wiser, fuller human being ... Tell yourself you will remember to
transform the negative into a positive light.

Active Imagination: Aligning Energies with a Positive Vision

Feel the space you now occupy ... fully relaxed ... yet there is
much potency ... like the atmosphere right before the morning
sun rises ... the dawn of a new day ... Very peaceful, yet
pregnant with potential ... Very quiet, yet charged with
possibility ... It is in this space that probabilities are created ...
This space is where the future takes shape ... This space is
very powerful ... Here, you can discover what's possible ...
you can shape what's probable ... This is where the future
dawns ...

Imagine that you are sitting in a magic theater. You have control behind the spotlight, and you can choose whatever you'd like to illuminate ... The light illuminates possibilities in the future, and you can shape what takes place by simply changing the act on the stage ... however you'd like to change it ... This is a powerfully magic space ... Take a moment to choose what you'd like to focus on ... It may be this day ... it may be the coming week ... it may be an important event ... You can focus the light in the immediate ... you can focus the light in the distant future ... Here, time stretches ... You can focus it on issues that are personal ... You can focus it on issues regarding your family, or your community, or even the world ... Choose what you'd like to focus on now ... ...

Focus the beam on the particular area that you would like to explore ... Create a scene ... Imagine how it might unfold ... Watch it on stage ... Witness what's so at the moment ... What's likely to unfold? ... What are the currents of energy? ... Let your imagination give detail to the scene ... Imagine it in full detail ... the different people involved ... What's taking place? ... How are you doing? ... The mood ... let yourself imagine it ... Like watching previews ... What unfolds? ... What's the quality of energy present? ... Create it ... imagine it ... listen deeply ... sense it ... feel it ... Watch carefully as your imagination brings you the possibilities ... Witness ...

Now go back to the beginning of the scene and shape it so it unfolds in the best possible way ... Imagine that it draws out the best in you ... and it draws out the best in everyone ... Let your imagination paint the most wonderful scene ... It's

so good, it glows ... Feel it ... let it sing ... Imagine it sparkling ...
Imagine it unfolding in a way that is really wonderful for
everyone ... joyous ... ...

Imagine it in detail ... feel it ... Now sense what ripples out as it
unfolds in this way ... Witness how it affects others ... See what
unfolds ... Notice how others experience it ... Make any
adjustments so that all that occurs is good for everyone, and for
the earth itself ... ...

Now, enter into the scene ... as though you could travel down
the light and enter into the scene ... be in it ... Feel it unfolding
around you ... Feel your body inside the situation ... the
smells ... the sounds ... the atmosphere ... Feel yourself in
it ... pretend you are there now ... These events are unfolding
around you ... Feel the excitement awakening inside you ... Feel
your heart sing in this situation ... ...

Now, move into the future and look back into this time you
have just been exploring ... Feel as though it has already
occurred ... it's become a memory ... Notice how life is after it
has all unfolded ... As you explore, if you come across anything
that needs an adjustment, make the adjustments, so that all that
unfolds is good for everyone it touches ... If you come across
any resistance, listen in ... discover the story ... Your intuition will
offer the insight needed ... Work with the vision till it settles
comfortably for everyone, and everyone looks forward to it ... ...

Now you can bring these energies into your present ... into
your life now ... Know that you are in alignment with these

energies ... Know that in working with these energies in this way, you have brought yourself into alignment with the possibilities ... You have energized these probabilities ... You intuitively will know just what is needed to make space for them to manifest ... Expect this to be the case ... Believe in the future ...

Acknowledge the very fact that you can imagine these energies makes them real ... Imagination is the stuff probabilities are made of ... Like energies attract like energies ... You are drawn into these experiences ... and all that is resonant with these experiences in the world is drawn toward you ... Know that this is so ... Notice if you are inclined to do anything to bring these energies into the world ... to plant them in your life ... If there's anything you want to express to another ... Notice what you might do to cultivate them ... Or, if there's anything you need to release to make space for them ...

Choose what you will commit yourself to ... Imagine doing it ... Know that in doing so, you bring this energy into the world ... you embody it ... you open to it ...

Count Out

Expect the best ... Offer your best ... Trust the future ... Just as the sun gives birth to a new day, imagination gives birth to the future ... With each exhalation of breath, know that these energies move out into the world ... With each inhalation of breath, you draw resonant circumstances into your experience ... Trust it ... Affinity is the way of the universe ...

Take time to go over any insights you have gained ... any

choices you have made ... Channel positive energy wherever it may be needed ... Appreciate the gifts life offers ...

Make yourself ready to come out to outer conscious levels ... Finish what you are doing ... Know that the energies exist, all you need do is act on them ... Know that you are now in alignment with these visions, and you will intuitively act in accord with them.

In a moment, I'm going to count from one to five. At the count of five, you will open your eyes, remembering all that you have experienced, feeling refreshed, revitalized, relaxed, and bringing with you the energies you have tapped, in full alignment with the best of your visions.

ONE—coming up slowly now ...

TWO—becoming more aware of the room around you ...

THREE—at the count of five, you will open your eyes, revitalized, refreshed, and relaxed, remembering all that you have experienced, and knowing you can return to these dimensions whenever you like ...

FOUR—coming up now ...

FIVE!—eyes open, revitalized, refreshed, and relaxed, open heart and spirit, ready and able to act on the energies you have tapped, trusting the future.

•6•

Tapping Universal Energies

For most of us, our natural inclination is to spend our energies primarily focused on our personal lives, our trials, and our tribulations. We tend to forget our connection to the earth, to the sky, to each other, to the life that is constantly percolating in and around us. When we forget our connection, we wind up feeling drained and isolated. When we remember it, we become energized, inspired, and feel supported by and a part of all that is around us. Running energy is a technique that you can use to stay connected in the midst of your activity, and it also offers continuous, easy access to your intuition.

Running energy as an individual practice is powerful. Running energy in a circle for the purpose of healing and weaving visions together is the most potent way to work with Applied Meditation.

Running Energy: Shifting Out of Ego Attachment

Running Energy moves us out of personal isolation into connection. When you run energy, you experience yourself as being part of, and held by, universal energy. In a seemingly magical way it enables you to embody the interconnectedness of life and your ordinary life fills with grace. You feel yourself in alignment with the flow of the natural world. The process itself is simple: imagine the energies of the earth and sky to be constantly moving through you, just as the air continually moves through you. Do not let its simplicity fool you; running energy can literally change your life. (The third track of the CD is a running energy meditation.)

A couple of years after I had begun working with the power of consciousness, I took a class at The Berkeley Psychic Institute where I learned this technique.[1] Until then, whenever I taught a full-day workshop, I would be so exhausted at the end of the day that I would not have the energy to cook dinner for myself. I would just collapse into bed. The next time I had to teach an all-day workshop, it occurred to me that there was all this energy around; I need not depend only on my own. Right before I started my class I meditated for a couple of minutes and envisioned the energy of the earth and sky moving through me. Then before I returned to an outer focus of attention, I made the suggestion to my inner self that the energy would continue to move through me in the same way throughout the day. When the workshop was over, I made dinner and went out dancing for the next four hours. The difference it made was astonishing; never again have I gotten drained from teaching because now I always run energy.

When I am running energy, I do not actually feel anything; it is just a picture I create in my mind—I am a visualizer. As with Mental Housecleaning, the results are profound and are felt in the midst of activities, not in the meditation itself. When I first applied the technique, I did not understand why it worked: I still expended as much physical energy as I ever had. In retrospect, I can see why in the past my teaching exhausted me. My ego had been too involved. Much of my energy was engaged with how people were hearing me and what they thought. The fact is that I have no control over how people hear me or what they are going to think—nor should I. All I can do is present the material in as clear a way as possible, respecting people's choices as to how they will respond. It is only natural for me to want both approval and agreement, but it confuses my clarity, drains my energy, and certainly does not help people hear me any better.

Before I started running energy in my classes, if I had information that I thought would help someone with a problem, I would restate it many different ways in order to convince them to follow my suggestions. Now, when I run energy, it does not occur to me to try to convince anybody of anything. Instead, I find myself communicating with greater clarity. My expression is precise because I am not caught up in the opinions of others. Running energy causes me to respect people's processes automatically because my ego is no longer separating us. Clear communication occurs because my personal feelings are not clogging up the process; it is not as though they go away, they are just no longer in the driver's seat.

Running energy moves you from an individual ego-separated perspective into a spirit-connected perspective. Your feelings move into the background and your intuition comes forward. Running energy is the single most effective technique for overcoming stress. Much stress grows out of isolation and feeling you have to fend for yourself. It is particularly helpful in difficult situations, like being around annoying relatives. If you run energy in the midst of such a situation you will surprise yourself, you might actually enjoy being with them.

Just as running energy reduces your need for approval, it also enables you to steer clear of negative energy. You will naturally avoid absorbing other people's energy. Many women suffer from this because we have been socialized to respond to other people's needs before our own. Running energy puts everything in perspective so that one can respond to both one's own needs and those of others. This is key whenever you are working with others, whether you are providing leadership, teaching, or healing.

Running energy is also valuable for living in alignment with your sense of greater purpose and meaning. It enables you to stay true to your intention, making it easy to sift through and know just what you should be paying attention to and what you should not. One client who had struggled for years with bulimia would run energy whenever she felt the compulsion to purge, and thereby maintained self-control. It is important to note that running energy can also be helpful in healing many bodily problems such as headaches, carpal tunnel syndrome, or even more severe conditions like epilepsy.

Sometimes it is useful to emphasize sky or earth energy. If ever you are stuck, lack vision, need creativity, or are depressed, bring through sky energy. If, on the other hand, you have lots of great ideas but trouble focusing, then bring in the earth energy.

When working with running energy, it is important to sit comfortably while keeping your spine as straight as possible. Running energy does not need an induction before working with it. It stands on its own. You can, however, run energy as a substitute for going into your meditative state with your relaxation symbols. This is an especially good way to enter meditation if you tend to fall asleep while meditating. Running energy will enable you to enter a deep state of consciousness, while at the same time remain alert. You can also use it in conjunction with your symbols, in which case you connect with the earth while relaxing your body, and connect with the sky while relaxing your mind.

What is essential about this practice is that energy, like breath, is constantly moving through you; you have created channels so that nothing gets stuck. When you use it in your daily life, before you start any activities, take a few moments to close your eyes and begin the energy moving. Then establish the intention by telling yourself that the energy will continue to move through you as you go about your activities. Throughout the day, occasionally pause for a moment to focus your attention on the energies moving through. With time, you will find that you will automatically run energy whenever you need to.

Running energy is helpful to make meetings more effective. For example, if your group is stuck on an issue and you cannot seem to bring it to resolution, stop the discussion for a few moments and have everyone draw in sky energy. Afterwards, you will find yourselves knowing how to move forward. Similarly, if the group seems to be working all over the agenda, unable to focus on one thing at a time, stop and draw up earth energy and ground yourselves.

Energy Circles: Concentrating Consciousness

Meditating in a group is exponentially more potent than when you are alone. When a whole group is meditating on the same thing at the same time it becomes even more powerful. It is as though everyone's deeper experience merges, dissolving isolation, heightening people's creative and intuitive capacities, and boosting influence on probabilities. I have named this process "Energy Circles."

I developed Energy Circles as a form for collective meditation over thirty years ago. It is so effective that it has not changed in all these years. It is a great way to unify people before everyone goes about a common task. It inspires a community spirit and invites both creativity and intuition to inform the work. The Circle causes everyone's energy to move into a deep resonance with one another.

People have been praying together for millennia. Energy Circles are similar to prayer circles.[2] What I really appreciate about the form is that it offers an easy way for diverse people to come together, whether the purpose is to align energies, gain insight, channel healing, or weave vision. They allow people who hold different religious/spiritual beliefs—or none at all—to tap the power of spirit together. Remember that coherent groups or bonded pairs are most effective in influencing the random event generators.

The form is as simple as running energy. People sit in a circle holding hands and a leader guides them into imagining earth and sky energy moving through themselves and then around the circle. Once all of this is happening, the leader brings the group's attention to the specific concerns people would like to focus on, or people take turns directing everyone's attention. Afterwards, it is both inspiring and helpful for people to share what they imagined as they focused on the issues.

You can use Circles in all kinds of settings. They can be large or small (two people or hundreds), and they can take as little as three or as long as thirty minutes. An Energy Circle allows us to align ourselves with our goals, energize events, channel healing, and gain intuitive insights that illuminate strategies for addressing concerns.

Energy Circles are useful to start a meeting or any kind of group activity, especially planning. It takes only a few minutes, yet will shorten your meeting overall because it establishes an energetic coherence enabling people to work together more effectively. I was in a group that was to do an all-day workshop, and, rather than having the usual drawn-out discussion in planning an event like this, we did a Circle. Every few moments one of us would throw out a question like, "How many people are there?" "What is the mood in the room?" "What different roles are we playing?" After the Circle, we shared what we had imagined—our visions wove together. Clear patterns emerged and we planned the day in about half an hour rather than the usual two or three hours.

It also got us aligned with our shared purpose and set the stage for a successful workshop.

Energy Circles can qualitatively change your life when used on a regular basis. They have been the central component in my Applied Meditation support groups for decades. Working consistently with one another for a length of time, we have come to develop an entirely new kind of relationship. We are intuitively attuned to each other, an attunement that grows with time. We witness one another's transformation from the inside out, instead of the other way around—an experience of knowing people in a wholly different way. Doing Circle work supports maintaining well-being no matter how challenging your life becomes. Energy Circles are also beneficial because using them clarifies what is most important to you and what is a positive approach for the issues you really care about. They become an invaluable resource for finding positive points of reference, which, in turn, creates an upbeat approach to life.

Circles have become the major source of support in my life. In fact, if it were not for them this book would never have been written. The effects of energizing and the insights gained are extremely helpful. For instance, my cat Madeline once developed a limp that I hoped would go away by itself. After a couple of days, it was still bothering her. I made an appointment with her vet following the next day's Circle. In the Energy Circle, we channeled healing energy to her. When I returned home, she was prancing around as if nothing had happened. Stories like this begin to occur frequently when you work with Circles. In addition to the mysterious ways that healing and intuition show up, you get to witness the creativity and humor intrinsic to inner consciousness. It lightens the heart.

Just as important to me is the uncanny sensation I get in the Circle itself; it is as if I am being fully supported by the energy and suspended in it. For the duration of the Circle, it feels as though I am relieved of carrying my own weight. Sometimes, it feels as if the whole room fills up with energy. Once, right in the middle of a Circle, an unopened bottle of wine sitting on the table next to us popped its cork. To me, the energy in which I am suspended feels as though it extends out beyond the space and time of the Circle and becomes an underlying support as I go through the activities of the week. Life gains buoyancy.

If you already meditate in a group context, start with a Circle. Otherwise, get some friends together and try it.

How Energy Circles Work

When doing an Energy Circle, sit comfortably and close enough to hold hands. Have lots of pillows available to prop your arms and hands so you can be comfortable for the duration. (For really long exploratory Circles, some elect to lie on the floor with their heads to the center.) When you do a Circle, one person should lead. This person guides everyone into imagining the earth and sky energies moving through them, and then moving around the Circle. The leader gives cues to each individual to take their turn and ask the group to focus on their specific concerns. These concerns can be personal, for loved ones, and about the larger world. Individuals can ask for as many as half a dozen issues.

Each request needs to be concise, positive, and in the present tense, or targeted to a specific time. Expressing the "whys" and "hows" is cumbersome, distracting, and evokes beta rather than deeper awareness. The principles for composing a request are the same form as making an affirmation. Before the Circle forms, it is good for people to briefly describe the general scenario of the concerns for which they will ask for energy. We frequently need help deciding how to state a request in brief and positive terms. Most of the time, we are more aware of what we do not want than what we do. Group members offer a fresh perspective and can help you figure out how to state an issue positively, providing a vision to move toward rather being stuck in reaction.

You can ask for energy for many issues. Because of the simultaneity of inner consciousness, it does not take long to focus on each request (maybe ten seconds or the duration of three full breaths). You can ask for energy on anything. Think of a challenge you would like support in, or a new habit you would like to reinforce, or a goal for which you are aiming. Channel energy to your neighborhood or peace in the world—the sky is the limit!

Psychic energy knows no boundaries, so we must create them. It is important to focus on one issue or person at a time, recentering between each; otherwise the energy from the last person or issue gets carried over to the next. Recentering is simple; it just means letting go of what you were imagining and focusing on the energy moving around the circle or on your breath. Recentering only takes a moment, but you need to remember to do it. When moving from one person to the next in the Circle, there should be a few moments between each person speaking so that people can be clear and ready to focus on the next person. It is good for the leader to reinforce the process by saying something like "grounded and open, earth and sky energies moving around and around …." Then the leader invites the next person to take a turn. This helps both maintain the momentum and gives people a moment to recenter themselves before moving their attention to the next person.

It is important to think of it as channeling energy—universal energy. Do not think of it as sending your energy; you need your energy, and others do not. A while ago, a counselor who worked primarily with people's emotions joined one of my groups. The first few Circles exhausted her.

When it was pointed out that she was to channel energy—as opposed to "personally being there" for each person—she found Circles energizing rather than draining.

Everyone has her own individual way of channeling and focusing energy. Some people experience a knowing that has no form, some experience bodily sensations, some hear song or tones, and many others visualize colors, or symbols, or miniature dramas. In whatever way you imagine a positive outcome for each request, this is what is right for you. Trust whatever occurs and play with it—if you get an image or a sensation, embellish upon it. If none comes to mind, create one and work with that. Your first impression is like the outline in a coloring book—when you color it in, it comes to life. Trust your process, and remember that creating it versus having it come to you are equivalent processes when working with inner consciousness.

If you ever imagine a scene or have sensations that do not feel good to you (that is, when things do not seem to be moving in a positive direction, or there is a constriction present), it is important to try to shift it as best you can so that you reorient the probabilities. Refrain from judging whether something is accurate in these dimensions; you do not know. And it is important to note that the subjective world is not the same as our objective experience. Meaning is usually found by the person who asked and not by the one who channeled. During the Circle, as with individual meditation, your beta consciousness is likely to discount what is occurring—it may seem hokey—that is okay. After you have experienced the power of Circles, the messages of your beta mind will subside.

After the Circle, it is good to share what each of you imagined. This sharing is always delightful. People love to hear issues about which they care deeply imagined in a positive light. If you work with Energy Circles in this way it will not take long before you experience the psychic nature of the imagination. After a Circle, you will feel as if all that had happened was just in your own head, with no connection to the outside world. It is only by taking the risk and expressing what happened that you get validation for your intuition. You never discover the significance of your imagining in the midst of the Circle—that only comes later through the feedback process. It may take a while before you become aware of what is going on in the Circle and are able to articulate it. Give yourself time to become comfortable with the process. Also, keep in mind that the language of inner consciousness is metaphoric.

It is crucial that you work with Energy Circles from a place of humility and ethics—this work is powerful and needs to be approached with reverence. See "The Ethics of Applied Meditation" in Chapter Five.

I think Circles are the best way to experience the power of the imagination. Most of us can name many issues in life to complain about and not as many visions of what we are cultivating. Without vision, we are perpetually stuck in the mire of the things about which we complain. The great power of Energy Circles is that they provide a means for creating vision, and further, ways to weave our visions together, reclaiming our interconnections. Meditation allows us to feel ourselves embedded in the greater reality of all that exists. When we come together in these states of awareness, we heal ourselves and our communities.*

---

* You'll find more details on how to work with Energy Circles on our website. If you would like help connecting with others in your area to do Energy Circle work contact us at circlework@toolsforchange.org.

Running Energy: Centering for the Day

Make yourself comfortable sitting with your back straight ... Focus on your breath ... Move your attention to the area around the base of your spine ... Feel the energy there ... Sense a core of magnetic energy there ... Imagine as though, as you exhale, you were to drop a cord of energy from this center down through the floor ... all the way down ... down into the earth ... Imagine that this cord of energy sinks down through the soil ... through the clay ... through the underground waters ... deeper and deeper through all the layers of the earth ... each exhalation carrying it down further and further ... way down until it settles ... in the center ... like an anchor ...

Imagine there's a magnetic connection between your center and the molten center of the earth ... Imagine as though gravity were to absorb any tensions or distractions ... anything you want to release and transform you can breathe it out and gravity draws it down and it is transformed in the earth, making nutrients for new life ... Breathe out anything you want to release ...

This energy cord can also bring earth energies up into your body ... just like the trees draw nutrients directly into themselves ... Imagine pulling up earth energy like you had roots ... draw earth energy up into your body ... however you experience this ... Feel earth energy ... feel it coming up into you and moving through your whole body ... grounding you in this present moment ... present in your body ... focused ... relaxed ... relaxing into the support of the earth ... Feel it ... This is your grounding cord. Whenever you ground yourself in this way, you can release anything to be transformed, and you can draw up earth energy ... the earth that has witnessed all of history ... When you draw up earth energy you always find yourself fully present ... wise ... focused ... relaxed ... supported with all the endurance, patience and courage that you need in the activities before you. When you are grounded you are centered ...

Now bring to your awareness the great spacious skies ... the stars ... the planets ... the radiance of the sun ... the magnetism of the moon ... the great skies ... The patterns of weather ... the winds ... the rains ... the snows ... the clouds ... the breezes ... all the patterns of weather ... Imagine sky energy funneling down into the top of your head ... pouring into your body ... moving through your whole body ... mingling with the energy of the earth and moving back out again ... either out through the top of your head, or out your hands or your feet, or out the grounding cord ... Let the sky energy come in and out continually just as breath moves in and out ... Imagine it ... however you experience it ... sense it ... feel it ... Feel yourself as spacious inside as the skies above ... sky and earth mixing together inside as they do all around you ... Whenever you bring sky energies through you in this way, you open to the vast possibilities that life offers ... Clear ... creative ... open ... insightful ...

Tell yourself that both the earth and the sky energy will continue to move through you as it's now moving through you throughout this day. Imagine moving through the day grounded, focused and clear. Expect this ...

Take time now to do any inner work ... Open your eyes when you are ready and inclined ... Take as much time as you like ... When you open your eyes, know that you will continue to be centered in this way throughout the day, more than equal to the challenges before you.

Energy Circle

The person designated to begin the Circle can suggest an approximation of the following.

Focusing on your breathing, breathing with your belly, breathing in calming energy, gathering any tensions and distractions, breathing them out and down your grounding cord ... sinking your grounding cord down into the center of the earth, all the way down through all the layers of the earth ... letting your grounding cord carry any tensions, any distractions into the ground to be transformed by the earth ...

Imagine that we are all a circle of trees—roots intermingling in the ground, drawing up earth energies, up our grounding cords, up our roots, into our bodies ... feeling the earth energy in our bodies ... feeling our connection to the earth, feeling attuned to the substance of which we're made ... feeling attuned to our bodies ... feeling the support of the earth below us, the nurturing energy of the earth, focused and relaxed ... Draw on the great wisdom of the earth which has witnessed all of history ... Earth energy offers sustenance and courage ... Feel Earth energy move through, magnetic connection between ourselves and the earth ... held by the earth ... Breathing with the earth ...

As we continue to breathe with the earth, let us move our attention to the sky to the air around us, as trees reach to the sky, feel the air around us, be aware of the vast sky above us, the patterns of weather, the radiant sun ... the luminous moon ... the planets ... the millions of stars ... the whole sky ... Open to the vastness of the skies. Imagine that these energies drop down through the tops of our heads. Bring the energy of the sky into our bodies, mixing it with the energy of the earth, let it move in and out continually, just as air moves in and out continually. However you imagine this to occur, feel yourself as open on the inside as the skies above ... Feel possibility, sky energy brings with it the spirit of the future, creativity, fresh perspectives ... open to it. As it moves through you, it cleanses and clears you ... As the energy continues to move through us in this manner, imagine it moves around the circle, as though it were moving in your left hand and out your right hand ... around and around, potent energy, magnetic energy ... building momentum as it moves around and around, getting stronger and stronger ... Feel the pulse of the energy ... the life of the universal energies moving around the circle, the energies of the earth and sky moving through us ... wisdom of the past, possibilities of the future all here now ... energy moving around and around ...

This energy supports each of us ... it brings insights ... It is the stuff probabilities are made of ... energy moving around and around ... energy that will continue to move around as we focus it on different issues to gain insight and align ourselves with the best of possibilities ... energizing the probabilities that benefit all beings ... powerful energies moving around and around, gaining momentum ...

Now the leader can lead people through a process of tuning to and aligning with their common purpose (then skip to the last line of this script) or suggest to the first person that she state what she would like energized. Then the first person asks one request at a time, saying "thank you, now recenter" after a moment of silence, before going on to the next. After that person's requests have been energized, the next person can imagine the energy moving around the Circle a couple of times and then say the following.

Recenter yourselves ... clear your awareness ... feel the energy of the earth and sky moving through you ... moving around the circle ... in one and out the other ... around and around ... powerful energy.

Then she can ask for whatever she wants energy focused on; then the next person does the same thing. Proceeding all the way around the circle in the same manner, going through the clearing process each time (i.e., when the next person to ask for energy is finished sending energy to the person before her, she leads the group in clearing their minds and feeling the energy continuing to move around the circle). When the last person's (the leader's) requests have been energized, the first person who requested energy can lead the following ending process.

Recentering yourselves ... feeling the energy moving around the circle ... go back over in your awareness what you sensed each time you channeled energy for each of us ... Finish anything you did not have time to finish earlier, having your last sensation be a positive one ... Take as much time as you need ...

Know that the energy we've generated will continue to move as we move on ... Open your eyes when you are feeling ready and inclined.

·7·

We Are All Healers

The regenerative healing process is one of life's greatest mysteries. To understand it rationally is like trying to understand colors with your ears. But just as your eyes know color, your deeper self knows healing. As we repossess our inner selves, we repossess healing powers. Traditional healers throughout the ages have entered altered states of consciousness (alpha and theta) to understand and heal ailments. Indigenous healers have long taught that life is healthy when in equilibrium and that disease is a result of imbalance in the material, emotional, and spiritual realms. They treat the whole person, family, or community by restoring balance to the situation.

Health results from living in harmony with yourself and your environment. To be healthy is to be in sync with life, with all the rhythms harmonizing: bodily functions with life activities, life activities in rhythm with community life, and community life harmonizing with the cycles of the earth. But living harmoniously in our modern high-tech world is an oxymoron. We are lucky if we can keep up. We can no longer assume that the air is clean, that our water is drinkable, or that food will give our body sustenance. It is as though society itself is carcinogenic.

The most pervasive health problems in the United States are related to stress and to what we ingest into our bodies.

Studies have shown that between 60 and 90 percent of the population's visits to the doctor are stress-related.[1] Our body's natural self-protective system, the immune system, is suppressed by the presence of chronic stress and environmental toxins, compounding our susceptibility to illness.[2] Mainstream society's solutions have been in the service of "efficiency" and the mechanistic world view described in Chapter Five.

Rather than addressing the causes of stress and disease in order to prevent illness or regain balance, three billion prescriptions are dispensed each year.[3] Instead of cleaning up the environment or supporting living healthy lives, high-tech medicine proposes to replace worn-out body parts, genetically screen out the "weakest" of us,[4] or even to reengineer us to adapt to unsafe environmental conditions![5]

Health is a sociopolitical issue, not a private one. What is called for is slowing down so that reflection is an intrinsic part of our culture, cleaning up our environment, and creating an accessible health-care system focused on healing. As we work toward these goals, we need to maintain our health as best we can. Understanding the entwined relationship of mind and body is crucial to our healing; inner consciousness has a major impact on the state of our bodies, regardless of our participation with the process. Your conscious participation with the processes perpetually transpiring between your mind and body may have more impact on your health and well-being than any other single change you make in your life.

From Machines to Living Beings

In the same way that the advent of rationalism took life out of the objective world, justifying its exploitation, so too has the body become divorced from the mind to become a machine that only the mechanic (doctor) understands.[6] You, who inhabit the body, are often treated as though you have nothing to do with the causes of disease, and nothing to do with the healing process either; environmental influences are rarely considered.

> Following the Cartesian approach (the idea that the body is a machine that can be understood completely in terms of the arrangement and functioning of its parts), medical science has limited itself to the attempt of understanding the biological mechanisms involved in an injury to various parts of the body. These mechanisms are studied from the point of view of cellular and molecular biology, leaving out all influences of nonbiological circumstances on biological processes.[7]

Researchers have now successfully sequenced the entire human genetic code, and claim that soon they will be able to predict and cure all diseases. The medical model defines health as the absence of disease, which gives you about as much understanding of it as defining exercise as the absence of rest. With the concentration on disease, health itself recedes over the horizon.

In our culture, physicians enjoy more moral authority than any other professional group. Yet the medical system itself is responsible for causing many health problems:

> The pain, dysfunction, disability, and anguish resulting from technical medical intervention now rival the morbidity due to traffic and industrial accidents and even war-related activities, and make the impact of medicine one of the most rapidly spreading epidemics of our time.[8]

> There are 2,000 deaths/year from unnecessary surgery; 7,000 deaths/year from medication errors in hospitals; 20,000 deaths/year from other errors in hospitals; 80,000 deaths/year from infections in hospitals; 106,000 deaths/year

from nonerror, adverse effects of medications—these total up to 225,000 deaths per year in the U.S. from iatrogenic causes which ranks these deaths as the No. 3 killer.[9]

Recent public health research provides evidence that in many ways, technical medical interventions have little or no positive effect on populations:

Life expectancy is no greater in regions that have more intensive medical care, the researchers find, and Medicare surveys find that their quality of care is no better.... Another recent study, on the distribution of newborn intensive-care specialists and the death rate among infants, reached a similar conclusion. A tripling of the numbers of these specialists did not result in any improvement in infant mortality.[10]

If we are to reclaim our own healing abilities, it is essential to wrest our belief away from the medical model and reclaim the natural healing powers that are our birthright. Much of the positive impact of medical treatment is due to the placebo effect—the patient's belief in the efficacy of treatment.

In 75 percent of all cases the usefulness of the prescribed medication is not in the active principles but in the faith that the patients have in the technology. In other ages people believed in miracles; today they believe in science, and so the medical ritual takes on the appropriate guise.[11]

Approximately 80 percent of the response to [antidepressant] medication was duplicated in placebo control groups .... Improvement at the highest doses of medication was not different from improvement at the lowest doses. The proportion of the drug response duplicated by placebo was significantly greater than the medication.[12]

In an experiment, Japanese children who were allergic to Japan's equivalent of poison oak were told by a doctor that he was going rub their arms with the noxious plant. Instead the doctor used benign elm leaves, but the children's skin blistered anyway. Conversely, when he said that he was rubbing their skin with benign elm leaves and actually rubbed it with the noxious plant, their skin did not blister.[13]

In another remarkable study of people having knee surgery for arthritis, one group thought they were undergoing surgery but actually only had an incision and the surgeon acted as though he was performing surgery. These patients fared as well as those who actually had the surgery![14]

Placebos have positive impacts when they cause people to expect improvement, but what happens when people are given a negative prognosis?

> Another study looked at the following train of events. They examined 4000 people who were feeling well and confirmed that 30 percent were clearly ill without being aware of it, and that 60 percent had latent diseases to which they were well adjusted. Only 10 percent were in clinically good health. The authors' conclusion: when these people who were feeling fine were informed of their clinical profile: that was all it took to transform 90 percent of them into patients and bring on in most of them the appearance or worsening of symptoms that they had ignored up to then.[15]

We have been taught to regard illness as a problem that only doctors have the expertise to understand and solve. Our complaint is often diagnosed with a four-syllable word that we cannot even pronounce, but we are given a play-by-play account of the progression of destruction the illness is likely to take through our bodies. We get all of the appropriate messages to keep us ill; knowing precisely what to expect, our bodies respond with disease.

Many doctors consider it their responsibility to tell their patients how much time they have left when they give a "terminal" diagnosis. The problem is that just such a pronouncement can set in motion a self-fulfilling prophecy in the patient. In one case a man was told that he had cancer of the esophagus and that it was 100 percent fatal. He died a few weeks after hearing his diagnosis. The autopsy revealed only a couple of spots of cancer on his liver and lung, but no trace of it on his esophagus and not enough cancer to kill him. His doctor later said that "he died with cancer not of it."[16]

We need to reclaim our faith in the resilience of life and our own ability to be attuned to and participate with what is taking place in our bodies. Like physics, medicine is now reframing some of its perspectives.

Over the last three decades of mind/body research, thousands of studies have revealed that imagery, meditation, biofeedback, and hypnosis help people in a wide variety of ways. For instance, it has been established that people are able to diminish blood loss and complications in surgery, side effects of chemotherapy, pain, and anxiety. With these approaches, in rigorous research trials people have been able to increase immune function, memory, fertility, and shift the positioning of breech babies. In addition, it has been demonstrated that people can promote healing of burns, cancer, strokes, alcoholism, high blood pressure, multiple sclerosis, asthma, wounds, fish skin disease, bulimia, and more.[17]

We have more knowledge about the condition of our bodies then any other source. According to several studies involving more than 25,000 people, "our own opinion about the state of our health is a better predictor than physical symptoms and objective factors, such as extensive exams, and laboratory tests, or behaviors such as cigarette smoking."[18]

If we learn to pay attention to that "knowing," we will have a deep sense of what is taking place. This knowledge is not rational; it is intuitive. It does not provide a diagnosis in the logical manner to which we are accustomed. For instance, one person using visualization to help him heal his cancer created a scenario with which he engaged daily. He imagined that his white blood cells were rabbits eating their way through a field of carrot cancer cells. One day as he was doing his routine visualization, he found that the rabbits could not find enough to eat. The next time he saw his oncologist, he was told that the cancer was gone.[19]

The concept of "spontaneous remission" does not invite an inquiry into the power of healing but instead makes it sound as though it was happenstance. Any transformation that has taken place in the ailing person's heart, soul, or life remains invisible. This reinforces the attitude that there can be no cure except through medical intervention. The medical model promotes beliefs that encourage suspicion of the body and of nature—the intrinsic healing powers of life itself are systematically ignored.

Making Miracles Commonplace

One of the most significant changes in my life since I have come to learn how to work with consciousness has been my own health. I used to feel that whenever I got sick it was something that had happened to me. I had to follow the doctor's instructions, go to bed, take medication, and wait until my illness left. I used to be sick an average of ten days a year. Now, I virtually never get sick for more than a day at a time. If I get the flu, I involve myself in passing it through my body very rapidly. I have learned that I can listen to my body, participate with my healing processes, and avoid responding to potential threats altogether.

Meditation slows us down, reduces stress, and creates an acutely receptive state of awareness through which we can sense the subtle messages of our bodies. The Inner Witness reveals when we are in balance and when we are not. All that is needed is to stop, breathe, and pay attention; then we can respond to messages our bodies give us. Like all work with Applied Meditation, when you can imagine what you want—that is, feel what it would actually be like—you can project it with the Active Imagination. When you cannot do this, an insight is required, so you then engage the Receptive Imagination, ask questions, and respond to the information you get.

When I was younger, I had a runny nose throughout every winter. During the winter after I learned the techniques of Silva Mind Control, when my sinuses started to react, I meditated, imagining my mucous membranes drying. I pictured that it was like cotton evaporating. I did this only four or five times. My sinuses cleared up, and I have not had this problem since. Until I learned to work with my imagination, I continually gave my body the message: "This runny nose will be here all winter"; it had never occurred to me to imagine the problem clearing up.

Effecting change with the power of consciousness works in direct proportion to how strongly you believe that it will work. The more you believe, the less confusing your inner messages will be; clear messages are directives to which your body can respond. The catch is that belief comes from experience. I recommend that you begin with modest experiments. Choose an issue that has little emotional charge so it is easy to give yourself a clear message. I focused on avoiding mosquito bites, imagining an impenetrable wall around me that the mosquitoes could not get through. That did not work—the mosquitoes did not seem to see the wall. I tried another approach. I imagined talking to my skin, telling it that when the mosquitoes came, that it and the rest of my body would be happier if we let them come and go without responding. This technique was successful, and from then on, whenever a mosquito bit me, a welt would appear for perhaps twenty minutes and then go away, and the bites never itched. It is experiences like this that build confidence in the power of inner consciousness.

The more you experience success, the stronger your faith in the power of your body/mind becomes. Eventually, with the accumulation of experience you will find yourself spontaneously giving clear messages—without premeditation—always expecting what you want. Instead of being a victim to whatever dangers may cross your path, you will be able to maintain your power.

Expecting what you want does not mean that you get to transform into having the body for which all of us have been conditioned to strive. Each of our bodies has differing abilities, yet the cultural messages are to be strong, beautiful, thin, and not too short or too tall. Health does not mean conforming to the norm, but being in alignment with the resilient life force energies moving through our bodies. To reclaim healing powers, we each need to affirm who we are and work with ourselves. Striving to be something you are not only removes you further from the attunement needed to maintain good health. With the Inner Witness present, you will be able to tell if you have succumbed to the conditioning that diminishes the integrity of your body. If you do, you can use Mental Housecleaning to shift into a healthier perspective. An appreciation of our bodies is necessary if we are to work with the great healing powers that reside within.

Three years after I began meditating, I had a profound experience that revealed the degree to which I had come to know the power of the mind/body and how much I had reclaimed mine. I was moving a refrigerator on a dolly, pulling it backwards down a driveway into the street. The driveway, rather than having the gradual decline I had expected, dropped from sidewalk level to street level very quickly. Suddenly, the refrigerator was pushing me—I was not pulling it—and then I tripped on a four-by-four. As I fell, I instantaneously called on healing powers. One would expect that the leverage created by the bars of the dolly and the corner of the four-by-four would have snapped the bones of my legs under the impact of the refrigerator. If I had responded with fear, expecting to hurt myself, my body would have responded by receiving the full impact, and my legs would have been crushed. Instead, when I landed on the pavement, I felt an incredible mushroom of energy holding up the refrigerator. Afterward, my legs did not hurt and that energy continued to buzz through me for the rest of the move we were making that day—as if I had drunk a few cappuccinos. And my legs never even bruised.

Lynn, a close friend of mine, had a similar experience on his motorcycle. He made a left turn in downtown traffic, not seeing a car coming toward him—nor did the driver see him. When Lynn realized what was happening, he stopped the bike and put his foot down on the pavement while scream-ing at the driver. The driver hit his brakes and the car's front tire stopped on top of Lynn's left foot. The moment Lynn saw the car approach his foot, he flashed a feeling and sense through his mind: "My foot is safe and sound and will stay healthy and strong." When the driver realized what had hap-pened, he backed up and the tire rolled off Lynn's foot. He shook it gingerly, discovered that his foot was not even sore, and proceeded to drive on.

Each of these examples demonstrates the power of setting intention with the Active Imagination because the last and therefore prevailing message the body received before possible injury was positive. Trusting the power of the body/mind to maintain itself leaves no space for the idea of being victimized. In a study of 152 cancer patients, "the most significant finding was that a positive attitude toward treatment was a better predictor of response to treatment than was the severity of the disease." The Simontons, who conducted this study, pioneered the use of visualization for addressing cancer; their patients have a survival rate twice the national norm.[20]

Whether positive or negative, our bodies are always responding to whatever images we hold in our imagination at any given moment. It is crucial to appreciate how much our bodies and minds are tied together. Notice what messages your mind is giving your body. Advertisers tell us: "Got a stuffy nose? Take a decongestant. Got indigestion? Take an antacid. Can't sleep? Take a sleeping pill. Can't cope? Take depression and anxiety medications." These messages promote total distrust in the body's ability to heal itself. We're led to believe that the innate wisdom of the body/mind simply does not exist.

The multibillion-dollar diet industry coupled with the prevalence of eating disorders reflects the contempt we have for our own bodies. Instead of believing in our bodies, many of us hate them because they are not the right size or shape. Most of us could use a little Mental Housecleaning.

The powers of the mind/body are not exotic; it is not as if only a few exceptional individuals are endowed with them. They sleep inside each of us and can be reawakened.

Hearing the Voices of Your Body

Spending time with our bodies while in meditation establishes conscious communication between body and mind. Tune in to the condition of your body regularly. Scan your body with your imagination. Witness if any area is calling your attention. This need not take long. Notice how your body feels and where energy seems to be—if there is too much or too little anywhere, or if the energy is getting stuck someplace. Then try to imagine it balancing out. You will find yourself able to respond to your body's needs before you get ill. Also focus on any areas that you are working toward healing, tune in, and sense how the process is going—give it a little added support.

When you are meditating on a health problem, strive to give your body a clear message of what you want. Imagine what it would be like to be healthy in that particular area. To find positive points of reference, think of areas in your body that are in good health, or remember times when you felt full of vitality or a time when healing happened easily. Endeavor to transfer this positive sense into the area of distress. If you cannot envision yourself as being healthy, then work with the Receptive Imagination. Imagine going inside and visiting with the area of your body that is having difficulty. Assume that you really can do this, and further, that it makes a difference. Talk to your body. Comfort it; talk with it and with the ailment.

Witnessing what happens when you strive to experience the area as healthy will offer you deep insight into what is taking place. You just have to pay close attention. If the vision of well-being you are trying to hold keeps reverting to the status quo, then your body is not ready to heal—there is likely to be a message to which you should attend. In the presence of the Inner Witness, you can both discover insights that help you heal, and just as importantly, you can also find peace with what is occurring in your body—make peace with yourself.

Energy Circles are a great way to work with health challenges. Other members of the Circle will offer insight and positive points of reference for your healing. Plus, you will gift your body with an energetic boost.[21]

Sickness is a result of imbalance. It is a message that something needs to change to enable you to regain balance. With any illness or pain, your body is talking to you—you need to listen. If you keep taking aspirin for headaches, but do not stop to discover why you have them, your body does not stop signaling you. Its reactions will get louder and louder until you can no longer ignore them. Down the road, you may find yourself with a condition that is much more difficult to heal.

Doctors spend their time looking for the symptoms of a disease, rarely acknowledging that illness itself is a symptom. Treating the symptom may bring comfort in the short run, but it is ultimately ineffective in regaining balance. Our automatic reaction whenever we get sick is that something is wrong with our bodies rather than with our lives. This discounts the wisdom of our bodies, for they are our early warning system. To reclaim our healing powers we must reclaim our illnesses.

> Might not the illness be the inevitable response of a healthy individual to a situation that is not? Aren't the digestive troubles, headaches, rheumatism, insomnia, and depressions that switchboard operators, key punch operators, assembly line workers, and electronics solderers suffer from, more than anything the "healthy" protests of an organism that cannot adjust to the violence done to it daily, at an eight hour stretch?[22]

Ill health is an invitation for introspection. If you listen deeply you will find what is out of harmony in your life. As suggested above, this can be done easily while meditating, by simply going inside your body and talking with the ailing part. Put your Receptive Imagination to work. Be inquisitive and imagine what this part of your body would say—let yourself make it up and you find out what is happening. You will discover simple things, some easier to respond to than others, like needing more rest, establishing a better eating pattern, or making a change in a relationship. The answers are often simple and may feel like something you already knew. There is a felt sense that the answer is right. The issue is what you are willing to do with the insight. Are you willing to act on it? If not, some negotiation is called for. Make an agreement with your body as to what you will do about it. Some of the messages are harder to respond to—they may be about your working environment, which is usually out of your control. If this is the case, at least you have discovered the specific cause of the problem and can take protective measures against it.

You must be careful not to blame yourself for getting sick and not to ignore the conditions of your life that need change. Placing all the blame on conditions outside of yourself entirely leaves you in a powerless position. The way out is to get rid of the detrimental influences and at the same time discover how it is that you collude with them. Your internal response to an event is as important as the event itself. Consider a situation in which the clothing of two people catches on fire. One person panics, runs, and fans the flames, severely burning herself. The other remains calm and consciously chooses to roll on the ground, thus smothering the fire and receiving only minor burns. The environment is increasingly full of substances that are hazardous to our health. Everyone exposed to carcinogenic substances does not develop cancer. No matter what is going on, despite how we may feel, we are not victims, but participants. Since we are participants, we can be creative in how we participate.

Often the problem itself provides a solution for something else. Ask the ailment what it is protecting you from. What are you getting out of it? Your immediate reaction to this question is likely to be defensive, but blame is not the issue here. Even the worst of things have their positive side. If you allow yourself to look under the surface, you can know what is true for you. Maybe your illness offers a much-needed rest, alleviation from overwhelming responsibility, a chance to mourn a loss, or a way out of a seemingly irresolvable situation. When you find out what the advantages are for you, you can take steps to get your needs met in other ways. Then you will be able to focus your energy effectively on healing yourself and your environment.

When meditating on healing, it is good to have a framework in which to work. Find a health-care provider with whom you can collaborate. Form a partnership, assert yourself, and make the provider work with you, not on you. Rather than asking her what is going to happen with the illness, find out what transpires physiologically in the healing process as opposed to the course of disease. Give yourself positive points of reference by reading about the subject or talking to people who have successfully healed themselves of a similar condition. Find an anatomy chart—you want to give your imagination food for thought.

Some years back, I was exposed to infectious hepatitis A. I have never liked having shots, and once again I wanted to prove to myself the power of my mind/body. I asked the nurse what gamma globulin shots actually do. She told me that gamma globulin is simply something that the body already produces to ward off disease. If I had little trust in my ability to protect myself, I would have gotten the shot. Instead, I wanted to exercise the powers I knew I had. I imagined my body producing gamma globulin overtime—armies were being created. I imagined little armies of gamma globulin marching through my blood and standing in formation around my liver creating an impenetrable fortress. It worked—I did not come down with the hepatitis, to which I had definitely been exposed. I once again confirmed my power to maintain my health, and thus my power was further increased. I am not recommending that you ignore medical opinion, but only that you bring yourself and the power of consciousness into the healing process, and further that you find out what healing might look like rather than be preoccupied with disease.

In fact we can actively and creatively participate in our

healing, becoming empowered to blend mainstream medicine and "alternative medicine" in ways suited to our needs.

Robin Roth, a health educator and client of mine, had con-
tracted hepatitis C, a serious, long-term, chronic, and dangerous disease affecting about four million people in the United
States alone. The standard medical treatment is unpleasant
and only offers a 50 percent chance of clearing the virus. Robin
was in a population that had an even lower chance of success—she was told 12 percent. She decided "If someone was
going to be in the 12 percent, why not me?"[23] Working closely
with me, she created an affirmation to make healing her prior-
ity and researched what healing her liver would entail.

Along with the standard medical treatment, she worked
with complementary healing practices to increase her chances
of becoming a sustained responder. I recorded a meditation
grounded in the language of her inner consciousness to help
her envision her healing process, both in her body and in all
that she was doing to complement her treatment. She used it
daily and it helped her stay on a healing path. Successful in
clearing the virus and healing her liver, Robin was so enthusi-
astic that she wanted to partner with us to produce a CD of
Applied Meditation that would support others in coping with
hepatitis C. People who are using the meditations on the CD
are better able to sleep at night, deal with the symptoms associated with the disease, and some seem to be experiencing an
improvement in the way their liver functions.*

Your Body Is Your Home

When working with Applied Meditation for healing cultivate
patience, particularly if you have quite a number of conditions
bothering you. It took time for your problems to develop, and
it will also take time for your body to develop and maintain
healthy habits. Your body has become accustomed to the

---

*See www.hepcmeditations.org for information on the CD.

problems, and it will need time to become accustomed to the solutions. It bears repeating here, honor what is true for your body, and do not impose what you think it ought to be from a superficial level. For myself, I was born with a bone condition, which brings with it some disabilities. It has never occurred to me to "heal" myself of this condition. It is simply part of who I am. Each of our bodies has its own limitations. This work is not about turning us all into superwoman or superman, but reclaiming our wholeness and being attuned to healing energies.

I relate to my whole self as conscious. Every cell in my body possesses intelligence. You do not need to explain to your cells how to replenish themselves. Consciousness moves along habitual grooves. Sometimes healing is simply a matter of re-educating your cells and telling them that the situation has changed.

This work is not a quick fix. You have to do your part in bringing about change. Keep the agreements that you make with your body. Often people discover that this is difficult because when in meditation one becomes aware of all the solutions. Inner consciousness does not have to contend with the limits of time. It offers everything that would facilitate a return to health. You may find yourself making lots of agreements. Then a week later, you find you haven't been keeping all of them. It is as if you tried to eat a banquet in one mouthful. If you find yourself not having kept all the agreements, the next time you meditate, discuss it with your body and choose a more manageable course of action so you can take it one bite at a time. Patience is likely to help. You will find that as you make the changes in your life, it becomes increasingly easy to hold a sense of well-being in the areas of your body that had been ailing you.

If you have a constant problem—chronic pain, for example—tell yourself that the pain is dissolving ever so slowly, that it is imperceptibly getting better, and over time it will be gone altogether. This way, you have not let your experience of the problem become a reflection of your inability to heal it; instead, you have allowed yourself to experience the problem while knowing that it is continually getting better.

Another approach to healing a recurring health issue is to focus on it at a time when it is not immediately affecting you. Do the necessary inner work ahead of time so when the need arises you are ready for it—the same principle as working with symbols. The first day of my monthly menstruation used to feel really awful. Once, I was scheduled to do a workshop on the day it was due to occur. I could not afford to be under the weather since I was working with a new group of people. I began talking to my uterus three weeks in advance. I was feeling fine at the time so it was believable that I would feel fine later. And, in fact, I did.

This approach is particularly useful because when you are feeling bad, you are not inclined to meditate at all, much less convince yourself that you could feel otherwise. The agent of change is belief. You want to be in a place to project what is believable. Somehow you figure out how to offer yourself a placebo. Trick yourself into believing, and you change your situation.

Notice if you are spending more energy thinking of the problem than you are focusing on its moving into a state of health. Your body simply is going to respond to the strongest messages. It's hard to focus more on the solution when you are experiencing the problem, but the important thing is the prevailing last message whenever the area of concern comes to mind. If you think of the problem, always have your last image be your recovery, and that will be the direction in which your body goes.

Do not focus on the problem to see if it has begun to heal yet. I learned this lesson well when trying to rid myself of headaches. The Silva Method teaches you to get rid of a headache by telling yourself in meditation that at the count of five your headache will be gone. Whenever I got a headache, I would do just that. Then when I returned to an outer focus of attention, it was only natural to check to see whether I was successful. I had just had a headache, and there it was as soon as I looked for it. It took me a while to realize what I was doing wrong: the question "Do I have a headache?" kept the thought form in my mind to which my body loyally responded. Now, whenever I get a headache, I meditate and tell myself that during the next half-hour the headache will gradually dissolve. Afterwards, it is okay that my headache is still there because I know it is going to take a while to go away. In a half-hour, I am occupied with other concerns, and my headache disappears in the same amount of time it takes to digest an aspirin.

Since your body is tied to your mind, it is important to bring your beliefs into conscious awareness. They pave the roads that your thoughts move over, leading you in very specific directions. Even though thoughts are subtle, you can become fully aware of them by taking the time to bring them to light. Being mindful of what you say to yourself as you move through your activities reveals them. What you are discovering is not reality, but your attitude about reality—and that you can change. Once you become aware of a negative attitude, you can use Mental Housecleaning and also transform the attitude into its opposite with an affirmation.

In all inner work, building positive points of reference is crucial. It is of equal importance to remember the resilience intrinsic to life. Regularly focus on the innate wisdom of your body. Build your confidence. Give yourself a placebo daily. Remember how your body healed in the past; acknowledge the ways it functions well.

If you are struggling with a life-threatening disease, it may seem impossible to have an image of yourself as healthy. You may wish for it passionately, but expecting it is another matter. Healing is only possible when you can sense what it would be like. The case may also be that healing is not about extending one's life, but about coming to peaceful terms with yourself and your life, which, in turn, is a preparation for death. I do not mean to imply that being given a medical prognosis of imminent death means your fate is sealed. Many people whom doctors "put in their graves" years ago are still alive and well. But in our youth-worshipping, death-denying culture, there is a way that we deny ourselves the ability to come to terms with the natural processes of our bodies—we will all die sometime.

If you cannot imagine being well in the area of your body that is afflicted, then you can use the resources of your inner consciousness to come to terms more easily with what is happening, discovering what you need in order to live in more comfort or come to a sense of completion with your life and let go. Working with inner consciousness offers a way to intimately know what is happening inside and what you need. It is truly profound when facing death. Inner consciousness not only offers healing, but it offers access to wisdom and knowing in the spiritual dimensions beyond the body.

Induction

Make yourself comfortable. Focus on your breathing ... Bring to awareness your symbol for physical relaxation ... Breathe through any tensions ... Feel breath release them ... Relax into the support of the earth ... Breathe. Breath carries life ... ...

When you are ready, bring to awareness your symbol for mental relaxation ... Breathe. Let your breath be the breeze that clears the sky of your mind ... Experience your mind opening into spacious awareness ... ...

Bring to awareness your symbol for emotional relaxation ... Breathe out any feelings that are tugging at you ... ... Acknowledge your goodness ... Offer yourself some loving kindness ... Feel your heart relaxing ... ...

When you are ready, bring to awareness your symbol for your creative, self-restoring center. Take a moment to acknowledge your gratitude ... Acknowledge the sanctity of life ... ...

Now take time to enhance your level of awareness by whatever method you choose. You can simply rest your awareness on your breath ... Or you may choose to go to a relaxing place, or

MEDITATIONS

listen deeply to the pulse of your own heart, or any other methods that you are inclined to work with to deepen your awareness ... Tell yourself you will be fully relaxed and alert throughout this meditation ... ...

Begin to finish what you are doing ... You are now consciously developing the intuitive skills you have always had. You are at your creative self-restoring center. Here the Inner Witness emerges and you discover a rich, beautiful landscape of receptivity and creativity. As you open, more and more of these energies flow through you. Just as using your muscles keeps your body strong and resilient, so too, working in your creative self-restoring center keeps your intuitive and healing powers fully accessible ... From here you discover the powers to heal yourself and others. Here you become a healer.

I am going to suggest several affirmations; if you wish to affirm them, repeat them to yourself, feeling as though they are fully true; knowing that in focusing on affirmations, you create patterns of energy that materialize in your experience.

Life is resilient; I believe in life ...

I trust my nature, I trust nature ...

I love my body; my body is resilient ...

The whole of my body/mind is healthy ...

I am fully present and mindful in each moment ... ...

I listen to my intuition ...

I always successfully protect myself ...

My life is in harmony with the life around me ...

My life is whole; my life is a part of the whole of life ...

Energy flows easily and clearly throughout the whole of my being ...

I am in harmony with the natural rhythms of life within and around me ...

I am always attuned to what is needed for healing to happen on all levels of being ...

I honor my body with care ...

I eat only those foods that nourish my body ...

I rest all I need to replenish my body ...

I exercise all I need to maintain my health and vitality ...

My body/mind is whole and fully attuned. My mind responds to the messages my body offers; my body responds to the messages my mind offers ...

I am resilient; I maintain balance amidst change ...

I trust the future ...

Take a moment and breathe in gratitude as you inhale ... and breathe out compassion as you exhale ... Gratitude to be alive; compassion for all life ... ...

Now take time to focus on any of your own affirmations or symbols. Know that in focusing on affirmations, you set energies in motion and you will find that the affirmations manifest in your experience. Expect this to be the case ... ...

Know that in focusing on affirmations, you have created patterns of energy that will move out into your life and materialize within and around you ...

In a moment, I am going to count on a descending scale from ten to one. At each descending count you will relax into yourself, into your body, more. As you relax, you become increasingly sensitive to the state of your being, to the state of your body. At the count of one, you will be fully attuned to the healing powers of life itself.

Ten, moving deeper now ... Nine, returning to yourself ... Breathing ... Eight, relaxing ... Seven, relaxing into your body ... Six, your body relaxing into the universal life energies that carry it ... Five, deeper and deeper ... Four, moving down ... Three, relaxing ... Two, very aware ... One, feel the expansive energies of life itself. Breathing ... here is where healing energy flows ... Here you experience the intimate connection of body and mind. You are fully attuned to what is so in your body.

Tell yourself you will remain alert throughout the whole of this meditation, and you will remember all that you experience.

Vitality of Life

Now sense vitality, imagine life force energy ... You may wish to imagine the radiance of the sun, imagining that you have a golden sun within you, emanating this life force energy ... brilliant energy that your life rides upon ... Or a spring of water that sparkles with the light of the sun dancing on the surface ... Radiant, resilient energy that is life, your life. Sense this spring of energy, the source of vitality ... However you experience it ... it's the continuous flow of being ... breath, heart, life moves through, life carries you ... animating who it is that you are.

Witness it ... Feel it. Sense it, as though your energy were coming up from an underground spring ... continually coming up ... continually moving, like a river that is never twice the same ... the continuous spontaneous flow of being ... the spirit of life itself ... sometimes quiet, sometimes loud ... Breathe it ... It breathes you ... Feel the continuous resilient life force energy ... However you sense it ... vibrant energy.

Feel it moving through every cell of your body infused with the pulse of life ... sometimes it is soft, sometimes it is surging ... resilient life energy always carries you ... Breathing you. Spontaneous, inexhaustible energy ... vibrant, radiant energy moving through you. Your life rides on it ... Feel it teeming in every cell of your body, through every pore, every organ ... energy ... Feel this energy's connection with all of life energy that permeates everything ... The glow of life.

The cells of which you are composed animated by life, vibrant with life ... cells continually being created, continually growing, as old ones die ... the continuous transformation of energy ... Life is fully resilient. It rejuvenates itself. Acknowledge this ... Feel the self-perpetuating, self-healing regenerative powers that your body has ... It continually renews itself ... Witness the innate intelligence that your body possesses, its ability to heal and regenerate itself ... Witness the intrinsic intelligence of every cell of which you are composed ...

Acknowledge the intelligence of life itself. Let yourself trust life ... Now create a symbol for all that you are experiencing. Create a symbol for vitality, for your health, for the vitality of life itself ... ... Know that whenever you bring this symbol to awareness it will move you into alignment with the life forces energy ... It will revitalize you, energize you ... Know that whenever you bring this symbol to mind it creates a channel to receive the information you need to regain your health and vitality ... Expect this ... Tell yourself this now ... Imagine that the energy of this symbol pours into the whole of your body ... ... Acknowledge your gratitude for the gift of life ... Acknowledge the gift that your body is.

Developing Rapport with Your Body

You are going to journey through your body ... Your imagination will transport you through your body's inner landscape. You will be able to experience directly the vitality in all the parts of your body. Imagine yourself very tiny, riding a pinpoint of light ...

light that illuminates the internal workings of your body ... Know that it is fine to simply make up what you imagine it to be like inside ... However your imagination depicts what is happening inside is what is true for you ...

Bring to mind your symbol for health and vitality and keep it in the background of your awareness as you explore the inner workings of your body; in doing so your symbol will enable you to fully experience the innate intelligence of each area within you.

Feel your bones ... Explore what they look like ... Imagine what they would feel like if you were to touch them with your fingertips ... Become aware of the strength, the durability of your bones, of the whole of your skeleton giving your body a frame to stand on ... Inside them your blood is created. Imagine blood being manufactured ...

Imagine the layers of muscles connecting your bones ... Be aware of the muscles' strength ... flexibility, their texture, their color, their tone ... Explore the whole of your musculature ... ...

Become aware of your heart, the rhythm of your pulse ... the sound of your heartbeat ... Witness your heart pumping blood, keeping it flowing throughout your whole body ... rivers moving through the landscape of your body ... Imagine moving through a vein and exploring your circulation ... blood bringing to each of the areas of your body what it needs and carrying away the wastes keeping your body in balance.

Feel the rhythm of breath, like waves rising and falling. Breath renews, cleanses, and sustains your body ... Breath is carried by blood ... Sense each cell of which you are composed breathing ... Breath carries life ... ...

Now become aware of your digestive system ... You may wish to imagine riding on a piece of food ... Go through the whole of your digestive system ... Notice its feel, its color, its sound. Experience your digestive system transforming food into energy; keeping every cell of your body well-nourished ... ...

Become aware of your reproductive system, its harmonious balance ... how it looks, how it feels, where it is in the cycle of life ... Appreciate sexuality as a celebration of life itself ...

Become aware of your brain, sense it, feel it ... Become aware of your spine ... aware of your nervous system branching out to the full reaches of your body ... Feel how alert and responsive your body is ... Imagine the networking of impulses throughout your nervous system keeping all your body parts in communication ... Feel how acutely aware your body is ... Acknowledge the intelligence residing within you ...

All of your senses are sharply attuned ... Explore your five senses, see them, feel them, fully sense them ... Take time to explore them ... ...

Imagine your lymphatic system; your immune system maintains the integrity of your body ... keeping your body safe and secure ... always on the lookout for and clearing away anything that does not belong ... maintaining the peace and well-being in the

landscape of your body so all parts can do their job
well ... ... Notice each of your glands producing the
appropriate fluids for all of your body to maintain
equilibrium ... Notice how each of your glands plays a role in
keeping your body in balance ... ...

Now explore on your own areas you have been through or
areas you have not yet gone into. Remember your symbol for
health and vitality and explore with it. Take time to do this
now ... ...

Take time to finish what you are doing ... Take a moment to
fully appreciate the nature of your body ... Feel its integrity ...
Believe in your body, make friends with it ... Feel how all the
areas in your body cooperate with one another. Your body is
always able to replenish itself, providing you with a good home
for yourself ... Love your body for the home it gives you.
Imagine offering it loving, healing energy ... As you breathe,
bring loving, healing energy into your body ... Acknowledge
your gratitude for the gift of life ...

Self-Healing

From this place be aware of the resilience intrinsic to life itself,
for life is healing, self-clearing, regenerative ... When you cut
your skin, it rebuilds itself of its own accord; your body knows
how to regenerate itself ... Acknowledge the self-healing
capabilities intrinsic to your body. Ailments are signposts
pointing towards what is healthful. Each problem contains
within itself the seeds of its own healing ... Remember times

when your body has healed itself ... Trust the nature of your body ... Your trust gives your cells added support for their healing work ... ...

Now become aware, fully aware, of the whole of your body, the position it is in ... the condition it is in ... the pulse of life percolating through ... Know that you are becoming as aware of your internal physical environment as you are of your external physical environment ... With your keen inner sense, become aware of any areas in your body that you would like to heal ... To promote and maintain good health, you can communicate with any area of your body ... You can hear its messages and discover what is needed to increase well-being ... Your body will hear new messages you offer ... Your body is loyal and responsive to whatever messages you give. Appreciate that this is true ...

Choose one particular area you would like to work on ... If you have a number of different areas, choose one, and know that you can work on others another time.

Imagine this part of your body; imagine what it looks like, what it feels like ... Be aware of the atmosphere in which it lives ... Be aware of the quality of energy present in it ... Use the story making capacities of your imagination. What mood is it in? ... Sense sounds, smells, colors, and textures ... Trust what occurs to you ... Let it all come through your imagination.

Sense the intelligence of this part of your body ... Imagine that it sends out a messenger to represent it ... Welcome the representative. Give yourself permission to pretend that indeed you can talk to this area. Let the child within you make up a story ... Talk to the messenger; listen to what it has to say about what is true for this part of your body ... Be sensitive to how it communicates, it might not be verbal, it could come in the form of direct knowing ... You might find yourself knowing at the same time that you are asking ... Pay keen attention to what occurs. Be receptive to whatever you sense. Trust what happens. Ask the messenger what is going on ... Be receptive to the area's experience ... ...

Ask if there is anything it is defending you against ... anything in your life it is protecting you from ... or what it wants protection from ... understanding happens ... ...

Come to ways that work to take care of needs ... Ask what it wants; sense what it has to say ... Ask it if there are particular exercises, foods, rest, or whatever that would be helpful ... Trust your sense ... ...

Decide if you are willing to give it what it wants ... Decide if there is anything you want from it and ask for it ... ... You can tell it how you feel, what you want ... You may need to re-educate the cells—tell them what is happening now or reassure them about the future ... ... You and your body may need to let go of some old habits to make ways for energies to move in new ways ... ...

Sense if the area is willing to give you what you want ... What agreements might you make so that you can cooperatively take care of one another? ... Compromise when need be ... Tell it what you are willing to do ... Be patient with one another ...

Endeavor to make life easier for one another ... Bring kindness into the scene. Breathe some kindness into the area ... Put any difficult feelings through your Mental Housecleaning device ... ...

Bring your symbol of health and vitality into the scene ... Ask the symbol if it has any light to shed on the healing of this area ... Breathe in healing. Breathe in vitality ... As you inhale, gather vital healing energy ... As you exhale send it to the area, shine it onto the messenger ... Feeling healing happen ... ...

Witness if there is any part of you that somehow is a little hesitant, not so sure this change is such a good thing. Talk with this part too. Imagine what it is you need to do to take care of that part of yourself ... Decide how you are going to act on this ... and imagine doing so.

Know that whenever you bring this symbol to mind, it will help your body in its healing process ... Know that this is so ... ...

Know that every day you are getting better ... Trust your ability to heal yourself to be in harmony with the whole of yourself and all that is around you ... ... Acknowledge your gratitude for the gift of life ...

Healing Attitudes

Here you can witness the patterns of your own consciousness. Here you witness what you tell yourself is so. Here your beliefs become sharp and clear. Not only are the patterns of your consciousness revealed to you here, but you can re-pattern your attitudes so consciousness moves only in positive directions. You can transform negative ideas and pave new roads for your consciousness—moving in a healthful direction ...

Focus on your breath. In the quiet of breath, just breathing, take a few moments to simply be with your body ... breathing and aware of your body ... Tune into your body ... witness what comes up for you ... ...

Notice what crosses your mind as you breathe and focus on your body. Breathe ... What comes to awareness as you are quietly with your body? Notice, are you glad to be with your body? ... Do you have aversion? ... Witness ... In the quiet as you rest your attention on your body, note what comes up for you ... ...

Witness your responses as you hear the following questions ... Witness if tension arises. Witness when you feel good. At the end of the meditation you will have time to transform attitudes and cultivate new ones that empower you to have a loving relationship with your body ...

As you move through your day, when do thoughts and feelings about your body come up? ... When you are dressing? ... When you are eating? ... When you are moving about? ... When you are with others? ... When you are resting? ... When you are exercising? ... Witness what is true for you ... ...

Do you ever talk to your body? ... What do you say? ... Are you friendly? ... What feelings are there? ... ... Are they wanting your body to be different than it is? ... What are you telling your body? ... ...

Explore your inclinations to care for your body ... ... What are your strengths? ... What limitations do you have to contend with? ... What are you always vulnerable to? ... What do you assume to be so? ... How do you care for your body? ... What do you assume the future holds for your body? ... ... Explore all this ... ...

Now transform any attitudes that are limiting with your Mental Housecleaning device, or ground them with your grounding cord, know the earth transforms them. Symbolize the attitudes and all their accompanying thoughts and feelings ... Tell yourself you are changing your approach ... and let the old assumptions go ... ...

Bring to awareness your symbol for vitality. Remember the resilient qualities of life itself. Offer your body loving kindness ... Have gratitude for your body, be generous toward your body ... ...

Now invite the specific beliefs and affirmations that assume health and well-being are as natural to your body as breathing ... Be specific ... ... Go back to the particular attitudes you just released and make beliefs that are life affirming ... Work with one at a time. Create specific affirmations that affirm your body ... ...

Breathe in these perspectives ... Get a feel for them ... Imagine going about your day holding these beliefs are true ... Believe in your ability to change. Believe in your body. Believe in your wellness ... Imagine exaggerating your belief. Stretch your faith; make it even greater ... Feel how your life will be after these changes have fully taken root ... ...

Notice what you can do in your life now, to seed this life-affirming perspective you are cultivating. Acknowledge your gratitude for the gift of life.

Creating a Healthful Routine: Food, Rest, and Exercise

You now occupy an extremely receptive and knowing state of awareness. You are now going to explore the life of your body. Acknowledge the fact that within you lies the knowledge of what you need to care for honor your body ... Bring your vitality symbol into your meditation and let it shed light on your exploration.

Food is sacred. Food nourishes your body. Some food your body will resonate with, some food your feelings may resonate with. Some foods may hum, some may scream ... Be aware of what part of you desires different foods. Simply bring a food into awareness; witness whether it's your body that desires what this particular food has to offer, or another aspect of yourself that desires this food ... Explore what parts of you desire the different foods in your life. Bring these to awareness one at a time. Imagine the food in detail and witness what occurs. Be in your body and feel what happens ... ...

When you are finished exploring the different foods, if there are foods that you are wanting with parts of yourself other than your body, talk to them and see how you can meet their needs in new ways, so you only eat those foods that your body wants ... ... Choose what you want to eat for healthful life, meeting the needs of all of yourself, your body, and your feelings. Notice if there are foods that your body wants that you have not been giving to it ... What food does your body want for optimal health and vitality? ... ...

Choose how you want to relate to food as you move through your daily routine ... If you have in any way been compulsive about food, breathe through it ... Mental Houseclean the pushy energy and forgive yourself ... ... Appreciate that food connects you to the whole community of life. To eat is a sacred act ... ...

Now take time to be aware of what your body needs in rest and relaxation on the one hand, and activity and exercise on the other ... Be in your body; how does it experience the rhythm of your life? ... Create a routine in your life that is balanced with vital activity and replenishing rest ... Imagine the optimal rhythm. Life thrives in rhythm. Offer your body what it needs to maintain optimal health ... ...

Decide what you are willing to do ... Make agreements with yourself. Imagine acting on your choices ... caring for your body, the home of yourself ... ... Acknowledge your gratitude for the gift of life ...

Count Out

The whole of your mind/body functions harmoniously ... as harmoniously as the whole of nature. Know that every time you meditate, you tap harmonizing energies and they heal you ... Review the lessons and insights you gained, any symbols you worked with ... Go over any agreements that you have made ... ...

Notice how acting on the knowing that you have come to is going to affect your life ... How it will affect your activities? ... Now notice how it will affect those around you ... Notice if any adjustments need to be made ... if anyone needs to be spoken to ... what support you have for these changes ... what support you will now be able to offer others.

Healing energy can be channeled from this state of awareness. Channel healing wherever you like. Imagine well-being. Hold yourself or another in the light of healing energy ... ...

Finish what you are doing ... Trust yourself, trust your body, trust your mind, trust nature. Trust life ...

In a moment I am going to count from one to five ... At the count of five, you will open your eyes remembering all that you have experienced ... feeling refreshed, revitalized, and relaxed.

ONE—becoming more aware of the room around you ...

TWO—coming up slowly now ...

THREE—at the count of five, you will open your eyes feeling relaxed, revitalized, and refreshed remembering all that you have experienced ...

FOUR—coming up now, bringing with you your sense of well-being ...

FIVE!—eyes open, feeling refreshed, revitalized, and relaxed, remembering all you have experienced ... having brought with you your sense of wholeness—open heart and spirit ... Healthy and resilient.

◆8◆

Making Your Life Work for You

There is a great elegance and mystery to the universe. It is as though all that exists is woven into a grand symphony of being—there is symmetry in constant flux from atoms to solar systems, from stardust to galaxies. Life is resilient; it self-regulates, it heals, and it recreates itself. Aware of it or not, we are held by the universe. It is in deep consciousness that we experience oneness. When we move *with* the unifying energy that runs through all that exists, our lives are harmonious. Life is in alignment, and there is a quality of grace present.

Western rationalism has separated us from the whole, alienating us from the innate wisdom of our bodies, as well as from the resilience intrinsic to consciousness itself. When we withdraw from the unifying life forces and constrict ourselves, we become rigid, disassociated, and unable to learn. Our lives become discordant—cut off from creative and healing energies. We are likely to act in ways harmful to ourselves and others, for we have lost touch with the sanctity of life.

How often do we try to ignore the back pain, the uncomfortable relationship, or the tedious job because we just cannot see a solution? We all have problems; we do not make them up, they are quite real. They originate in the world in which we live and in the conditions of our lives, both past and present. Contradictions exist everywhere in spite of the connectedness of all that is—contradictions between our need to experience peace and the challenges we have to contend with in our everyday lives; contradictions caused by our unresolved feelings, ignored lessons, or outdated beliefs, or between the complacent and courageous sides of ourselves.

If we rely exclusively on rational thinking for solving problems, we compound them. Rational beta consciousness makes us feel as if time is speeding, leaving no room for inner consciousness to surface. On the run we do not stop and reflect. Beta thinking categorizes, sorts, and separates. Beta consciousness would have us believe that only one side of a contradiction can be true, rather than both. Having a linear cause-and-effect orientation, it assumes that the key to making change is in discovering the origin of problems. This, in turn, causes a preoccupation with the negative; if we are not careful, we find that we put all of our attention on what we *do not want* rather than on what we *do want.*

Some people continually revisit the past, searching for the origins of their suffering. They believe that in order to solve their problems, they need to understand what went wrong in their childhood. Looking back may make one feel more at ease with current limitations, but this is likely to reinforce them rather than resolve them. Understanding why it is the way it is does not reveal how it could be different. I approach issues from the opposite orientation. Whatever the issue, suffering can be lessened if one asks oneself what one wants instead. *We need a vision for which to strive.* Without one, the problem itself is the only point of reference, and therefore holds a monopoly on the issue. No matter how well one understands a problem, it gets replicated. As we have learned, our behavior and our bodies are always loyal to the images we hold in our minds. Without a positive vision of the issue, there is no change for the better. Working with the holistic aspects of consciousness is more effective in alleviating suffering than relying on rationalism; it opens the imagination and offers vision.

The Fundamentals of Applied Meditation

You need the spacious awareness of the Inner Witness to reveal what is really taking place. The Inner Witness notices when you are beginning to shut down. And just as important, it recognizes insights and openings that emerge as the Active and Receptive Imaginations dance together. I believe that focusing on a vision of how you would like things to be orients you in a positive direction and moves you forward. This is the work of the Active Imagination. But this visioning process is not as linear as it might seem. When you work with a vision in the presence of the Inner Witness, you discover what does not quite fit, what is not plausible, or if the vision reverts back to the status quo. You also witness how others respond. All of this is in the dance. What is important is not the product of the vision, but the witnessing of the dance.

The imagination is multidimensional. It is the aspect of consciousness we employ to give shape to our aspirations, and it is simultaneously the medium of intuitive information. More than that, it is the stuff of which probabilities are made. Appreciating this means that what we can and what we cannot imagine takes on profound significance. We both discover and create reality through witnessing the play of the imagination. Your Active Imagination (setting intent with creative projection) is entwined with your Receptive Imagination (intuition and learning). It is not as though you work with one and then when you are done, you go on to the next. They operate simultaneously in a dance of creativity and intuition that is all played out in the presence of the Inner Witness.

As I indicated previously, the most profound work with inner consciousness is witnessing what you cannot imagine;

that is when your projection keeps reverting to the status quo. This is crucial information. Contrary to the commonly held view of the imagination, in Applied Meditation, it is the window into reality. The display of whatever you are working on metaphorically represents the current state of affairs and reveals both subjective and objective limitations. Use the story-making capacities of the Receptive Imagination to find where openings lie. In the process, your intuition will offer crucial information, and you will find that the Inner Witness recognizes it when it appears. The Inner Witness always grounds you in the recognition of what is taking place and what is needed to move into alignment with life force energies.

The Continuum of Change

Life is in a constant state of change. Because of our awareness of this, we know that things could be different. Change carries possibility. The contradiction between the real and the ideal causes creativity to emerge and inspires the visionary within each of us to wake up.

The continuum begins with a recognition that conditions do not have to be as they are. Here, the Inner Witness recognizes that you can either shift your attitude or change the conditions themselves. This opens you to new possibilities. Rather than resisting and wearing blinders, you have expanded your view.

As you move along the continuum, you will no longer find yourself reacting or shutting down, but instead feeling proactive and open. With new possibilities apparent, you now have resources that your Active Imagination can use to set a positive intent. Whether you shift your attitude or discover an alternative, you can then imagine embodying it. As you do, it becomes increasingly clear. At the point when the new way remains steady in your imagination, change is imminent.

During the process, you continually witness *how* you imagine the embodiment of the change you desire. Watching this reveals where attention is called for. You discover what internal shifts will move you out of the old patterns that tend to keep you replicating the very circumstances you are trying to transform. You will also find yourself intuitively wanting to make particular changes, maybe a subtle shift in your attitude or perhaps a major change in your life—all this will be revealed in the dance of your imagination.

What you focus on is the reality you perpetuate. This does not mean that you should compel yourself to always to be positive. The act of forcing goes against the flow. Denial cuts one off from vital energy and it keeps intuitive knowledge out of view. Only in openness can healing and creativity take place. You cannot relax and be in denial at the same time because in open awareness problems needing your attention naturally surface. Repressing negative emotions will lead to compulsive behavior or addiction. When we are not centered inside our selves, we compulsively eat, clean, constantly socialize (as if there is no choice), or maybe numb ourselves with alcohol or television. The longer our problems go unaddressed, the more neurotic we become, and the original issues get buried under all the side effects of the compulsive behavior.

Consciousness, like the body, naturally heals when given the space to do so. The gift of the Inner Witness is that it recognizes when we are beginning to shut down. This awareness is where our true freedom lies. The Witness offers space so we have room to live with difficulties without shutting down. There is room to choose how to respond instead of simply reacting. Unlike beta consciousness, in spacious awareness, time expands. In the space created, the Witness recognizes where imbalance lies; it catches flashes of insight and it hears the soft voice of intuition. We do not need to *do* anything for the Inner Witness to come forth; it is as natural to consciousness as breath is to the body. In fact, all we need to do is stop doing. Make space, take a deep breath, and relax into wholeness.

Sometimes you might find yourself having a hard time with an issue, and creating a positive vision seems inconceivable and irrelevant. In meditation, simply sit with the difficulty. As you do so, you witness the web of energy patterns holding it in place. In the presence of the Inner Witness, you will be able to see multiple dimensions at play, learning to be at peace with the issue as it is rather than struggling against it. In spacious awareness you are able to see the difficulties more as a multidimensional set of relationships. You can find a loose end in the web and give it a tug, catalyzing an energetic shift in the entire situation.

Notice if you are preoccupied with the past or caught in avoidance. If you are, then use Mental Housecleaning to create space for inner consciousness to work. This will make room for fresh perspective to arise. When experiencing pain, one usually reacts with tension; yet, breathing into pain is what alleviates it. Breath heals on all levels of experience. As you focus on breath, you find that it invites the Inner Witness. In the presence of the Inner Witness, just be with the situation as it is. Do not do anything with it; breathe and share presence with it. Breathe; create space in yourself and in the scene—letting it be as it is; letting yourself be as you are. Listen deeply. Ask yourself what is good in the circumstance. You may find what it is in your inner landscape that is energetically congruent with the external problem; then you can then use Mental Housecleaning to make room for transformation.

The new realities you discover become the ingredients for your Active Imagination to conjure up a desirable vision, which may include a new attitude and/or a completely different circumstance. In the beginning, your projection is likely to feel as though it is not quite plausible. It has an elusive feel to it, as though it is just beyond your grasp. Your vision keeps reverting back to your current experience. When you imagine the desirable experience, it might feel like wishful fancy. This is when your current experience is the only one that seems possible. *Working in the gap between your vision and your experience is the heart of Applied Meditation.* As you stretch your imagination into new possibilities, you will be able to witness the nuances of how your imagination depicts your projection. This reveals exactly where attention is needed to cultivate conditions amenable to change. Einstein tells us, "No problem can be solved from the consciousness that created it. We must learn to see the world anew."

The Receptive Imagination Incites Change

Engage with the Receptive Imagination whenever your vision is not plausible or you simply have no vision because the difficulty screams too loudly. Imagine the situation itself becoming personified; imagine that it has an intelligence of its own, and then converse with it. If tension arises, just return to your breath and breathe through your tension; release it and simply witness. When you are ready again, work with the Receptive Imagination, let yourself be playful. With a really troubling issue, it might take many meditation sittings before you are able to fully work with the Receptive Imagination.

Be patient and give yourself the time you need. The Inner Witness provides a spaciousness in which the Receptive Imagination can play. To see the situation anew, shake up the scene, turn it upside down, imagine everyone switching roles, or displaying traits opposite to their usual way of being. Open up your imagination, shake everything up, and see where all the pieces land. Change is constant, so play with the energy, and discover what might emerge.

Recently, I had many more responsibilities than I had time to carry out. I meditated on the problem. An image of an hourglass came into my awareness. This hourglass was narrow not just in the center, but in four places. No sand could get through; as I sat with the image, the hourglass transformed into a trunk of an old cottonwood tree from my childhood. When I was young, I used to go to this tree to commune with it and with myself. It always held a magical quality for me. In its presence, I had a visceral feeling of rootedness and the knowledge that time would carry me, rather than having me run after it. In that meditation, I relearned the lesson: listen in and time opens out. As the day unfolded, I was able to move through it in a relaxed and effective manner.

As you work, you will have insights that are in alignment with your intention. Though it is likely to feel awkward, when you act on the insights, you will find that your original vision becomes increasingly plausible. You gradually see what it would be like more clearly and at the same time the old patterns have begun to dissolve. Eventually your vision no longer reverts to the old way of being. When you reach the point where you can imagine your new reality vividly—believing that it is plausible and feeling what it would be like—change has gained momentum. You no longer view your old experience in the same way. You are now expecting conditions to be different.

Witnessing the dance that takes place on the continuum of change reveals where attention is needed. Sometimes it is inside of us and sometimes it is outside—usually attention is needed in both. When you strive to focus on a desirable vision, anything that obstructs it is not a reflection of the limitations of your imagination. On the contrary, it points to the very conditions that are blocking change, whether that is something inside or out. Again, it is what you cannot imagine that points to where you need to work.

Beliefs Are Our Roadmaps

During the process of projecting a vision of the future, you might witness messages getting provoked like, "I'll get rejected if I do that!" The message is likely to be familiar, as well as show how you have been colluding with the limitations that you strive to overcome. This is where the past enters the scene. You work with it in this context because it blocks your ability to clearly imagine the future. Whatever messages you give yourself that discount the possibility of your vision are the messages that are keeping you from experiencing the new reality. Use the Receptive Imagination to personify the messenger and negotiate with it. You might imagine a cartoon character. Ask it what it is protecting you from. As you engage in the story, you will find new ways to care for yourself. It is important to inform your deeper self that life has changed and that now a more positive experience is available. Offer it a new perspective. Notice what you might do differently. As always, make clear agreements with yourself and stick to them.

We can be thankful that inner consciousness is noncritical. Our behavior is loyal to our inner messages, and our inner consciousness is accepting of the new messages offered. You will find that the old beliefs are amenable to change. This process may broach the same issues that people seek in classic therapeutic settings. Rather than scrutinizing or analyzing, take advantage of the fact that inner consciousness is suggestible and transform limiting inner messages. Explaining why you are stuck is irrelevant; what is needed is the establishment of a new belief providing you with a new footing. This puts you on the road of transformation. It is a totally different process than reaching into the past in search of what is wrong. As you transform the obstructing inner messages, you will find that your original vision becomes increasingly clear. (Or something may be revealed in the process that causes you to want to shift the vision.)

Though you do not want to delve into your past for what is wrong, you do want to be mindful of the beliefs embedded in your thinking. They are the conclusions we have drawn in the past. Just because you drew a particular conclusion as a result of what happened previously does not mean it still applies. Circumstances have often changed. What may have been a good conclusion before is now a limiting belief. It is our beliefs through which we interpret all that comes to our awareness; they control what comes into view and shape what we anticipate. Even intuition is loyal to belief as people who believe there is no such thing as ESP demonstrate by achieving below chance scores (see page 92). If we are not mindful, we take our beliefs for granted.

Beliefs are the maps we use to navigate our lives. You want to be sure that yours are not outdated. Only certain landscapes can be viewed from a particular road. Some beliefs are functional and constructive, while others perpetuate problems you would probably prefer to leave behind. In this case, it is time to reroute yourself. Consciousness always moves along roads paved by habitual beliefs. We act out of habit. That is fine if the road takes you in the direction you want to go, but if it does not, then you need to blaze a new trail upon which your consciousness can travel.

Outdated beliefs attract circumstances that we would each rather not experience. We find ourselves replaying the same old dramas and, worse, we pass them on to our children, and they cycle through from one generation to the next. If you find yourself caught in trying to distinguish between a belief and reality, do not worry. Reality is constantly changing and you can influence the course of change.

Seth suggests:

> In those areas in which you are dissatisfied, you feel that you are powerless, or that your will is paralyzed, or that conditions continue despite what you think of as your intent. Yet if you pay attention to your own quite conscious thoughts, you will find that you are concentrating upon precisely those negative aspects that so appall you. You are hypnotizing yourself quite effectively, and so reinforcing the situation.

You may say, horrified, "What can I do? I am hypnotizing myself into my overweight condition (or my loneliness, or my poor health)?" Yet in other facets of your life, you may be hypnotizing yourself into wealth, accomplishment, satisfaction—and here you do not complain. The same issues are involved. The same principles are operating. In those positive life situations, you are certain of your initiative. There is no doubt. Your beliefs become reality.

Now: in the unsatisfactory aspects, you must understand this: there is also no doubt. You are utterly convinced that you are sick, or poor, or lonely, or spiritually opaque, or unhappy. The results, then, as easily and effortlessly follow. Natural hypnosis, in the terms given here, operates as well in one case as in the other.

What should you do, then? First of all, you must realize that you are the hypnotist. You must seize the initiative here as you have in other positive aspects of your life. Whatever the superficial reasons for your beliefs, you must say:

"For a certain amount of time I will momentarily suspend what I believe in this area, and willfully accept the belief I want. I will pretend that I am under hypnosis, with myself as hypnotist and subject. For that time, desire and belief will be one. There will be no conflict because I do this willingly. For this period I will completely alter my old beliefs. Even though I sit quietly, in my mind I will act as if the belief I want were mine completely."

At this point, do not think of the future, but only of the present. If you are overweight, insert the weight that you think is ideal for you while you are following this exercise. Imagine that you are healthy if you have the belief that you are not. If you are lonely, believe that you are filled with the feeling of companionship instead. Realize that you are exerting your initiative to imagine such situations. Here there can be no comparison with your normal situation. Use visual data, or words—whatever is most natural to you. And again, no more than ten minutes is required.

If you do this faithfully, within a month you will find the new conditions materializing in your experience. Your neurological structure will respond automatically. The unconscious will be aroused, bringing its great powers to bear, bringing you the new results. Do not try to overdo this, to go through the entire day worrying about beliefs, for example. This can only cause you to contrast what you have with what you want. Forget the exercise when it is completed. You will find yourself with impulses that arrive in line with these newly inserted beliefs, and then it is up to you to act on these and not ignore them.[1]

There is nothing mysterious or hidden about our beliefs. They are constantly present. When we make an effort to look, it is surprising how apparent they become. Years ago, I made a commitment to myself to discover my own racist attitudes. Aware that I had grown up in a racist society, I knew there was no way that I did not have some racist assumptions. Our inner landscape is a reflection of the outer world. I found underlying attitudes that had been invisible to me because I had always taken them for granted rather than choosing to notice them. For example, I discovered that it had never been fully plausible to me that there were people of color who ran governments. It was an understandable attitude since my experience had shown me only white people in positions of power. The belief was subtle, but also obvious when I chose to look.

Be mindful of your internal dialogue, for it is a continual stream of suggestions. Being aware of it reveals all of your beliefs and attitudes, both positive and negative. Your Inner Witness will reveal the messages you give yourself. You can discover negativity by simply noticing if whatever you are thinking or feeling is life-affirming. Is it moving or static? Is it open or constricting? Notice when your thoughts are repetitious; when your mind is closed, there is no opening for insights to break the unsatisfactory cycle. Fresh perspectives are excluded by your belief and will go unnoticed. Typical of this kind of thinking is having clarity about all the reasons why something is wrong and only focusing on why it is the way it is. There is no room to recognize positive qualities or possibilities. It is easy to discover these thoughts if you hear yourself using all-inclusive terms such as "cannot," "never," "always," "nobody," "every," and so on. Reorient yourself. Notice yourself saying "can't" and change it to "have not been able to." If you say "always," change it to "usually." These simple changes will enable you to recognize new perspectives, and you will find your situation becoming flexible and amenable to change.

You can also reveal negative beliefs by reviewing the affirmations listed in this book and witnessing your responses to them. Like working with projecting a positive vision with your Active Imagination, affirmations provoke unnoticed beliefs.

Bring your negative beliefs out into the light and then use your Mental Housecleaning device to transform them, thus enabling you to open to fresh experience and act in new ways. When you are not acting from the old beliefs, they simply become background echoes, eventually fading altogether, because you have withdrawn their lifeblood. Without action they die.

It is important to bring to light the beliefs that need to be updated. But do not fall into the trap of only looking for what is wrong in your beliefs. It is at least as important to notice positive resources that you would like to cultivate. For instance, if you have a complacent and a courageous side, you can give your courageous side a winning edge by cultivating beliefs that strengthen it. Think of moments when you have taken risks or stepped up to a challenge. What did you assume at the time? Think of role models who you see as courageous. What beliefs do you imagine they have? What if you look at the world through the glasses of these beliefs? You can breathe even more life into them.

What are your positive resources, what do you love about yourself, about life, what makes you feel graced? These are beliefs that you might want to cultivate. Witness what happens when your Active and Receptive Imaginations dance with these beliefs. Listen deeply, what impulses arrive? Let it make your heart smile. When you cultivate positive, desirable beliefs, they take root in your life.

Materializing your imaginings takes a conscientious act of will—if you are not conscientious, you will find yourself behaving in the same old way. We are creatures of habit; if we do not choose to act differently, we simply behave in known familiar ways. Consciousness moves along the well-beaten paths it is used to using. When you set yourself on a new path, with commitment, change happens. With an act of will, choose to start anew. Because beliefs are born out of experience, it is good to do something that is symbolically in line with the new belief. New actions create new experience deepening the new belief. If you are trying to get over being shy, make yourself strike up a conversation with someone. If you tend to isolate yourself, take a class, develop new skills, or learn to tango! You have nothing to lose but your old habits.

At first, it will feel awkward, but with time, the new path will become as familiar as the old, and you can move your creative will onto other more challenging areas. You now have enough experience to solidify the new beliefs and they will remain on their own. Action is the lifeblood of belief. If at times you find yourself returning to old patterns, do not interpret it as a sign of failure; quite the contrary, if you weren't changing you wouldn't notice the backslide. In the past, that behavior was normal, and you did not see it. Give yourself a break and be patient—it all takes time. Whenever you discover yourself in old patterns, just focus on the new patterns and choose to act with their power. Let your Inner Witness be your guide.

Being Attuned to What Is True

Often, when you try to imagine a desirable experience, the obstacles that arise are actually a reflection of objective conditions that need to be overcome in order to make space for the ideal to be cultivated. Do not worry if what arises is rooted in objective conditions or outdated beliefs. You work with it in the same way as you do in addressing worries. You engage the Receptive Imagination to find the places that are amenable to change. Witness which of the imaginings you are playing with do not revert back to the status quo. Again, the imagination is the medium of psychic awareness. Play with the scenes and see what images are constricting and what images easily settle into a new configuration. This will both give you a vision you can work with and point to strategies you can use in your life.

As mentioned previously, intuition is not pushy—you have to choose to notice it. If you never shine the light of awareness into the area of concern, then intuitive knowing will not be revealed. Engaging the story-making capacities of the Receptive Imagination in the presence of the Inner Witness provides the context for discovering the operative energies in any circumstance on which you choose to focus. You will gain insight into exactly what is needed to change your perspective or conditions. In the presence of the Inner Witness, you recognize the answers. If you are unable to find an opening for a new configuration of energy, then you will be able to discover lessons needed to be at peace with current reality rather than struggling against it.

Consider the prayer "Grant me the serenity to accept the things I cannot change; to change the things I can; and the wisdom to know the difference." Witnessing as the Receptive and Active Imaginations dance together will enable you to do just that.

When you work with the Receptive Imagination, dialoguing with personified obstacles or beliefs, it is important to be mindful and witness your attitude. Are you coming from a clear, open, and receptive place, or is an emotional charge present? Your intention and anticipation dictate what appears in view and what unfolds. Doing your meditation work in the presence of the Inner Witness will reveal if you have digressed into an approach that is shutting down rather than one that is opening up. Always work in the presence of the Inner Witness so that you can see when you are opening up and when you are moving into constriction.

In spacious awareness, you have freedom, you can choose, you can be true to your deepest aspirations, and you can come into full integrity with yourself and others. In wholeness, healing happens and great possibilities are illuminated. When you keep the Inner Witness present, you safeguard yourself from getting caught in narrow self-interest that creates problems both for yourself and others.

When we open to deep consciousness, we move into alignment with the flow of life force energy. Compassion arises, healing happens, and creativity inspires us to join with others to create our world anew. Not at cross purposes with the resilience of life, we are open to the relations in which we are embedded. In meditation we reconnect with all that is.

Induction

Focus on your breathing ... Let your breath be full and easy ... each breath rolling through your body like waves caressing you into deeper and deeper states of relaxation ... Bring to awareness your symbol for physical relaxation ... Feel your body relax more and more into the support of the earth ...

As your body continues to relax, bring to awareness your symbol for mental relaxation ... Feel your mind relaxing into its natural state of spaciousness ... Let your breath be like the breeze that clears the air ... clear your mind ... Your mind is as spacious as the skies ... lots of room for whatever thoughts cross the sky of your mind ... your mind relaxes . . .

As your mind continues to relax, bring to awareness your symbol for emotional relaxation ... Give yourself permission to emotionally relax ... Let all the feelings that may be pushing or pulling you drop down into the ground by the sheer weight of themselves ... Breathe them out ... Let it all go down into the ground to be transformed in the soil ... Feel your heart getting lighter ... open ... Offer yourself some appreciation ... Tell yourself about your goodness ... Offer yourself

MEDITATIONS

loving kindness ... Feel your heart relax into its natural state of generosity and compassion, as though it smiles ...

As your heart continues to relax, bring to awareness your symbol for your creative, self-restoring center ... Acknowledge what you feel grateful about ... acknowledge the sanctity of life ... This is your creative, self-restoring center ... In this place you are connected to all that is ... In this place you can feel your connection to all that is ... Here, your Inner Witness is present ... your imagination is free ... your intuition is keen ... your creativity is ready ...

As you hear the sounds of these words, you can feel yourself moving into an even deeper state of awareness ... Feel yourself relaxing into an enhanced level of awareness with each exhalation ... Feel yourself moving deeper into yourself, deep down where healing and creativity flows ... Your consciousness knows just where it needs to go and is settling into that place now ... Trust consciousness ...

To enliven this space you now occupy, focus on your breath ... As though your awareness were to rest on your breath ... Your breath renews you ... Every moment breath brings life ... Settle into your breath ... Let yourself be carried by the rhythm of breath ... Extend your awareness, imagine as though the universe was also carried by breath ... ... Breath is universal ...

Affirmations attune you to express their energies in the world. Feel the potential of the following affirmations, pretend they are already manifest. Feel yourself open to their powers. Feel them awaken energy inside you ...

I believe in myself ...

I trust my awareness ...

I trust my experience ...

I am acutely attuned to my intuitive impulses ...

A spring of creativity continually flows through me and out into the world ...

I am visionary and courageous ...

I am fully present and mindful in each moment ...

My beliefs are grounded in the present ...

I am aware of all that I say to myself and always move my consciousness in positive directions ...

My attitudes are constructive, they enable me to be clear and open in the present situation ...

I welcome the lessons I need to meet the challenges life offers ...

I am curious and always learning ...

Every day my wisdom deepens ...

My feelings flow easily and clearly throughout my being ...

I perceive the true source of discord both within and around me and know where to direct my energy to create harmony ...

I am always attuned to what is needed for healing to happen on all levels of being ...

I always make clear choices ...

My life is full of love and laughter in all my relations ...

I celebrate belonging to the community of life ...

My increasing personal power is for making this world a more harmonious place to live for all beings ...

I am resilient; I maintain balance amidst change ...

I trust the future ...

Now take a moment and breathe in gratitude as you inhale ... and breathe out compassion as you exhale ... Gratitude to be alive; compassion for all life ... ...

Know that in focusing on these affirmations you have evoked deep powers. These energies are materializing in your experience. Take time now to focus on any of your own affirmations, symbols or beliefs you have been working with. Experience how it is to embody the energies you cultivate. Take this time to do any inner work of your choosing ... ...

Know that in focusing on these energies, you set clear intention and your consciousness travels in these directions. This energy is magnetic and attracts resonant events into your experience ... Trust that all of this is so.

Getting Free: Moving from Impasse to Insight

Now bring to awareness a problem you choose to work on for this meditation—an area in your life you would like to be different. Remember times when this concern has been present. Recreate these times ... Notice the atmosphere in which this problem thrives ... the qualities present ... your sense of self, the current of energy ... the motives present ... which aspect of yourself is prominent ... others that might be involved ... Bring all of this to awareness in the light of the Inner Witness.

Now let the qualities of this problem coalesce into a symbol ... Now put the symbol through your Mental Housecleaning device. Sense all the troublesome, tangled-up, heavy, stiff straining energy draining out—soon to be gone altogether ... Expect it.

Now project yourself into a time of the future—do not worry about where or when it is, simply experience a time in the future in which you are living in a liberated way ... liberated from that familiar concern from the past. Do not worry about how or when this comes about, just experience yourself living in a new independent way—this area of your life has become easy ... What used to be the wished-for is now real. Feel what this is like ... Notice the atmosphere of this time, the quality of this new time, your sense of self ... Resolution has already occurred ... Pretend this is so, imagine it, exaggerate it ... ... What does your life feel like? ... Your routine ... ... your relations ... ... What does it all feel like? ... Give it more detail, more life, embellish on the feel of living in this liberated way ... Create the scenes in detail—the smells, the tastes, the textures, create it in full detail ... If your vision is inviting, be with it and ignore what I am about to say. Instead, experience this transformed time.

If the time is not so inviting, or you have not been able to imagine a time in the future that is liberated and problem-free, then recreate the scenes in which the issue comes alive ... ... Turn it upside down, shift it around, imagine that people trade roles ... ... Shake up the scenes, imagine the energy reconfigures ... Talk to the characters ... ... Invite the problem-symbol to enter the scene ... Talk to it now, imagine it has personality and communicates with you. It may communicate with words or direct knowingness—trust your imagination. Ask it what it is doing ... what it offers your life ... what it is protecting you from ... how it is feeling ... what it believes ... what it teaches ... what it wants ... Tell it how you are feeling, what you want ... Negotiate so you can approach the issue in a new and open way ... ...

Harvest the energy. Create a symbol for this time of living in this new way, whether it be in the future or a new approach now, create a symbol. Create a symbol of this new way of being, an easier way of being ... Imagine that this symbol is charged with knowingness, knowingness of resolution. Imagine it hovering above your body and beginning to pour its energy into your body ... however you imagine that ... Breathe it in ... Feel resolution-energy pouring through the whole of your body ... re-educating the cells of which you are physically composed ... If any area has trouble receiving the energy, imagine asking what it wants in order to open to this new way of being ... ...

Make agreements with the reticent areas of your body ... Feel them receive as much of the energy as they are currently willing to ... Sense your body empowered by the energy, charged with this liberating energy ... Feel yourself embody this new way of being ...

Now let the empowering energy of the symbol shine into your mind. Breathe, feel the energy. As though you were breathing light, shine the light of this new way onto all of your ideas ... onto all your beliefs ... However you imagine this to occur. What does the world look like when you view it through this energy? ... If any voices or ideas pop up, unwilling to take it in, sense what it is they want ... Negotiate ... Make agreements ... Let the energy spread through the whole of your mind ... ...

Feel your mind full of resolution, believing in this new way ... Now let the energy of the symbol spread through your emotional self. Breathe, open your heart to the energy ... Breathe it into your heart ... Immerse all of your feelings with the energy. If there is any feeling that does not receive the energy so easily, ask what is needed ... Imagine doing what you are willing to ... Let your heart smile, as it basks in this energy. Celebrate this new energy ... ...

Feel your whole emotional self charged with this energy ... Now let it spread out and flow through your spirit, let the energy emanate from your spirit ... The whole of your being filled with the energy. Breathe it ... Your whole self vibrates in a new way. Imagine the energy sings and dances ...

Now if you wish to gain further insights you can bring back one of the original problematic scenes, bring it back into your awareness ... Now ask your solution symbol what to do about the situation. Let yourself know what to do to empower yourself, to change the quality of the situation ... to move forward in new ways ... ...

Acknowledge what you have learned ... Is there anything you need to do to cultivate the energy? ... Notice how your life will feel as you act on this new energy ... Is there anything you want to do to symbolically root the energy in your experience? ... Notice how all of this will affect others ... Be aware of people in your life who will support you in this change ... ...

Give yourself permission to believe in change, to believe in yourself and your ability to change ... The very fact that you have imagined these things makes them possible ... The energy exists. It is possible; it is probable; it is your choice.

Liberating Yourself: Transforming Defeating Messages

Focus your energy now on this moment, right here, right now ... Realize that you always live in present time ... Focus on breath ... It grounds you in this moment, in present time ... The present is your place of power ... Each moment is gifted with the next. It is always your present moment where you effect change both inside and outside of yourself ... Reside in the knowledge of this ... Breathe ... Right now, right here, is the accumulation of all of your past experience and all of your aspirations ... Your power is always in the present ...

You always act out of your inner messages ... Know that consciousness is fluid, flexible, and amenable to change. It welcomes new messages.

You are now going to work on an attitude that is limiting ... an attitude that perpetuates a way of being that you know you need no longer carry ... Knowing that things can be better than that outdated attitude allows, knowing that you can act in more liberating, open ways ... Your consciousness is now at a very creative dimension where you create new realities ... Pick one particular attitude you would like to transform ... Bring to awareness the belief that you have chosen to change.

Imagine a specific time when this attitude is informing the scene If a number come to mind, pick one ... Imagine stepping into the scene ... Notice how you are feeling ... Notice all the details of the scene ... Notice the atmosphere ... Now imagine as though the attitude is like clothing that does not fit anymore. Take off the constricting garb, take off the belief ... Breathe a sigh of relief ... Put it through your Mental Housecleaning device ... ...

Breathe ... Feel the release, the opening. Let your body, your mind, your feelings and spirit be released from the old belief. It is gone now ... Feel how much more comfortable you are now ... You have chosen to reroute your consciousness ... Tell yourself that now is your point of power ... that now things are different ... This was an idea about reality, not reality itself ... The present is different ... The future is different ... Know that this is so ... ...

In the present moment, you can repaint the past, you can recreate the future. Now is your point of power. Imagine whatever manner occurs to you, change the scene you have experienced so that it feels good, so it includes what you now know ... Put on new clothing, create a liberated situation ... You might want to create an atmosphere that is the opposite of the one you felt earlier. Create the opposite atmosphere, the opposite feelings, the opposite thoughts ... Adjust the scene until it fits just right ... ... What new beliefs are informing the scene? ... There is a quality of freshness, openness now ... Notice how this is ... What happens now? ... ...

If any other scenes arise from this old attitude, change them as you changed the first scene ... Know that replacing constricting imagery in your consciousness you leave old patterns behind ... You create space to act in liberating ways. In doing so, you have changed the future. Consciousness is powerful, flexible, and fluid ... Now is your point of power ...

Notice if there are anticipations of the future that need to be cleared out ... Use your Mental Housecleaning device to make space for this empowered way of being ... ... Each time you inhale, gather the empowering energy ... As you exhale, direct it into the whole of your past ... Fill up all the wounds until you find yourself standing fully present on the steady ground of your new experience, now ... ...

Your new belief is fully rooted ... Now experience this newfound self ... Know that you have changed ... How does it feel? ... What are you inclined to do ? ... ... What unfolds? ... Breathe life into the vision ... ...

Now, create an image, a symbol representing this new way of being ... This symbol will enable you to act in new ways that are fully coherent with this empowered way of being ... Know that if ever you find yourself acting in old ways, you can bring this symbol to awareness and it will inspire you to embody this new way ... ...

Ask your symbol to come into awareness spontaneously whenever you need it ... Know that this new way of being is soon to become as familiar as the old. Change has already happened. Thank your symbol, go over any agreements you have made and acknowledge yourself for making this change. Now all you have to do is act on it. Welcome change.

Know that you have left your past behind and created the future of your choice, for now is your point of power ... Know that this is so.

Receptive Imagination Offers a Gift of Insight

You are now centered at a deep level of awareness, relaxed and alert ... This is where you can witness intuition speaking through your imagination ... Here, your intuition is ready to offer you insight and knowing ... Choose a specific concern you would like to work on now, an issue that you would like to deepen your understanding of ... ...

Bring it to awareness ... Remember the times when this concern has been alive for you ... Replay these times in your awareness now ... You may want to choose one and witness what happens ... Replay the scene ... witness the feelings that arise ... the mood ... Imagine the scene unfolding ... just witness it ... ...

If tension arises, breathe through it ... let it go down into the ground and transform in the earth ... Witness the scene ... Notice the quality of energy present ... in you ... If there are others there, witness the quality of energy in them ... and between people ... What intentions are present? ... Where is energy moving? ... Notice if it is stuck anywhere ... If it is, breathe through it ...

Now, imagine as though all the energy wrapped around this concern were to roll up into a symbol, a character, a representative of some sort ... Imagine it ... Make it up ... This representative has an intelligence of its own and brings the gift of insight ... Greet it ... Converse with it. It has its own way of communicating ... Listen ... listen deeply ... It offers a gift of insight by using your imagination to reveal truth ... Imagine the representative's experience ... What is the story here? ... Imagine what this concern has to say ... It may not communicate verbally ... it may offer a quiet knowing, or it may offer pictures, or symbols—a metaphor.

Ask it what you would like to know ... Notice what you experience as you ask, for answers are often instantaneous ... What does the concern want? ... What is it protecting? ... What do you want? ... How might you work together? ... What might you each offer one another? ... Appreciate the offerings ... Remember, if tension arises, breathe it out and let it be transformed ... be forgiving ... See yourself in a positive light ... See the concern in a positive light ... Breathe through any constriction ... Let it drop into the ground to be transformed in the earth ...

What is the gift here ... what is the lesson offered? ... Feel yourself opening to the lesson ... Feel yourself equal to the challenge ... Appreciate the offerings ... Trust your experience ... Feel the shift of energy as you embody this knowing ... Imagine what you are inclined to do ... what offering you may make to the world ...

Now, as you breathe, breathe out a sense of well-being ... of peace ... Channel this energy wherever it may be needed ... Imagine acting on it ... imagine it spreading ... well-being ...

Thank the concern for the gift it has brought you ...

Count Out

As the energies you have been focusing on manifest in you and around you, notice how they will affect others ... Make any adjustments that might be needed ... Note if there is anything that needs to be communicated to anyone ... Hold a vision that increases well-being for everyone.

Acknowledge any insights you have gained and choices you have made ... Acknowledge how you may act on them in your life ... Appreciate the gift of life ... ...

Make yourself ready to come out to outer conscious levels now, bringing with you the insights you have discovered, ready and able to act on them in your life, and knowing you can return to these dimensions whenever you like.

In a moment, I'm going to count from one to five. At the count of five, you will open your eyes, revitalized, refreshed, relaxed, remembering all that you have experienced and bringing with you the energies you have tapped, ready and able to act on them.

ONE—coming up slowly now ...

TWO—becoming more aware of the room around you ...

THREE—at the count of five you will open your eyes, feeling revitalized, refreshed, relaxed ...

FOUR—coming up now ...

FIVE!—eyes open, revitalized, refreshed, relaxed, ready and able to act on the energies you have tapped.

◆9◆

Spirit Lives in Relationship

This book takes you on a journey that begins in the world inside, but now we are going to move out into the world we share. If you have been working with the first part of this book, you have likely begun to reclaim a sense of wholeness in your meditations. Now the challenge is to experience the wholeness in the world.

Western rationalism has conditioned us into a mechanical, linear worldview so that we tend to think in terms of separate objects, individual personalities, and goals to be achieved rather than the dynamic processes (relationships) created between us. We find ourselves alienated in a dispirited world. Thinking of ourselves as isolated, we lose track of our connection to the larger picture. This way of seeing makes us oblivious both to healing energy and to the multiple energy currents that shape situations we face. Yet this separateness is only an illusion; there are alternative worldviews that embody a sense of both connection and completeness.

Previously, we saw that the world is animate, that energy connects us, and that we are related on varied and deep levels. One image that stands out for me is the robot programmed to move randomly that spent an inordinate amount of time in the proximity of the baby chicks with which it was imprinted. This shows us that spirit infuses the inanimate world. The world itself is alive with spirit. This is the normal way of seeing for most indigenous societies, but modern cultures have lost sight of the presence of spirit in our everyday lives. We have been cut off from meaning. New developments in whole systems theory, physics, and biology give us a different perspective. As Joanna Macy describes:

> By shifting their focus to relationships instead of separate entities, scientists made an amazing discovery—amazing at least to the mainstream Western mind. They discovered that nature is self-organizing. Or rather, assuming that to be the case, they set about discerning the principles by which this self-organizing occurs. They found these principles or system properties to be awesomely elegant in their simplicity and constancy throughout the observable universe, from sub-organic to biological and ecological systems, and mental and social systems, as well.[1]

These principles reanimate our view of the world; they help us to focus on matters between us. Taken as a whole they allow us to see life as a dynamic dance of structure and process; to experience the unfolding of meaning from seemingly separate elements. Macy relates four characteristics that are found in all self-organizing systems:

> 1. Each system is a whole, irreducible to its parts. Its unique character derives from the synergistic interplay between its components generating "emergent properties" and new possibilities, which are not predictable from the character of the separate parts.
> 2. Through the flow of energy, matter, and information, open systems maintain their balance; they self-stabilize .... This is how we maintain our body temperature or heal from a cut.

3. Open systems both maintain their balance amidst the flux, and evolve in complexity. When challenges from the environment persist, they either fall apart or adapt by reorganizing around new, more responsive norms.

4. Another word for "system" is "holon," which is whole in its own right, comprised of subsystems , and simultaneously an integral part of a larger system. Thus holons form systems within systems, fields within fields. Each shift in "holonic" level, be it from atom to molecule, cell to organ, person to family—generates emergent properties that are irreducible to the capacities of the separate components.[2]

This systems view points to subtle connections that go beyond what we have been taught is normal. We previously saw that, conscious of it or not, we are psychically attuned to exterior reality.

Larry Dossey, in his exploration of the nonlocal mind, describes a particularly fascinating study showing how antic-ipation mysteriously impacts outcome. Do you ever remember feeling you were being watched, and then you turned, and indeed someone from the other side of the room was looking right at you? How did you know? This question has intrigued researchers who performed numerous studies where one person in a room was stared at by others in another room who intermittently and randomly watched the subject on a closed circuit television monitor. When researchers asked the subjects to tell them when they felt they were being watched, people proved to be fairly accurate at detecting when this was occurring.

Then the research took an interesting turn. Instead of ask-ing those being watched how they felt, they were hooked up to a computer that measured the electrical activity on their skin, which is an indicator of physiological arousal. These experiments showed that the people who were being stared at had heightened electrical activity in their skin during the very same periods they were being watched.

This line of research takes on an even more fascinating dimension. The experiments were repeated by two other investigators, one of whom believed in the existence of the nonlocal mind, while the other was a skeptic. The skeptic's experiment showed no evidence of nonlocal mind, and the other researcher's experiment proved that it does exist. These two scientists decided to collaborate on a study. They employed a rigorous double blind protocol. They worked from the same location, with the same equipment, and the same pool of people. The only difference between the two trials was that they were carried out by investigators who expected different results. No one knew who was in which group. The subjects that the skeptical researcher worked with showed no change in physiology when watched. Conversely, the group with which the believing investigator worked showed significant electrical activity in the skin during the periods of staring. Biologist Rupert Sheldrake has developed a theory that might explain what took place:

> The theory of morphic fields says that self-organizing systems, like social groups, have a field that links the members of the group together. Flocks of birds have morphic fields around them, which is why when the flock turns they can all turn practically simultaneously, without bumping into each other ... Fields are invisible—you can't see the gravitational field that connects the moon to the earth, but yet the earth pulls the moon and the moon pulls the earth, which is why it affects the tides. My theory is that there are fields around social groups and between people and their pets, and it's these fields that act as a channel for communication.[3]

Could it be that in the awareness experiments described above, a morphic field is created between each researcher and their subjects? It is as though we are held by energy fields as real as the air we breathe. There is congruence between what takes place and what we anticipate. The chameleon changes color to merge with the landscape. Take a moment and imagine that the world is a chameleon in the environment of the mind—not each of our minds, but the sum total of all of our minds. What kind of energy field are we collectively creating?

Culture Is the Air We Breathe and the Water in which We Swim

In the U.S., we have been conditioned to believe we are separate and fully independent from one another. Many of us do not experience ourselves as embedded in a larger community—instead, we feel we have to fend for ourselves. When we have problems we take the dualistic point of view and affix blame. Whether we blame ourselves or others, we have objectified and separated everything, thwarting our ability to see the full picture. When we blame others for our problems, we relegate ourselves to a powerless victim position or we blame ourselves and feel inadequate to make change. We do not acknowledge the relationships we are in, or the multiple dynamics that make our problems or can be employed to solve them. We feel alone, and find ourselves striving to meet fictitious images of what we should look like and own for a fulfilled life. Add the violence pervasive on television, in video games, and in the movies, and we have a lethal mixture.

Children are continual reminders of the joy of being alive. Watching a toddler in the midst of discovery will bring a smile to anyone. Childhood is the time full of pranks and play, magic and mystery. I believe that a society's quality of life is measured by the well-being of its children.

In the US they are not doing well, and one reflection of the state of the children's and youth's spirit is the rate of suicide attempts and deaths: In the ten years between '87 and '97 there were more suicide deaths by people five to twenty-five years old (approximately 55,000) than the total U.S. combat deaths in the ten years of the Vietnam War (47,355). Death by suicide in this age group is currently the third highest cause of death ahead of homicides. Even more disheartening is the fact that the number of suicide attempts has remained constant around 700,000/year.[4]

The image of a child committing suicide horrifies the heart, but in fact, it is congruent with the larger context in which it is taking place. Former Secretary of Health and Human Services Donna Shalala tells us: "In our country today, the greatest threat to the lives of children and adolescents is not disease or starvation or abandonment, but the terrible reality of violence."

Other members of the family are subject to violence as well: annually, there are nearly five million partner rapes and physical assaults against women by an intimate partner, while there are approximately 800,000 similar acts of violence perpetrated against men.[5]

This violence takes place in our private worlds, where we are hidden from one another with no extended family or community to which to turn. In other times and other cultures people have turned to their elders. In the United States, more than one and a half million of our elders are in nursing homes.[6] Our grief is not heard; our wounds are not seen. The greatest threat to our well-being is not a terrorist living halfway across the globe, but what we have become to one another on a daily basis. We live in a war zone. When the violence is hidden in the privacy of strict, culturally imposed silence ("it is none of my business"), it is made invisible. There is no place in which the heart can act and we lose our ability to care for one another.

Caring is a natural reflex of the heart. When we see another in need, we respond spontaneously. When faced with a major disaster, there is always an outpouring of support.

Note the groundswell of response that happened after 9/11. People rise to the occasion. Everyone pitches in to help. There is a palpable feeling in the air when people see their fates tied together. Everything is seen in a larger context and pettiness falls away. People put their individual concerns aside. A generosity of spirit fills the air. Everyone counts. In such an atmosphere, people let down their guard and are generous with one another. When everybody knows they belong, buoyancy is created.

We humans are intrinsically social beings. We need to belong. There are no conditions in which we thrive more than in a loving family and community. I believe that when we are deprived of our natural habitat, we go berserk.

If the events of September 11, 2001, have taught us anything, we learned that we are not separate and immune from the rest of the world. What if we experience in the United States what has taken place in Argentina, when the banks locked the doors and froze everyone's accounts?[7] To whom would you turn to survive? Who would turn to you? If we cannot answer this with "lots of people," we need to start building communities now—communities woven strong with the fiber of loving relationships. This is the way to achieve homeland security. For us to make community, we need to break the silence. We need to change this. Everyone's life counts.

When we are in an energetic field of violence, coercion, and control, we find ourselves in one kind of territory; if we are in an atmosphere of shared care we are in quite another. Love and care create energy fields we would all prefer to live in. What if we could rely on one another all the time? We are called to create community, move out of isolation, and connect with one another instead of fearing each other. Doing so not only will save children's lives, it will save our own. Studies show us that people who live in community have intimate relationships, serve the larger good, live longer, and have more fulfilling lives.[8] We need to take the time for each other—our survival depends on it.

The question becomes—how do we create fields of energy that lift all of us up? This is challenging given the condition of the world. Just like pain, our first reaction is to pull back. Hearts are soft, sensitive organs; we put up shields to protect ourselves. We do not share our vulnerabilities. The problem is that it is this very sharing that opens the heart. Peace is more than the absence of war.

Over the past decade, I have consulted with many organizations seeking to become multicultural and more equitable. I have also worked closely with agencies that provide support for victims of domestic violence. This heartfelt work addresses a great need—as you might imagine from the statistics above. The sobering irony is that I have found more distrust among women in this arena than in any other setting. In one organization, when we conducted our initial interviews, we asked people to describe the agency's culture. Women used terms like: "the Gestapo," "people disappearing," or "getting chewed up and spit out." This was not a description of the conditions that battered women had to contend with, but their description of relations inside the agency!

I believe that unless we are very mindful, we take on the energies in which we are immersed on a daily basis. It is difficult to maintain a belief in humanity when picking up the wounded after battle. But this is exactly what we need to learn to do. The Inner Witness will be of great help because in spacious awareness we can both hold the enormity of suffering and continue to keep the heart open.

Denial causes us to shut down, dissociate, and deaden ourselves; we cut ourselves off from fullness of being. The opposite—connecting to our deepest truths and to each other—holds the promise of healing: creating energy fields that glow with authentic loving energy. Whether we experience violence directly in our lives or not, we need to create a fresh atmosphere of truth in which our culture can breathe.

Occasionally in meditations, we are asked to go to an imaginary place that is peaceful and serene. Usually people imagine being in a beautiful natural setting. For most of us, when we imagine a peaceful place, there are no people there. It is time for us to turn this around; create peace with each other. It does not take rocket science to realize what we want. Ask yourself which moments that you have shared with others have made your heart sing. Even if they have been few and infrequent, what is important is not how many you have had, or how long they lasted, but to recall how it felt at the time. When we look deeply, we can discover what kind of atmosphere made the feelings possible, focusing on what took place between people. These are the environments we want to create. They teach us how to weave strong webs of connection.

We are all equipped with what it takes—big hearts. It does not take new technology, but it does take commitment, time, and patience. The rewards are wholeness and authentic relations with ourselves, our families, and our communities— and saved lives.

Circles Cultivate Big Hearts and Weave Strong Communities

What we focus on is what we get. We need visions from which to draw—visions that affirm our common humanity and visions that reflect our full diversity. (For more tips on drawing out diversity in Circles, see Chapter 11, especially "Weaving Trust" and "Circling.") As with all inner consciousness work, one needs to find positive points of reference. We can create contexts that inspire the heart. One way is to host a gathering for people to share their stories, because personal story always touches the heart.

I suggest that you invite a few friends, your family, or even a few families from the neighborhood to come together and share. Intergenerational groups are great. Explain that the reason to get together is to enjoy one another, get to know each other more deeply, and have meaningful connections. For those who have been meditating with others, expand your practice to include sharing heart stories as described below.

Sit in a circle together—in a circle everyone is equal and all voices count. Go around and take turns sharing stories of positive moments in your lives. They need not be particularly profound, just moments that have made the heart smile— short stories or long ones. Share moments that made your heart smile in regards to your children or other loved ones; share stories about someone in your life you consider a role model—someone with a great big heart. Stories have their own pace to them, so these stories are for the sharing, not to get to the point or punch line.

You can share stories about receiving or offering kindness, courage, or reconciliation, or love. You want stories, not reports—descriptions, not explanations. Tell about times that portray the best of what it means to be human. These stories will lift everyone's spirits and build a positive field.

These stories take listening with heart. Usually five or ten minutes is an ample amount of time for each person. Some circles choose never to interrupt; others may prefer to be able to occasionally ask questions that elicit more details, further drawing out one another's stories. For instance, ask, "What was that like?" or "What made that possible?" Do not respond to other's stories with your own opinion or experience. Listen—soak in the stories and feel them in your heart. Let them just hang in the air. Bear witness to them. Keep the storyteller the focus of attention. Discussions create a different kind of energy field.

If the group is larger or the stories longer than the evening can hold, break down into smaller groups so that everyone gets time to tell their whole story. Then come back into a full circle and share the shining moments and the hope that they inspire. People will feel uplifted after hearing these stories. The room will fill with lots of positive points of reference.

After the stories, do an Energy Circle in which each of you can ask for the specific qualities you would like to cultivate in your lives now. This will plant more heart energy into your life.

When we surround ourselves with these stories, they create another kind of energy field—one in which new habits of the heart will take root. If you continue to interact in this way, you will develop deep bonds. The energy field you create with this kind of sharing is durable. It will weather the storms. It invites deeply honest communication. There is room to share our vulnerabilities and space to work through conflict. In these settings you can reflect together on bigger questions that we all face.

In addition to creating contexts that build life-affirming fields of energy, I believe it is also necessary to reflect upon the cultural norms by which we in the United States tend to live—the values beneath our actions. As we have seen in earlier chapters, negative beliefs that go unnoticed produce experiences that we do not want. When they are brought to the surface we can do some Mental Housecleaning. And with mindfulness, we can withdraw their lifeblood by simply not acting on them.

The Corrosion of Our Relationships

The very fact that we are endowed with life means we are embedded in a web of mutually interdependent relations. We each have our place in the web. However, in mainstream culture, instead of experiencing mutuality we often find ourselves feeling as though we are up against one another—having to fend for ourselves. Competition renders us oblivious to the web of relations in which we are all embedded. It acts like acid on the fabric of our culture, eating away at the bonds that connect us. Instead of encouraging generosity, competition fosters an attitude that individual well-being is attained despite one another, not because of one another.

As a result, deep inside most of us is a gnawing sensation that tells us, "I am not good enough." We constantly feel that we have to prove ourselves to justify the life that is already ours. When we feel as though we are part of the human condition rather than apart from it, we naturally act out of a sense of mutuality, and our lives fill with meaning.

Competitive conditioning has penetrated deep into all of our psyches. Our thoughts are riddled with either/or oppositional thinking that is perpetually preoccupied with comparisons. Watch yourself for feelings that tell you that you are better than someone else or not as good as another. If you prefer tulips to daisies, does this mean that a tulip is better? This competitive thinking is so pervasive we tend not to recognize it. For example, in a gathering, after someone has been especially inspiring, the next person invariably begins with "That's a hard act to follow."

Being mindful and witnessing what beliefs are shaping our interactions and consciously choosing the values we want to live by is essential. If we take social codes as facts of life, and they are not serving us, they become invisible bars that imprison us.

All ideas lead somewhere. The eternal question: Are they taking you where you want to go? Be mindful of the choices you make. Notice if they move you into connection with people or farther away from others. What values are they rooted in? What motivation is driving you? Notice which orientation opens the heart to shared concern and mutuality, and which leads you to ignore others in pursuit of your own agenda. Notice if you believe that your words are more or less important than what others say, or when you get caught up in evaluating others.

Observing when we constrict or censor ourselves will reveal the areas that need to be examined. Additionally, if we look for and express what we appreciate in others instead of looking for problems with them, we will find ourselves opening to and celebrating one another. If you find yourself moving away from, rather than toward others, stop, breathe, and remember your connectedness in the web. Again, meditation will be of great help. Sit in the quiet of meditation and bring yourself back to your own self. Doing so will enable you to discover what is true for you and not just how you are conditioned to behave. Breathe, be with yourself, and offer yourself kindness. When we slow down, stop striving, stop trying to prove things and get places; when we just stop and breathe, life opens into wholeness. We accept ourselves; we accept others. Further, we welcome each other. When we start there, the only place to go is curiosity, creativity, and celebration.

Opening to Authentic Relations

Love is a relational experience. In my opinion, love and power over relationships are antithetical. In the latter, we dissociate from ourselves and one another. We vacate, doing great harm to ourselves and others.

In this country, we have inherited a culture born of bloodshed. The wealth we have amassed has not been born out of fair deals. People were killed, kidnapped, and exploited—the heart does not enjoy these kinds of scenes. It shuts down, causing denial; genocide and slavery are covered with terms like "Manifest Destiny," "the American way of life," "freedom," and "progress." I do not believe those who were on the receiving end consider it "progress." No one likes to acknowledge that their comforts have been made possible through the suffering of others. We in the United States have inherited a culture that denies us the freedom to be real, real in the expression of whatever we are feeling—joy or sorrow. Suppression is not conscious, but it is in the field.

Mainstream culture shapes what is considered appropriate to express publicly and what is considered private (no one else's business). In this paradigm, to show care is to risk being labeled sentimental, to be principled is to be called impractical, to be honest is considered vulgar, and to have humor is seen as a betrayal of authority. Mab Segrest, in her book, *My Mama's Dead Squirrel*, tells the story of a time when her mother gave a tea party. Unbeknownst to her mother, there was a dead squirrel right in the middle of the living room couch! The party continued for hours, but no one said or did anything about the squirrel.[9]

We are expected to be polite, be nice, and stay cool, calm, and collected. Image has replaced authenticity. It is a real challenge to have meaningful relationships within these norms. We are expected to hide vulnerabilities and cover our mistakes.

How can we have open, caring relationships if we cannot be real? Having a meditation practice enables us to stop, reflect, and notice what is percolating in our heart. Then we can take the risk and be authentic, which, in turn, awakens the hearts of others. If tension arises, stop for a moment and breathe together. Compassion arises naturally when the heart is in the forefront and involved in our actions. Residing in our larger humanity, we remember our own fallibility and have empathy for others, even those with whom we disagree.

In the same way that you strive to be mindful of internal constriction, strive to be mindful of what you pull back from in relationships. Sit with it and allow insight to arise. In meditation, put yourself in the other person's shoes. Invite your Receptive Imagination to play with the situation to learn what it has to offer. Inner consciousness provides clear understanding, and inspires empathy. Notice what happened and what you think, feel, and need regarding the matter. The heart does not rush. Patience enables us to slow down, take a full breath, and take in the whole of a situation. Creating space for truth to come forth makes the field open to heart talk. Widening horizons, wisdom emerges. Then our relations fill with meaning, love, and laughter.

The heart lives in connectedness; it is forgiving. We no longer need to play out roles or defend positions. When we are not trying to prove anything or be anybody, we can just take pleasure in one another. Deep listening and being heard ensures that everyone's experience can be honored. Just viewing one another with compassion makes the field open to heart talk. We weave a caring field and develop enduring relationships.

How do we apply all this when differences in perspectives and needs arise in our daily interactions with each other?

I have been conducting mediations for conflict resolution for many years. I always begin with a centering exercise (my way of naming what we are doing without using the term "meditation"). I ask people to settle into themselves and find that place inside where they can sit in their truth, while at the same time they can listen openly to the other. The rational mind cannot do this, it is hardwired to either/or thinking. But inner consciousness can embrace wholeness; this is the place where the heart lives.

Take a moment and reflect together. If you have a regular meditation practice, it is easy to let go of the striving and sink into the present moment. You can find your own truth, as well as the openness to listen to the truths of others. In any gathering, start with a few moments of shared breathing—this will establish a common energy field. As you have discovered by now, when we sink below the chatter of beta mind, both heart and clarity are there.

In the quiet, notice what actually is happening for you. Through what beliefs are you viewing the situation? What feelings are present and what do you need? Imagine what is happening for the others involved, and what they are likely to believe, feel, and need. Wherever you come across tension in yourself or others breathe compassion into the scene.

When our energy is constricted, fear is present and, often, anger is on top of it. These energies bring dissociation, alienation, and separation. If you stop to focus on the breath and sit in the presence of the Inner Witness, you will make space for the experience of wholeness to return. Your individual truth becomes apparent, and you begin to see the truths of those with whom you are in conflict.

In spacious awareness, compassion will emerge and you will find courage to stay present with what is taking place. You will make room for your feelings and have empathy for others who are involved. In spacious awareness, we can continue to be connected with others instead of withdrawing or lashing out. We find ourselves inspired to move into deeper connection. Where you have fears, express them and let people support you. Though you might feel alone, you are not. This is an act of bravery that often gives others permission to share their fears. In vulnerability, our hearts touch.

When meditating on a distressing situation and tension arises, think of something that makes your heart sing. Flowers do it for me. I think of them and my heart just smiles—I cannot help it. For you, it might be your grandmother, a song, or a run in a park with your dog. Whatever makes your heart sing, bring it to awareness. Let your singing heart help you stay present with the situation you find distressing. Breathe and be with it. Sit in a place of openness and of inquiry. In openness, new approaches emerge. Heart Song, which is the last meditation on the CD, guides you through this practice.

Meditation opens the heart and allows us to bring the openness into those places in our families and communities that are wounded. In the act of healing, we all get to return to wholeness. In the words of the great Buddhist monk and peacemaker, Thich Nhat Hanh:

To understand ourselves, we must learn to practice the way of nonduality. We should not fight our anger, because anger is our self, a part of our self. Anger is of an organic nature, like love. We have to take good care of anger. And because it is an organic entity, an organic phenomenon, it is possible to transform it into another organic entity. The garbage can be transformed back into compost, into lettuce and into cucumber. Don't despise anger. Don't fight your anger, and don't suppress your anger. Learn the tender way of taking care of your anger, and transform it into the energy of understanding and compassion.[10]

I am not saying it is easy. I get caught in the mire of conditioning more often than I like to admit. But I am saying that the answers to the malaise in our culture lie inside each of us, all we need to do is bring out the answers and share. Look for the positive, be honest about our troubles, and share care. This, too, is not rocket science, nor is it a quick fix. It is not a new technique; it is slowing down and being together in our nakedness.

In Wholeness We All Belong

As we can witness wholeness in our meditations, we also can in our lives. Just what does "wholeness" mean? There is no dissociation; there is forgiveness of self and others. Everybody matters, everybody counts. All that is, simply is. In wholeness, there is no scapegoat, no blame, no shame. In wholeness we can share our vulnerabilities. There is honesty, there is integrity, and there is respect for the sanctity of life.

To be in wholeness means to sink into the diversity of life experience, of cultural background, of physical ability. Wholeness means it is all of our responsibility to make the world right, as opposed to none of our business. Wholeness means we each are good. It means you are already good enough, it means we each belong. It is beyond adding up all our parts, it is beyond inclusion, to embracing difference. It embodies that which we do not yet know.

In the words of theologian Barbara Holmes:

> Perhaps in ways that we don't yet understand, the struggle for justice on many fronts is an embodiment of a holistic and fragmented community. This community would not be the logical outcome of progressive movements toward an ascertainable external goal, but would be the sum of past, present and future expectations and disappointments. The community we call beloved becomes all that we can and cannot conceive, all that lies beyond the horizon of our apprehension, but is available to us as part of the matrix of wholeness.[11]

It is about sinking into the implicate order that Bohm wrote about. It is about accepting responsibility for all that is and acknowledging that we can never know all that is. Moving from struggling for our piece of the pie, we work so that everyone's needs are be met. It means cultivating peace. Peace makes wholeness. Wholeness makes peace.

Induction

Focus on your breathing ... Let your breath be full and easy ... Bring to awareness your symbol for physical relaxation ... Tell your body it can relax now ... Feel your body relaxing more and more with each exhalation of breath ... Send your breath through any areas of tension ... feel them releasing ... Feel yourself relaxing more and more into the support of the earth.

When you are ready, bring to awareness your symbol for mental relaxation ... Let your breath be like the breeze that clears the air ... Let your breath clear your mind ... and your mind relaxes into its natural state of spaciousness ... As spacious as the skies ... lots of room for whatever thoughts may cross the sky of your mind ... Your mind opens ... is relaxed and alert ...

When you are ready, bring to awareness your symbol for emotional relaxation ... Breathe out and release any feelings that are pushing or pulling at you ... Breathe them out ... let them drop down into the ground and transform in the earth ... Give yourself permission to emotionally relax ... Take a moment to appreciate your goodness ... Offer yourself loving kindness ... Feel your heart

opening ... Sense your heart relaxing into its natural state of
generosity and compassion ... ...

Bring to awareness your symbol for your creative, self-restoring
center ... Take a moment and appreciate what you hold
sacred ... what you cherish ... Remember your gratitude ...
Life is sacred ... This is your creative, self-restoring center.
Here, you are held in vast awareness ... The Inner Witness is
present ... receptivity is present ... creativity is present ...
Here, you tap healing energy ... you can channel this healing
wherever you choose ... This is your creative, self-restoring
center.

Bring to awareness loved ones in your life ... Invite them to join
you in this meditation ... You may want to bring in others too ...
Take a few moments to share presence with each
other ... Send them some loving energy, however you imagine
doing this, with color, light, music, or simply good intent. Fill the
space between you with generosity and loving energy ...
Imagine that there are vibrant ribbons of energy that move
between you ... You are all held up in a great net of
energy ... Lives entwined in loving energy ... Imagine it ... The
energy connects with others too ... Feel it. Breath carries
connection from one to another ... Imagine it ... ...

I am now going to suggest a number of affirmations. If you wish
to affirm them, repeat them to yourself after me, feel as though
they're already true. Know that in focusing on affirmations you
align yourself with patterns of energy the affirmations materialize
in your experience ...

I honor the integrity of all people and all life ...

I open my heart to the present moment ...

I listen deeply to others ...

All my relationships are filled with empathy, and mutual care ...

I trust the support of others ...

I am patient with all people ...

I trust my experience and express my truth ...

I believe in myself, I believe in my family and friends, we believe in our community; there is a free flow of support among everyone ...

We reside in the care we have for one another ...

I am a cooperative person ...

My feelings flow easily and clearly throughout my being ...

I am honest with myself and others ...

I express my feelings in constructive ways ...

I cultivate strong community ...

I am sensitive to the needs of others ...

I am always attuned to what is needed for healing to happen on all levels of being ...

My life is full of love and laughter in all my relations ...

I celebrate belonging to the community of life ...

I am visionary and courageous ...

My increasing personal power is for making this world a more harmonious place to live for all beings ...

I am resilient; I maintain balance amidst change ...

I contribute my best to making peace ...

I trust the future ...

Know that in focusing on affirmations you have created patterns of energy that will manifest in your life and you will find yourself acting in accordance with the affirmations.

Now imagine yourself being in a mountainous place, a meadow in the mountains with a lake in the center of the meadow ... Imagine being by a mountain lake in a very peaceful meadow ... You can see the sky reflected in the lake, the trees, the mountains reflected in this lake. A very peaceful crystal clear mountain lake ... If you like, you can invite others to be with you in this beautiful place ...

Notice a welcoming quality of this place ... It welcomes you, others, spirits; this is a welcoming place. Imagine the scenery around you ... Experience the sights and sounds ... the colors and smells ... textures, the quality in the air ... the silence, the movement, the freshness of this place ... Imagine all the plants that grow here, the animals and insects that live here—all a part of this place ... aware of the water, the mountains around you, as though the meadow were cradling you ... ... Notice that the lake is very still and very quiet—crystal clear.

You can look down into the lake and see the bottom of the
lake ... This is a very magical lake. It can help bring peace in
your life and relationships. It will clear you and refresh your
life. To work its magic, gather up all of what has been going
on in your day-to-day activities—all that makes you spin your
wheels ... As you inhale gather it ... Symbolically roll it up,
and as you exhale, toss it all into the water and the lake will
transform the energy ... It will all disappear into the lake to be
transformed ... All the different things that stress you out and
make you spin, keep throwing them into the lake ...
Symbolize them and throw them into the lake. Responsibilities
that you have ... feelings that you have ... relations with
friends, family ... things that you have done ... things that you
have not yet done ... throw it all into the lake to be cleansed,
transformed ...

Each time you toss something into the lake, you will find
yourself feeling lighter and becoming more and more
present ... Feel the relief ... Watch the splash as it hits the
surface of the water ... Watch the ripples of the water rolling
out over the surface of the lake ... Watch all that you throw
in dissolve and disappear into the depths of the lake ... ...

After there is no more to throw in, watch the surface slowly
come to a very quiet state once again. Know that as the lake
becomes calm, at the same time, the whole of your inner
dimension becomes calm and quiet and as clear as the water of
the mountain lake ... Know that your relationships invite peace
and clarity now ... You will be able to see into the depths of

yourself, into your relationship, into beingness itself, as clearly as you are able to see into the depths of the lake. Let this calming process occur. Breathe calm, each breath clears you ... ...

In tune with the clarity and peacefulness of this mountain lake, imagine the same quality of peacefulness and receptive reflection residing inside of you ... Breathe it in ... so peaceful you reflect clearly. Feel that peace within you ... Know that as you feel this peace within you, you are able to be fully receptive and perceive clearly whatever is going on around you. Just as the mountain lake reflects clearly, you can listen; see clearly ... a very accurate reflection of what is going on around you is created in your consciousness. Notice the quality within yourself as you are able to listen receptively, and your reflections are clear and acute, true reflections. In this place, you can truly appreciate others in their full being.

When you are able to be quiet in yourself, quiet as a mountain lake, you can be aware of the needs and offerings of those around you ... of the needs and offerings of the environment around you ... you can hear them ... and be aware of your own needs and your own offerings ... aware of the great exchange of energy that is always moving.

Integrity of Life

This mountain meadow is a very quiet and peaceful place, yet full of life, thriving, teeming with life ... the meadow is full of life, the lake is full of life, even the air is full of life ... Imagine all the life in this place, the pulse of life, all the different plants and

animals ... Feel the energy that vibrates out of the different forms
of life here ... each unique, each with an integrity of its own ...
each being distinct in and of itself, yet part of the whole ... Life
is breathing in all that lives here ... ...

Imagine strands of luminous energy that connect each life form
as it is in relationship with others that live here ... many strands
of energy exchange that support the web of life.
And all provide some of its strength. Each has its spot in the
web ... ...

Now, draw your focus into yourself. Let your awareness move
deeper and deeper inside yourself. As you breathe, become
aware of the quality of energy that emanates from your
center ... The essence of who you are, the tone of your
personality, whatever that means to you ... Just as other people
seem to have a tone, imagine yours ... Be very receptive and
listen to the tone of your being. However you sense this ...
Listen ... Feel. Be aware. Experience the very tone of your
being, the center out of which all your life force energies spring
... ...

Acknowledge the dignity of your being, just as every form of life
has an integrity of its own, so too, your being has an integrity of
its own ... Life breathes in you ... Honor your integrity,
appreciate yourself, believe in who you are. Love yourself as
you love life itself ... Know that the person you are is fully
complete, whole, you are enough being who you are ... You
are so uniquely who you are, the tone of your being is so you
that it can't be compared with anyone else. Acknowledge the

dignity of your way of expressing life. Not another form, not another person, nothing expresses life as you do ... Only you have this particular tone, this particular quality ... only you express life in this way. Feel the integrity of life being expressed through you ... You give it form; you give it shape in your own characteristic way. Honor yourself ... Honor the life breath brings ... ...

Trust yourself, knowing that you are a complete, full being, you are enough ... Imagine that this sense of fullness, the tone of your being forms waves as you breathe ... Feel them roll through your whole being, returning you to yourself. Breathe ... Relax into the being that you are ... ...

Imagine that these waves roll through any areas in your life where you felt you were not good enough, where you felt inadequate ... Fill up these areas ... As they fill, imagine yourself feeling whole in these scenes ... Let the waves roll through and fill any holes within you, and fill any holes in your life, returning you to your sense of wholeness ... The integrity of your being, the tone of your being shines out ... ...

Now extend your awareness to include the other people in your life. Focus in on one person at a time and be aware that they, too, have a tone to themselves that is uniquely theirs ... Each person has a quality that is uniquely theirs, just as you do ... Life is being expressed through them in their own way ... Each person has integrity of their own. Each person is different ... To compare one tone to another is fully irrelevant, like comparing one particular musical note to another.

Acknowledge the integrity of all the different people in your life
... ...

Witness the wonder when you put everyone together ... What
gets woven? ... Everyone has a place on the web ... all
connected ... ...

Now extend your awareness to include all the different life
forms. All the diversity in life on the earth ... each form of life
has integrity of its own. Each entity by the very fact that it's
alive has integrity of its own ... giving shape to the life flowing
through it, giving shape to life itself ... All that lives is sacred
...

Bathe in the knowingness that your life deserves the space that
you have on the earth. By affirming your integrity, you affirm the
integrity of all life ... You deserve the space you occupy: Let
yourself fully occupy the space that is yours ... Breathe. Take up
your space on the web ... ...

Do not occupy more space than is yours, crowding others, but
do not shrink from the space that is yours either ... Fully occupy
your life, in this time in this place, honoring the integrity of who
you are ... As you do, you inspire others to treat you with
integrity ... Honor the integrity of your life ... Honor your
intelligence, let yourself be confident ...

Experience yourself moving through the activities of your life
filling up the space that's yours ... Imagine expressing life
through your own unique tone and quality, different than

anyone who ever has been or shall be, your life has integrity of its own ... Only you can express life the way that you do.

Just as the sun radiates light, heat, warmth, let your center radiate who it is that you are, creating your space in the world, contributing your gift to the world ... Only you can fill the space ... Only you offer this gift ... ...

Know that there is a space for everyone to fill, for everyone has a unique quality. Honor the integrity of all those with whom you come in contact ... each person ... each form of life ... People celebrate one another.

Crystal Clear Communication

Know that this reflective mountain lake is like a crystal ball—you can watch whole scenarios unfold in it. You can observe scenarios unfold before you; as you do, they will become crystal clear. Just as water reveals the true colors of a stone, you can now discover the true colors of any relationship ... Choose one particular relationship you would like to work on, a relationship that is troubling you, something that is going on between you and another person that concerns you ...

Replay particularly significant scenes that took place between you ... Let the lake reflect them back to you ... Witness the interactions as they replay before you ... Watch them as though you were watching a movie of somebody else's drama ... Notice the atmosphere between you, all the details of the scene, as though you have control of the film and you can rewind it. Go back and freeze the frames in which the particular things that happened bothered you. Just make note of those things ... exactly what took place that bothered you ... If tension arises breathe through it and feel it release ... ...

Now focus into your own self. Witness what feelings surfaced as all of this unfolded ... ... Notice what you believed to be true ... What did you tell yourself ... When have you been in a similar situation? ... ...

Breathe. Bring yourself into present time ... Bring wisdom to the scene, breathe out reactivity ... This time is a different time; it is not all the same as before ... Notice what you might be doing that is contributing to the situation ... Witness. Notice what you need ... Acknowledge what you might offer to transform the situation ... ...

Imagine putting aside your experience for a moment. Release it. Breathe ... Clear yourself, recenter yourself ... You can see the depths of the lake clearly—crystal clear ...

Focus on the magic of the reflective lake and let it reflect what you imagine to be the experience of the other person or persons in the interaction ... Rerun these same scenes, witness what unfolds from the other person's perspective ... Imagine what is true for the other ... If there is more than one other involved, focus in on one person at a time and witness what is true for each ... Put yourself in their shoes ... ... Watch the scene through their eyes ... Replay it, note the frames that bothered the other ... ... Imagine what is true for the other ... ... Sense what is in their heart ... Focus in on each person involved and discover what might be true for them. Listen with heart ... ... Imagine what others need ... ...

Now imagine there being room to take into account everyone's needs ... ...

When you see it unfold in a way that feels good to each of you, imagine entering into the scene. Fill the scene with deep listening and heart ... Sense how it is to be in it, to experience it ... ... See if compromises need to be made ... How does it unfold? ... Feel what it's like ... ...

Notice what you need to do to bring this vision into your relationship ... What do you need to communicate, and act on to make for positive transformation? ...

Heart Song

Now bring to awareness whatever makes your heart sing ... It may be music ... it may be a loving moment with another ... it may be a place ... it may be a moment of creativity or inspiration ... Moments of generosity ... It may be a child ... Bring to awareness what makes your heart sing, or quietly smile ... Whatever makes your heart sing or smile, bring it to awareness now ... Let it all dance in your awareness ... ...

If there are any scenes that attract your attention, focus in on one ... Recreate it; remember the details ... Let it make your heart open wide all over again ... Breathe ... breathe all of this into your heart ... Fill your heart with this energy ... Breathe it in

... Let it open your heart ... your heart smiles, sings ... opens wide ...

Now, bring to awareness what in particular has been distressing you of late. If there's a person or situation that's been distressing you or maybe a feeling inside that's come up for you lately ... Remember a scene in which it is present. Recreate it now ... imagine it ... If tension arises, breathe through it ... Release it into the ground to be transformed in the soil ... Remember the good energy in your heart ... breathe heart energy ... breathe your heart song into the scene ... Breathe out the tension and breathe heart energy right into the scene ... As best you can, fill the scene with heart energy, however you imagine doing this ... If tension arises, breathe compassion into yourself ... Breathe compassion into the scene ... Keep doing this until you can keep your heart open and witness the situation with compassion ... Breathe ... Release tension into the ground ... Breathe ... breathe compassion for yourself ... for others ... Be in peace ... Be in peace with the scene ... Let yourself breathe and be with the situation ... Offer loving kindness to the situation ... See yourself in a positive light ... Be forgiving ...

Look deeply into your heart ... Witness what you really need ... Reassure your whole self ... Offer each aspect of yourself loving kindness ... ...

See others in a positive light ... Be forgiving ... Have compassion for everyone ... What is the gift of the situation? ... ...

Breathe ... let your heart sing again ... Notice what might open the situation up ... What you might say or do ... Imagine it ...

Make heart connections between you and any others present ... Make the connections from heart to heart ... make them be filled with loving energy ... Weave loving energy between you ... Imagine it ... intend it ... feel it ... ...

Breathe this energy into your life ... Imagine what you may want to do or say ... Imagine doing it ... saying it ... Sense the shift of energy ...

Breathe loving energy wherever you'd like to channel it ... wherever it's needed ... in the world, in yourself ... healing ... Channel it where it's needed ... ...

Acknowledge and appreciate the gifts of life ... what makes your heart sing ...

Count Out

Finishing what you are doing make yourself ready to come out to outer conscious levels ... ...

Before returning to an outer focus of attention we are going to breathe healing into our hearts and world. Take a few moments and generate loving energy in your heart. You may do this by remembering loving moments, or drawing on the quality of compassion ... However you are inclined, imagine that your heart opens to love and compassion ...

Now breathe them out and channel them wherever they may be needed ... With each exhalation, breathe them out and offer them wherever they are needed ... Cultivate fields of this wonderful energy in your family ... in your community ... in the world ... wherever they are needed ... Healing happens ... breathing compassion, love, generosity ... Imagine it sings, it shines ... ...

Acknowledge the fact that the very process of your being able to imagine all that you have makes it possible ... makes it probable ... Let yourself believe in the goodness of people ... ...

Go over any choices you have made ... energies you have become attuned to ... Tell yourself you will intuitively act in accordance with these energies ... ...

In a moment, I am going to count from one to five ... at the count of five, you will open your eyes feeling revitalized, refreshed, and relaxed ... remembering all that you experienced ... ready and able to act on the energies you have evoked ... heart open and strong.

ONE—coming up slowly now ...

TWO—becoming more aware of the room around you ...

THREE—at the count of five, you will open your eyes, revitalized, refreshed, and relaxed ...

FOUR—coming up now ...

FIVE!—eyes open, feeling revitalized, refreshed, and relaxed, remembering all that you have experienced, ready and able to act on the energies you have evoked.

•10•

The World in Which We Live

In Openness Resilience Arises

Every day we are assaulted by news that takes our breath away, news that causes us to recoil and recede into ourselves. Although in the past people have felt that the world was coming to an end, ours is the first generation to live with the possibility that we might annihilate all life, whether it be from nuclear holocaust, global warming, pollution, or over-consumption. While the planet itself feels as though it sits on a precipice, information about all the problems comes at us at such a speed, in such great quantities, it overwhelms us, dumbs us down, and finally it numbs us out.

The possibility that there may be no future is an awareness that is hard to hold. It is a possibility so painful to contemplate that we try in thousands of ways to blot it out.

The issues are so huge, it seems like we can't have a meaningful impact. It is hard to face our feelings of grief, guilt and loss so we shut down.

But the degree to which we shut down is the degree to which we are not alive. Earlier in this book, I talked about the ways in which a mechanistic world view, individualism, consumerism and mass media have held us in a dream of separation from ourselves, each other, the planet and spirit. The world is calling on us to awaken out of this dream to come back to life in all its fullness. How do we open to the challenges facing the world and step into our role in its healing?

This is no small task, but when we open to the state of the world, we awaken, come alive, and become resilient. Breathing into pain opens space for healing and deepens understandings. Breath grounds us in the present, and we find a pathway to peace, to truth, and to what needs to change. Mindfulness reveals when constriction takes hold so we can then choose to open. This opening is not a process of pushing, pulling, or quick fixes—it is emergent. The solutions become apparent as we open and respond to the truths of our times. Meditation allows us to move out of reactivity; rather than turning away and shutting down, we expand into wholeness. As we do so, we can each find our unique response to the times.

The world sits in such a delicate balance that the acts of any one of us might tip the balance. This is a time that is full of opportunity to create ways of living that hold the promise of sustaining humanity and the planet through millennia. The choice is upon the generations alive right now—that is us, all of us.

Be mindful as you read. You may want to run energy to stay centered (see Chapter Six). Vision how you would like the world to be. It is vision that provides guidance and inspiration as we each do our part in turning the tide. After each paragraph close your eyes, breathe, and let your deep self hear. It is our deepest selves that can get us through these times. Breathe, feel yourself alive, part of this great living earth that offers us home; part of humanity in all its great diversity. Feel yourself belonging.

Being Present to What Is Happening in the World

Western culture's emphasis on rational thinking has led us to act as though we are separate from one another and the rest of nature. This false dualism has wreaked havoc on the world, splitting the self from nature, from the body, and from others, and has allowed economic growth to be the sole indicator of success. It has allowed colonization of indigenous people first inside Europe and then in the rest of the world. It has allowed the creation of a system where some were slaves and some owners.

There is nothing excluded in wholeness, but working in beta linear consciousness, modern economists have coined a term that allows economic activity to be split off from its consequences. "Externalities" refer to the "side effects" of making profit in any particular venture. Externalities are not included in calculations of profit and loss, whether they are environmental or human costs. It is a fancy term used to avoid responsibility. As long as we think of the following consequences as "externalities," we abdicate our ability to secure the future.

Only in wholeness can we act with integrity. People brought about the following conditions, but it is not too late to turn the tide. People make history; in wholeness we can act with integrity to remake it.

Some say that the trees are the lungs of the earth. If externalities are counted, then just one ninety-nine-cent hamburger costs fifty-five square feet of rainforest.[1] Imagine standing next to a big empty football field; notice its size. Now fill it with tropical trees, and birds, and all sorts of critters. Imagine the sounds of the forest and the moisture in the air. Feel the breath of the earth. Now imagine it full of birds calling, monkeys swinging, vines growing. Now let your heart know that every single second all this life is destroyed in the process of turning forests into grassland for cattle.[2]

We are losing our farmlands too; it takes nature three thousand years to create the soil needed to plant a crop. Fertile lands are disappearing while the deserts grow by ten million hectares a year—about the size of 17,000 football fields![3]

Whether in China, Brazil, or Africa, millions of plants, people, and animals have lost their home to the encroaching sands.[4]

The coral reefs are dying, taking with them all the glittering life that makes its home there. If global warming continues, all the reefs will be dead in twenty years. Glaciers melt and the oceans rise. By the end of the century all glaciers will be gone; islands and coastline everywhere will be swallowed by the sea.[5]

The web of life is under assault. Species are disappearing one thousand times faster than the natural rate of extinction. The fabulous diversity of species that share this wondrous planet that gives us home is under assault: birds' songs will never be heard again, flowers will never be seen again, and insects and whales will be gone forever. Frogs and tigers may come to live only in fairy tales. At the present rate, every year 50,000 species disappear and by the turn of this century it is estimated that half of all species will be gone.[6]

And humanity is not faring much better. As biological diversity is being destroyed, so is cultural diversity. Of six thousand languages currently spoken around the world, only three hundred are being taught to children. Within a generation or two, none of the people from those cultures will have a direct connection to their history.[7] With the languages gone, the cultures disappear. McDonald's, Nike, Coca-Cola, Sony, Microsoft, and IBM are now the most recognized names on the planet.

The current economic system concentrates wealth, a process that makes for fewer and fewer rich people and more and more poor. One-fifth of the world's population lives on less than $1 a day.[8] On the other side, the richest fifth consume 84 percent of its resources.[9] The assets of the three richest individuals in the world are equal to those of the 48 poorest countries.[10] One-fifth of U.S. citizens cannot meet basic needs.[11] The top 1 percent in the United States owns more wealth than the bottom 94 percent combined.

Compensation for CEOs has skyrocketed, while regular wages have fallen for workers. For every dollar a company worker makes, its CEO receives over $400.[12] As layoffs multiply, Manpower—a temp agency—has become the biggest employer in the United States.[13]

In a globalized economy trillions of dollars slosh across boarders daily. Investors have transformed the world into a global casino. Money is protected with free trade agreements while it gobbles up resources at an unprecedented rate. Growth and "progress" are used as justification for these "externalities." The imbalance causes more and more instability as this tendency accelerates. Cancer grows in total disregard for its environment. The transnational corporations operate in the same manner. Economic globalization rests on concepts that can only hold meaning to cold, calculating linear (beta) consciousness. Economic profits for the shareholders have become the sole criteria of success. The heart has a wider view.

Two of the "externalities" that have the corporate powers-that-be frightened are peak oil and global climate change.[14] Either one of these trends could drastically change life as we know it. Global climate change threatens mass disruptions for all life on the planet;[15] at the same time, we now have reached (or will in the next few years) the peak of oil production.[16] Until now oil production has matched the increase in demand. Those days are over. It costs more and more to extract oil because there is less and less of it. The "externalities" are crashing in on us catalyzing a domino effect, from food shortages caused by lack of fuel and oil-derived fertilizer to massive unemployment associated with an economic downturn. Without oil we cannot fuel industrial society— our culture as it is now is doomed. These two phenomena are deeply interconnected by the addiction we have to material goods and cheap energy. Dale Allen Pfeiffer describes the predicament of our times:

Like the withdrawal symptoms endured by an addict, the effects of the coming petroleum crisis will ravage the American body politic and work necessary but painful changes in the life of the entire human community. Just as that inexorable withdrawal closes in on us, we're acquiring a new awareness of the damage already done by the petroleum addiction itself. Peak Oil is the crisis of getting off petroleum; climate change is the almost-irreversible legacy of two hundred years of fossil fuel pollution ...

Corruption, income inequity, narco-traffic, money-laundering, the warfare state, loss of civil liberties, imperial overstretch, racism, and the constant recourse to violence as a tool of domestic and international policy—all the ailments of the republic are interconnected. At their center is an oil economy bound to militarism by the petrodollar money system. Change that system, and the other problems become far more amenable to rational reform.[17]

In the name of "progress," the self-regulating and self-healing processes of the earth and our societies have been stripped away. The earth suffers while fewer and fewer get access to more and more, and the rest of us lose what little security we had. The vast majority of people on the planet would not choose this state of affairs. The gross inequities I have described above can only be perpetuated by coercion and manipulation.

This profit-driven system maintains an awesome apparatus of propaganda which generates false needs; a legal and regulatory infrastructure with "free trade agreements" and the World Trade Organization (WTO) which now make it against the law to meet local needs if it cuts into corporate profits; and military might that is used when the first two strategies fail. It thrives on economic blackmail or plain bribery—if your livelihood is at stake, you tend to play by the rules of the game. This is as true for individuals and communities as it is for nations.

The nonmilitary arm of this profiteering has been recently revealed by John Perkins. The profiteers describe themselves as Economic Hitmen who cheat nations around the world out of huge sums of money. They funnel money from international development and aid organizations into the pockets of transnational corporations and wealthy individuals. As Perkins said, "They play a game as old as empire, but one that has taken on new and terrifying dimensions during this time of globalization."[18] These players have been the means by which international finance and aid has been used to control small and developing nations. When that fails, the CIA or the military are called in to enforce the rules.

As Perkins said, the game is not new. In 1935, General Smedley D. Butler testified before a congressional committee regarding his thirty-three-year Marine Corps career:

> I spent most of my time being a high-class muscle man for big business, for Wall Street and for the bankers. In short, I was a racketeer for capitalism ... Like all members of the military profession, I never had an original thought until I left the service ... I obeyed the orders of the higher-ups .... I helped make Mexico and especially Tampico safe for American oil interests in 1914. I helped make Haiti and Cuba a decent place for the National City Bank boys to collect revenues in. I helped in the raping of half a dozen Central American republics for the benefit of Wall Street.
>
> The record of racketeering is long. I helped purify Nicaragua for the international banking house of Brown Brothers in 1909 to 1912. I brought light to the Dominican Republic for American sugar interests in 1916. I helped get Honduras "right" for American fruit companies in 1903. In China in 1927, I helped see to it that Standard Oil went its way unmolested. U.S. military power was used to establish

the ground rules within which American business could operate.[19]

In the second part of the twentieth century, the game continued with new intensity. Chile, Congo, Haiti, and Guatemala, and sixteen others have had freely elected democracies that fell victim to U.S. intervention (often carried out by the CIA).[20] Military regimes were supported in their place. Phillip Agee, ex-CIA operative said, "There have been more than one million killed—direct victims of the United States' harsh policies."[21]

Thomas Freidman laid out the relation of militarization and globalization:

> To ignore the role of military security in an era of economic and information growth is like forgetting the importance of oxygen to our breathing .... Indeed McDonald's cannot flourish without MacDonald Douglas, the designer of the U.S. Air Force F-15. And the hidden fist that keeps the world safe for Silicon Valley's technology to flourish is called the U.S. Army, Air Force, Navy, and Marine Corps. And these fighting forces and institutions are paid for by American tax dollars.[22]

The costs of the global corporate agenda, which places trade and profit above human or environmental needs, have come back home to the United States as budgets for human services get cut and environmental regulations get slashed. In the United States, prisons are popping up everywhere as school budgets decrease. Police are immune to prosecution if they kill innocent people, and incarceration rates are skyrocketing despite the fact that crime has gone down. Over 1.8 million people are currently imprisoned in the United States. Our country is seen as protecting freedom but has the highest per capita incarceration rate in the history of the world.[23]

Citizens are being asked to give up our rights in the name of the "war on terrorism." Untold numbers of innocent people are detained or killed both inside the country and out in this mistaken approach toward assuring security. One month after September 11, 2001, Thich Nhat Hanh's words spun around the Internet, appealing to our highest sensibilities:

> Terror is in the human heart. We must remove this terror from the heart. Destroying the human heart, both physically and psychologically, is what we should avoid. The root of terrorism should be identified so that it can be removed. The root of terrorism is misunderstanding, hatred, and violence.

> This root cannot be located by the military. Bombs and missiles cannot reach it, let alone destroy it. Only with the practice of calming and looking deeply can our insight reveal and identify this root. Only with the practice of deep listening and compassion can it be transformed and removed ....

> Only understanding and compassion can dissolve violence and hatred .... Acting without understanding, acting out of hatred, violence, and fear, we help sow more terror, bringing terror to the homes of others and bringing back terror to our own homes ....

> Everyone has the seed of awakening and insight within his or her heart. Let us help each other touch these seeds in ourselves so that everyone could have the courage to speak out.[24]

We can share the earth's abundance in equitable and sustainable ways that honor the natural world. The U.N. Human Development Report tells us that $210 billion would be enough both to solve the world's most pressing environmental problems ($140 billion) and to eradicate absolute poverty worldwide ($70 billion).[25] The United States has already spent twice that in the Iraq war.[26] We have the money and the know-how, we just need the will.

The World Reflected Inside

The pseudo-surplus of capitalism leaves us unfulfilled. Competition and advertising combine to create needs that can never be satisfied. We become enslaved by the need for more. Those of us who have credit go deeper and deeper into the hole; those of us who have jobs become afraid to leave them. Materialism itself becomes a trap.

Freedom has come to mean we can get whatever we want. But the more we have, the more we become paralyzed. We get trapped by our fear of losing what we have and build walls around our houses. We are afraid of losing our jobs for fear that we will not be able to keep those houses. In 1820 when Big Soldier, an Osage chief, politely refused to become a part of "American Civilization" he said:

> I see and admire your manner of living, your good warm houses; your extensive fields of corn, your gardens, your cows, oxen, workhorses, wagons, and thousands of machines, that I know not the use of. I see that you are able to clothe yourselves even from weeds and grasses. In short, you can do almost what you choose. You whites possess the power of subduing almost every animal to your use. You are surrounded by slaves. Everything about you is in chains and you are slaves yourselves. I fear if I exchange my pursuits for yours, I too should become a slave.[27]

Out there, alone, fending for ourselves, we cannot afford to be disapproved of or to be exposed. Our individuality never gets expressed as we squelch anything we think or feel that is out of line. In school and work, our creativity and spontaneity never get a chance. Our values imprison us, and our fear of disapproval is the guard that keeps us in jail. We have traded in subjective autonomy for the American myth of objective autonomy. A common deception rooted in individualism is that if everyone becomes self-aware and self-responsible, then society will no longer be askew. Again the sole focus is on "me." We need to move our attention out and become aware of what is taking place around us. Individualism is a cancer; it makes us oblivious of the relations in which we are both embedded and dependent. We have all been indoctrinated into the system.

When we relax and meditate, our natural connectedness arises and we remember our gratitude. When we remember our connectedness, we can relax into the web of life that holds us all. We can raise our voices and claim our passions.

The paradox is that the more we are able to be in deep connection with ourselves and others, the more we are able to become autonomous.

Holographic Life

There is an opportunity to awaken to the possibility of transformation: "Awareness is the moment when we arise with eyes encrusted from self-induced dreams of control, domination, victimization, and self-hatred to catch a dream of the divine in the face of the other.["][28]

When we find ourselves upset about what is taking place in the world, it is a reminder that we are, indeed, interconnected. Though we may feel isolated, overwhelmed, or disconnected from what is taking place, whether we acknowledge it or not, we are each a part of the whole and there is no escape. When we shut down, we weaken the whole. If reality is an intricate, interconnected hologram, then we cannot turn away from any one part of it without damaging its integrity.

Conversely, as we open, we facilitate the circulation of energy, making room for the self-correcting, self-regulating, healing processes intrinsic to open systems. When challenges persist, open systems either evolve or fall apart. It is truly awesome to think that by cultivating a generous heart, we not only feel better, but we impact the whole world. Even relaxation is not a private experience! Open and you heal the world—what great powers reside in each and all of us!

I started this chapter noting that relaxing without going into denial, when focused on the state of the world, is a daunting task! It is as though we are being asked to be open in the face of our torturer. This takes a gigantic heart; I have to admit, it is a heart bigger than I possess. The process is like working with an affirmation. You would not need an affirmation if it were already true; an affirmation simply orients you to a desirable direction. Mindfulness helps us move into openness so we can witness suffering without withdrawing and shutting down. In receptivity, we talk to the issues facing us; we do not turn our back to them, but instead we imagine the stories that might carry us through.

We are called to bear witness: To bring peace to a war zone means keeping a peaceful heart in the midst of the fire. The current times call us to step into the fire. This is an immense challenge and a great act of courage. Envisioning peace in a quiet natural setting is not such a difficult task. Envisioning peace when you are informed of the issues that are fueling war is not at all easy.

If we believe that we are victims, we abdicate our power and feel as though life happens to us. Victim mentality dwells on hopelessness, sometimes with a righteous tinge. We have been socialized to think that we are separate, and that the source of our problems is purely external or our own fault. In either case, we are expected to solve them on our own—no wonder it is so overwhelming!

But we are not separate. We are deeply connected, and

our fates are entwined. We cannot deny the devastation. The good thing is that as we feel it, we come alive to our interconnections, and we open to awesome powers. The key is to feel what is true and align with the resilience of life to turn the tide. We can call on feelings as fierce as a mother who protects her young.

Some people believe they cannot contribute to the world until they have "gotten themselves together." Others believe that they cannot attend to themselves because the world itself is in such dire straights that it needs all of their waking attention. We cannot "get ourselves together" separate from being in the world anymore than we can help the world while ignoring our own needs. *Just as we breathe in and out, we work on the inside and we work on the outside. One cannot breathe in one direction.*

Our hearts have been torn by dissociation from the earth and one another. The most powerful way I know to heal the rupture is to come to sense our inter-being, a word that Thich Nhat Hanh uses to name our true state of interconnection and interdependence.[29] Meditate on interbeing: life is woven together, as we breathe out, the trees breathe in. Follow your breath into the air and through the plants. Follow the water you drink though your body and back into the body of the earth. Witness the food you eat—its growth, the soil it came from, and the many hands that brought it to your table. We live interbeing with each breath. With others, contemplate interbeing and share your sensations and visions; you will gain a wealth of alternative points of reference to supplant the limited ideas we have of ourselves as isolated beings.

We have been conditioned to think there is no point in embarking on a course of action unless we know that we will be successful. The scientific rational approach instructs us to carefully inspect all ideas and not to proceed until there is no doubt and the efficacy of the approach has been proven. All ideas are suspect until they have weathered thorough debate. The heart, however, does not function this way. It moves us to action when whatever we care about is in peril. Whether we are successful at turning the tide is not the question to be asked, for we cannot know. We only know that we have an invitation to come alive. Responding to the call that lives in our hearts, we join with millions of others; that is the gift itself.[30]

Answers emerge as we walk together.

Signs of Hope

Every day, people love, give birth, plant gardens, sing, dance, create, play, take time with one another, and pause in a busy schedule to watch a flight of birds. When we take the time to breathe, life pulses around and through us. Every day, people act on faith and hope. The decision to embrace life, one moment at a time, is steadily moving all of us toward the possibilities of new ways of being with one another and the earth. Signs of hope are everywhere.

This sense of a new time emerging is being felt by many. For some, it is captured by the phrase "paradigm shift," for others it is changing the cultural dream. Recently, some have said it is the rise of creativity over control. Joanna Macy calls it the "Great Turning." She says that a revolution is underway as people begin to realize that all of our needs can be met without destroying our world.

> We have the technical knowledge, the communication tools, and material resources to grow enough food, ensure clean air and water, and meet rational energy needs.

> Future generations, if there is a livable world for them, will look back at the epochal transition we are making to a life-sustaining society. And they may well call this the time of the Great Turning. It is happening now. Whether or not it is

recognized by the corporate-controlled media, the Great Turning is a reality. Although we cannot know yet if it will take hold in time for humans and other complex life forms to survive, we can know that it is under way. And it is gaining momentum, through the actions of countless individuals and groups around the world. To see this as the larger context of our lives clears our vision and summons our courage.[31]

There are three dimensions of this Great Turning: The first is holding actions that slow destruction of the earth and her peoples, the second is making structural analysis and beginning the creation of life sustaining institutions, and the third is a profound transformation of consciousness.

Actions to slow the damage to Earth and its beings are perhaps the most visible expression of the Great Turning. These activities include all the political, legislative, and legal work required to reduce destruction, as well as direct actions—blockades, boycotts, civil disobedience, and other forms of refusal.

Around the globe, people are resisting destruction: Mothers who lose children to violence organize to provide solace to one another, whether in Detroit or Buenos Aires; people band together to defend forests from untrammeled cutting to keep farmland from being flooded, and to protect the earth from being scarred by toxins, coal mines or nuclear waste. In cities and towns across the country, people working for environmental justice are planting grasses to clean toxic soil, documenting the use of lead in paints and pipes of local schools, and battling waves and winds to clean birds and wildlife suffocated by oil spills. In India, half a million farmers protested against Cargill to protect their traditional way of saving seed from one year to the next—an ancestral practice that secures each generation's survival.[32]

Women around the world hold vigils for peace—inspired by the courage of Latin American, South African, Israeli, and

Palestinian women, Women in Black, and the Mothers of the Disappeared. Their powerful but silent presence bears witness to alternatives to war. The persistent and imaginative protests against the World Bank, the World Trade Organization, and other trade institutions are among the most visible of these kinds of activities. Less dramatic but equally courageous are the people who have come forward to testify about the corruption in corporate America and in the U.S. government.

The analysis of structural causes and the creation of structural alternatives, says Macy, is the second dimension of the Great Turning:

> In order for us to free ourselves and our planet from the damage being inflicted by the Industrial Growth Society, we must understand its dynamics. We must understand the tacit agreements that create obscene wealth for a few, while progressively impoverishing the rest. What are the interlocking causes that indenture us to an insatiable economy that uses our Earth as both supply house and sewer? ... When we see how this system operates, we are less tempted to demonize the politicians and corporate CEOs who are in bondage to it. And for all the apparent might of the Industrial Growth Society, we can also see its fragility—how dependent it is on our obedience, and how doomed it is to devour itself. In addition to learning how the present system works, we are also creating structural alternatives. In countless localities, like green shoots pushing up through the rubble, new social and economic arrangements are sprouting. Not waiting for our national or state politicos to catch up with us, we are banding together, and taking action in our own communities. Flowing from our creativity and collaboration on behalf of life, these actions may look marginal, but they hold the seeds for the future.[33]

Every spring, hundreds of thousands of people inside our nation's cities plant gardens, restoring the earth and their own sense of self-sufficiency. Young people are challenging car culture by critical mass bike rallies and converting old school buses into bio-diesel transport.[34]

Alternatives ways of living are emerging around the world: In Columbia, Gaviotas is a community that is a hotbed of inventions for sustainability. For three decades, Gaviotans—peasants, scientists, artists, and former street kids—have struggled to build an oasis of imagination and sustainability in the remote, barren savannas of eastern Colombia, an area ravaged by political terror. They have planted millions of trees, regenerating the rainforest. They farm organically and use wind and solar power. Every family enjoys free housing, community meals, and schooling. There are no weapons, no police, no jail. There is no mayor.[35]

In a small German village called Stuyerburg, Lebensgarten, once a slave labor munitions factory for the Nazi regime, has been converted into a multigenerational ecological village. In Detroit, neighborhood groups are turning abandoned houses into homes for teen mothers, using principles of sustainable architecture.[36] Neighborhoods in Argentina form cooperatives in the wake of a collapsed economy. These cooperatives produce food, medicine, and goods necessary for daily life.[37] In the United States, urban communities (rich and poor) form direct relationships with small farms, creating community-supported agriculture, bypassing the distribution channels of mega-agribusiness.[38]

These activities are happening in backyards, village squares, bus stops, and on the Internet, where people make connections that are reshaping our world. New sources of information flow around the mainstream. Independent Media Centers have appeared in cities and communities around the world.[39] They and other media and technology initiatives provide an infrastructure for unfiltered news that is more global than the mainstream media.[40]

Indigenous people of all continents are reclaiming their cultures and ways of being, not in selfish ingrown ways, but in service of the planet itself. In Ecuador, a complete and autonomous education system is growing out of indigenous peoples' working together to preserve their way of life and to come to the global community on their terms. The Intercultural Bilingual Education system is 2800 schools strong in which children learn first in their traditional language and then in Spanish. They are recovering orally-based knowledge that has survived and been maintained in indigenous people's daily life. They are educating new professionals who are committed to putting indigenous knowledge into practice."[41]

Restorative Justice is taking root in many of our cities as a community-based way of dealing with people who commit criminal acts. Justice Works and the Zen Peacemakers work with prisoners to create peace and dignity within the prison system and to support people when they are released. And in the Indian state of Kerala, for nearly forty years almost three hundred murderers have lived in an open prison, without fences, armed guards, or surveillance towers. In all its years of functioning, there has been only one repeat offender and one escapee.[42]

These structural alternatives cannot take root and survive without our adopting values to sustain them—this is the third dimension of the Great Turning.

They must mirror what we want and how we relate to Earth and each other. They arise as grief for our world, giving the lie to old paradigm notions of rugged individualism, the essential separateness of the self. They spring up as glad response to breakthroughs in scientific thought, as reductionism and materialism give way to evidence of a living universe. And they come to pass in the resurgence of wisdom traditions, reminding us again that our world is a sacred whole, worthy of adoration and service.

Systems thinking, deep ecology, liberation theology, Creation Spirituality, shamanism, eco-psychology, and earth-based spiritual practices are all palpable evidence of this shift. Over the past century, there has been an influx—and by now a real groundswell—of Eastern religious thought and Buddhist practice in the West. Within Judaism, Christianity, and Islam, underground streams are emerging that express devotion to the living Earth. Everywhere, people are embracing holistic health, spiritual healing, and ways of understanding that harkens back to times before classical Western science.[43]

The Great Turning is built on trusting our true inner natures and all that exists. May we bring the great powers that live inside our hearts and spirits out into the world. It is in our hearts and our spirits that healing happens.

Induction

Breathing with your belly, bring to your awareness your symbol for physical relaxation and feel the whole of your body relax ... Breathe through tension, release it into the ground ... Relax into the support of the earth ... ...

When you are ready, bring to awareness your symbol for mental relaxation. Extend your awareness to include the vast reaches of the sky, the sky that extends out forever ... Feel your mind relax into its natural state of spaciousness, as spacious as the skies ... ...

Now bring in your symbol for emotional relaxation. Let go of the "shoulds." Just as you can relax into the support of the earth, you can relax into the support of the community ... Relaxing into the web-work of life, the net of relationships of which you are a part, support your life ... ... Imagine that your heart relaxes into its natural state of love and compassion. However you experience this, breathe love and compassion. As you relax emotionally, your heart opens ... love and compassion arise ... ...

Bring to awareness your symbol for your creative, self-restoring center, where your expanding awareness flows ... ... Here your heart opens and deep knowing grows ... Here you can listen to the whispering of spirit ... Here you can bear witness to what is true ... This is where visions are born. And you can join in creating the world anew ... This is where healing and creativity arise ... Here you discover all that you need to heal and create the world anew ...

Take a moment to honor what you hold sacred ... Remember your gratitude for the gift of life ... It is a gift to be alive ... part of the whole and the whole lives inside ... held in interbeing ... ...

If you would like, you can invite spirits to accompany you in this work ... beings of the past or future, or beings who occupy different life forms ... If you would like, invite them to accompany you ... Welcome them ... ...

Feel your heart and spirit ready for the work you are about to embark on.

I am going to suggest several affirmations; if you wish to affirm them, repeat them to yourself after me, feeling as though they are fully true.

I believe in people ...

I celebrate belonging to the community of life ...

I relax into interbeing ...

I believe in my family and friends ...

We believe in our community; there is a free flow of support among us in creating change ...

I honor the integrity of all people and all life ...

I am visionary and courageous ...

I am aware of the impact of all of my actions and I act with respect to all beings ...

I cultivate a joyous and generous heart ...

Time is generous, I relax into the moment and it carries me ...

I am always attuned to what is needed for healing to happen on all levels of being ...

I am glad to honor the earth with good care ...

All my relationships are filled with empathy, and mutual care ...

A spring of creativity continually moves through us ...

We offer our gifts to healing the world ...

We gain strength from our connection to the peoples of the world ...

We have confidence in our ability to care for the world ...

We learn from the past and welcome the future ...

We work to bring about a positive future ...

Take a moment and breathe in gratitude as you inhale ... and breathe out compassion as you exhale ... Gratitude to be alive; compassion for all life ... all life on the planet ... ...

Know that in focusing on affirmations you evoke powers from the depths of beingness itself, powers that manifest both within and around you. In focusing on affirmations, you cause yourself to align your energies with them, and you will discover yourself acting out of these very powers you have evoked ...

Listen very carefully to all that is said letting the words draw up your deepest knowing, knowing from the depths of life itself.

From Holding to Opening into Interbeing

Feel that as you are relaxed, you are open ... your body opens ... your mind opens ... your feelings open ... Enjoy this open state ... Breathe out and feel openness ... Find that place within you where you feel strong, and open ... fully receptive in your strength ... receptivity being your strength.

Let your awareness ride on your breath, your breath brings release, you open ... Breathe. In openness you experience wholeness ... With each exhalation, feel yourself relaxing into your natural state of wholeness ... openness ...

Experience openness allowing movement ... Breath is easy ... in openness there is fluidity ... fluid motion moving through you ... welcoming newness ... It's this fluidity that gives you strength ... supple ... Shutting down brings rigidity, when you constrict and turn away from your experience, you fragment and weaken yourself—energy no longer flows through. Feel the power of flexibility ... Wholeness is not static, it is always in motion ...

In mindfulness, witness when constriction arises ... All you need to do is breathe through and openness returns ... As long as you are supple and open, you are carried by life force energies ... Breathe, feel that you can open further as you breathe. Breathe and feel your life open ...

Breathe life energy into any aspects of your being that have gotten rigid ... ... Breathe life into those places that need it ... Feel them breathe and become open, supple, fluid again ... Let go and life carries you ...

Tune in to your body and notice if there are any holding patterns ... Send breath there ... Breathe through and opening happens. With intention, aim your breath wherever you like ... Feel opening happen. Breathe. Wholeness is a natural fluid state ... ...

Extend your awareness to your environment ... Extend this openness to the life that is around you ... Watch your breath roll through you and into the trees ... Out of the trees and into other beings ... Breath weaves life. Interbeing ... ...

Sense the many relations that connected to ... Family ... Others in your life ...

Bring to awareness the food you eat ... those who worked to bring food to your table ... You might want to tune to one kind of food ... Imagine it alive and growing in the place from which it came ... What nourished it to grow into its being? ... Imagine all that took place that brought the food to your plate ... the hands it has passed through ... Community, exchange of energy ... Interbeing. Witness it ... ...

Imagine the different things that you do moving out and
touching others on the web ... Just as breath weaves life, all
activity weaves the web of being ... Awesome ... All held in
the web ... All making the web. Imagine letting go into the web
... ...

If you come across any tension breathe through it ... Breathe.
Feel your body softening, letting go and relaxing into the
support of community ... Feel yourself getting stronger and
stronger as you relax into interbeing ... ...

Become aware of your mind. Notice if you have any beliefs
that have become rigid, or dogmatic, beliefs you hold onto
tightly ... If you come across any, breathe through and release
them, Mental Houseclean them ... Plant beliefs that inspire
opening and trust ... Notice if you have cynical ideas that say
nothing will change anyway ... Notice any beliefs that tell
you that you have to fend for yourself, you have to defend
yourself ... Beliefs that tell you not to trust your own nature ...
not to trust nature ... Breathe them out ...

Remember the intelligence intrinsic to life itself, trust it, know that
this intelligence moves through you too ... ...

Send to your mind opening energy. Let your ideas be supple
resilient and strong ... Remember times you have felt most open
and blessed to be alive .... . Breathe in this energy ... Feel it
infuse your whole belief system with connectedness, gratitude
to be alive ... ... Feel the climate of your mind be open and
relaxed, resilient and strong ... Imagine that ideas grow and

reach up to the sky ... Feel curiosity awakening ... Openness that welcomes insight to appear ... ...

Now become aware of the emotional climate of your life. Notice any feelings in your emotional life that are tight, constricted, alienated ... feelings of separation or loneliness, areas in your emotional life that have become parched and dry ... or brittle and bitter ... or cold and icy. Scan your life and notice if any of these feelings come out in the different circumstances ... feelings that no longer receive the nurturance of others, of life itself, feelings that close you off and move you into further isolation, feelings that are dense, hard ... Breathe through them. Offer yourself loving kindness ... ... Feel your heart breathe. Remember times that have inspired your heart to sing ... ... Feel your heart open ... ...

Give yourself permission to be warm-hearted, to be light-hearted ... If any beliefs crop up that stop you transform them as you did the others earlier ... ...

Everyone has warm spots inside them. Give yourself permission to touch the warmth of others, to receive the warmth of others ... Feel yourself soften, appreciate each other ... Fill the hardness with softness ... Moisten the dry spots with the love of life ... Let yourself feel your gladness to be alive ... open to life, open to others ...

As you open, your spirit lightens. Feel the spirit of life percolating through. Let your spirit be open too ... Let the openness extend to include all the people in your life ... Let yourself be supported, flexible, a part of the life of the community you live in ... Just as your heart pulses with life, feel your community pulsing with life ... Alive.

Like breathing in and out, you receive from others and you give to others, life holds all ... ... Flood yourself with the good feelings of community life ... Breathe out any feelings of isolation ... ...

Now look out into this coming week. Imagine the events unfolding ... Witness if you tighten up, hold on, alienate yourself, or separate yourself anywhere. Witness your tendencies ... ... Breathe openness into yourself in the scenes ... Let the energy ground you in interbeing ...

Notice how in doing so you find yourself with more energy, no longer expending it to hold on ... as you open creativity, curiosity, and compassion all flow ... Interbeing, exchange between you and community. The web is strong ... ... You get your strength from community, no longer using up energy in separation, instead relaxing into life's natural state of interbeing ...

Create a symbol for this experience ... Tell yourself you will remember to bring it to awareness if ever you find yourself shutting down. In doing so, you open to the resilience of life and it lifts you up.

Toward a Balanced World: Distinguishing between Cravings and Needs

Feel yourself in a very quiet place inside of yourself. Be in your own presence ... Breathe ... Reside in your own energy in this moment, breathing quietly ... Simply be present with yourself ... here in this moment ...

Give yourself permission to feel your feelings ... Be aware of all your feelings of desire and all your feelings of satisfaction which come and go like patterns of weather. Witness the flow of feelings through your experience ... Notice how desire shows up in the landscape of your experience ... Witness where desire is awakened in your life ... ...

Now let the desires, the "shoulds," the "coulds," all of them, soak into the ground ... Let yourself relax into the life that percolates through you ... Become aware of the resilience of life ... the continual renewal of life ... transforming energies constantly, the resilience, the renewal, the transformation ... Life itself is abundant, it naturally renews itself ... Let yourself relax into trusting life itself ... Experiencing the intelligence of life, the self-clearing, self-healing capacities intrinsic to all life ... Sense this self-healing intelligence inside you ... Trust it ... ...

Now bring back to your awareness those things you discovered as you scanned the landscape of your life. With the knowingness of life itself you will discover what is good for your life and what is not. Bring to mind one desire, be it a food, a thing, a type of relationship or activity ... Choose one

desire or habit to explore ... If there are many choose one
now, knowing you can explore others another time ...
Bring it into the light of awareness. Witness. Remember
moments when this desire is alive in you ... Notice its
dimensions ... ... Now notice what feelings resonate with this
desire ... Notice what each feeling is rooted in ... ... Notice
the quality of the feelings involved ... Do they clamor or are
they soft? ... Imagine their shape, are they round or
sharp? ... Do they connect you with the harmonizing resilient
forces of nature? ... or do they feed alienation? ... Witness
what is so with this desire ... ... If you discover harmonizing
energy, let yourself rest in gratitude ...

If you discover sharp, driven, hardened or discordant energy—
qualities that likely take you away from the quiet presence inside,
then you have found a craving ... When you fulfill a craving you
only feed more want—there is no satisfaction to be found ...
Witness what is true for you ... ... If you find craving, imagine
that there is a shell around it ... Imagine cracking it off ... inside
you will discover a true need ... It may be different than the
original desire, but this need can be satisfied ... ... Witness what
is true for you ... ... Breathe through the energy ... Imagine that
the shell is transformed in the soil, and feel yourself relax, let the
discordant energy soak down into the ground ...

Bring the qualities of generosity and gratitude in to the scene.
Remember times these qualities have been present in
your experience ... Experience these qualities now ...
Generosity ... Gratitude ... ... Breathe these qualities into the

scene ... Imagine the feelings and situations that have been present absorbing the qualities of generosity and gratitude ... Witness transformation taking place ...

Witness how what you have been focusing on impacts other life. Broaden your view and witness what is the case ... Notice where balance is found and everyone's needs are met ... the earth is honored ... ...

Now look out over the rest of the landscape of your life, notice the difference between your cravings and your needs ... ...

Transform the cravings and honor the needs ... Notice what part of yourself is desiring. If it resonates with life, or if it is a craving in compensation for disconnection ... If you run across craving, let it be transformed by going through its surface and discovering what is inside ... what true need is inside ... Honor your true needs. Let go of the cravings ... Bring in gratitude and generosity, these qualities heal. Mental Houseclean the old habits. Know that in doing so you are creating space to be even more attuned to what is healthful for yourself and others, for life itself ... ...

Life becomes simple and satisfying with generosity and gratitude. Know that you fully deserve to have your needs met ... Notice how as you honor your needs, you feel more connected to all the life within and around you ... Notice the choices you can make to honor your needs.

Imagine a daily routine based on these choices ... Honoring your needs, doing your part in keeping the place you occupy on the web strong and resilient ... ... Feel gratitude to be alive. Know that in honoring only your needs you create room for others' true needs to be met too, for you have taken only your fair share ... Honor the sanctity of all life ...

Keeping the Faith

As you hear the sounds of these words, feel yourself going deeper and deeper into the universal realms out of which all life springs ... Feel yourself relaxing into the resilient support of the web of life. With each word you hear, you are becoming increasingly attuned to the connectedness of life, the mutuality of life ... With the sounds of these words moving through your awareness, your consciousness expands. From your usual individual awareness into greater universal consciousness ... Give yourself permission to enter into your natural state of fluid connectedness ...

Feel the rhythms of life percolating through you ... the pulse of life, the breath of life, the hum of life ... Knowing life percolates through all creatures, through all people ...

Sense the universal breath—what we breathe out, the plants breathe in ... what the plants breathe out, we breathe in. Energy constantly supporting, transforming, moving—universal breath interweaves all that lives upon the earth ...

Feel the great synchrony of the universe. The movement of electrons, the movement of planets, all in synchrony ... Let your tensions be washed away by waves of universality ... Feel yourself sinking deeper into the support of life itself ...

Experience the fluidity of life ... everything moving, carried by time ... day into night, season to season, year to year. History is alive ... Each generation gives life to the next ... generation to generation to generation ... Each generation dreams and struggles for a better life for the next, history in the making ...

Remember those who passed before who cared ... living, breathing beings devoted to life, dedicated their lives to the struggle for humanity ... Remember them now ... ...

They live on in the spirit of humanity ... Summon up the courage of those who passed before ... Breathe in courage ... empowering ourselves, the spirit of humanity lives and breathes in us now ... Let our ancestors rejoice in our rising to the times ... ... Aroused, together we take up the call, make history, create the future ...

Feel life percolate through everyone; life regenerates itself. Life endowed us with life; now we are called to preserve life itself ... We are part of the Great Turning, the great healing ...

Give yourself permission to experience the fullness of your devotion to life, feel it in the depths of your heart, your soul, your whole being ... Allow yourself to care ... Remember the special moments in your life, times when your heart was warmed ... celebrations ... shared joys ... shared love ... majestic landscapes ... the wonder of life itself. Remember what makes your heart sing ... Feel your passion for life ... ...

Let your feelings merge with the feelings of others who have a passion for life ... passion ignites passion ... ever-widening passion for the protection of life ... everyone caring ... forming a great wave of humanity to change the course of history; history is alive within us ... Together we have great healing powers, together we transform ourselves and the world ... We make room for healing to happen ... ...

Remembering the powers, the power of people united, the power of life itself ... healing powers are all around and within us ... Let all the pain, the rage of yours, of the earth's, let it transform itself into a great healing force, a force as fierce as a mother protecting her young ... ...

Let the power of life surge through you. Breathe it ... Feel it in your heart ... pulsing life ... empowering you. Feel it uplift you ... arousing you ... Aroused, humanity forms a great moving wave ... Passion for life carries us, empowers us to emancipate life itself ... to create a future where the dignity of all life is respected ... where the life of every single baby of every kind is honored. Our ancestors rejoice as we answer the call of history, protecting the claim of life itself ...

You have your life to offer, you make a difference. You are alive in this great time ... Feel purpose ... Feel passion, the power of life lives within you ... Feel yourself a part of the great struggle, healing powers move through you ... Listen to your heart ... Listen to your convictions ... Listen to your instincts ... What cries out to you? ... ...

Give yourself permission to struggle for what you believe in ... Remember, there are many who share your cares ... joining together, feel how much more powerful you are, everyone is, as we're joined together ... Believe in our power. Feel it ... Together we can make a difference ... We are making a difference already ... Life always wins in the end, grass grows up through concrete and reaches for the sky ... Life regenerates itself, life always wins in the end ...

Feel your connection with life itself ... with other creatures ... with the plant world ... with other peoples ... ... We all create a great wave of life protecting life, securing it for the next generations ... Imagine that humanity pulls through, the spirit of humanity lives on and each generation continues to dream and to struggle for the next generation ... trusting the future, keeping the faith ... Let yourself be empowered by life itself ... and we'll heal the future.

Count Out

Begin to finish what you are doing and go over all the insights you have had and choices you have made ... Breathe out, and project these visions into your life. Set the stage for action ... ... Breathe and draw in these powers. Embody them ... Live into the changes you are making ... ...

Appreciate all the energies, spirits, and your own good will for accompanying you through your inner work ... Thank you for your inner work.

Make yourself ready to come out to outer conscious levels ...

In a moment I'm going to count from one to five ... At the count of five, you will open your eyes, remembering all that you have experienced ... feeling refreshed, revitalized, and relaxed, having brought with you the energies you became attuned to, ready and able to act on them.

ONE—becoming more aware of the room around you ...

TWO—coming up slowly now ...

THREE—at the count of five, you will open your eyes feeling relaxed, revitalized, and refreshed, remembering all that you have experienced ...

FOUR—coming up now bringing with you what you have experienced ...

FIVE!—eyes open, feeling refreshed, revitalized, and relaxed, remembering all that you have experienced, feeling a sense of well-being, ready and able to act on the energies to which you have attuned yourself.

•11•

Reclaiming Wholeness in Our World Secures the Future: Circles Are Our Safety Nets

Black Elk, an Oglala Sioux medicine man, tells us, "The Power of the World always works in circles, and everything tries to be round ... The sky is round, and I have heard that the earth is round like a ball, and so are the stars. The wind, in its greatest power, whirls ... and so it is in everything where power moves."[1]

I visualize wholeness as round; it is not a pyramid or a square, but a sphere or a circle. Sitting together in Circle, people come into resonance with each other and the forces of the universe.

Harrison Owen tells us, "When the circle of caring people is established; emergent order manifests, automatically, no problem, on cue. And the circle is important. Good stuff simply does not happen in squares and rows, or if it does, it is much slower and less satisfying."[2]

Circles create relationships where energy moves and spirit comes to life. Each person is needed to make a whole, and each person is held by the whole. We take joy in one another and hold each other in our grief. We think together, envision together, and offer one another courage to bring our values into our work and community. In a Circle, we weave new ways of being and find ways to reclaim ancient wisdom.

Meditating together, we generate an energy field that lifts us all up. Doing so, we create openings that touch the heart and help us to cope with the issues that arise. With mindfulness, we can let go of the turmoil of the day and be present. The strength of other people's compassionate witness and their intuition helps us to face issues that are especially charged. We can unravel patterns of energy and catch flashes of insight that might otherwise be dismissed. We ascertain how to overcome our limitations and move into liberated ways of being. In a Circle, we discover patterns of energy in the stories that people "make up." When we see the same patterns emerge, it is difficult to dismiss. We build faith in inner knowing.

Bring a decision you face to Circle and everyone can take an imaginary journey, exploring the different paths you are considering. They will offer pieces of information that bring your options into clearer focus. Then when you have chosen a direction, you can work with the Active Imagination both to increase the probability of it unfolding in positive ways and to set clearly-aimed intent. Remember the evidence that people in loving relationships or cohesive groups are most effective at influencing possibilities in each other's lives.

Circles can help us to reconnect to the natural world. Taking regular imaginal journeys together through inner dimensions can bring us into a deeper rapport with what we usually see as without consciousness. Maybe a tree on the corner is having a hard time growing. In Circle, you can go in, channel positive energy and sense what might help. Alone this feels crazy; together, you will find patterns in your imaginings that reveal what will help.

Circles help us reweave community on very practical levels. For example, if your neighbors have been violent with each other, in a Circle, you can meditate, channel healing, and imagine what can be said or done to shift the situation. Now, you might decide to accompany each other to talk with them. The world is a hologram—going inside helps us to become attuned and better connected with each other.

We live longer, happier lives when we are surrounded by many loving relationships. But love does not appear on command. Working with meditation, story, and truth-telling in a Circle creates a field that invites love to develop. Re-patterning our consciousness, we connect heart-to-heart and claim the world together and live into a new dream. In a Circle, the solutions to the challenges we face become clearer, whether they are personal, social, or political. We develop the kinds of relationships needed to accompany one another through life's celebrations and struggles—going to the doctor or the school board together, or to the house down the street from which we have heard screams. We can take care of each other even when we are in despair.

One of my students from Arizona who leads a Circle called me recently to share the joy that she and members of her community had experienced. She told me how upset they were about the war and the nightly roar of military jets overhead on their practice missions. Wishing for a place to share their fears, and feeling a need to express this in a peaceful way, the community gathered together and walked silently through town to the river. There they formed a Circle to draw on the power of peace. The local news announced that the Peace Walk would be a yearly event— this was in a town where the military was the prime employer. Everyone in the group was energized and amazed at the palpable strength and love that was present. They had planted seeds for the future in sacred Circle.

As the institutions that have supported us crumble, we turn to each other for sustenance. *We are one another's security.* In Circle, we hold each other day-to-day. When crisis strikes, we can turn to one another. Circles that bring people together across lines of difference are the strongest. These are the ones that will discover the ways we can create just and sustainable communities.

The times call for a weaving of Circles. When they inter-
lock, they create a living safety net. Circles offer the most
promise for securing the future. Rather than watching "life" on
television, let us knit Circles, sit in council,[3] meditate, share
heart stories, grapple with what to do about a troubling situation, study together, or conjure up public actions on which to
act. In Circles, we are carried by and carry the Great Turning.

Morphic Organizing

We engage in the Great Turning with each act that breaks the
mold. Each individual and small group that begins to
transform their lives and each new experiment in social
relations has ripple effects that spread far beyond the
immediate situation. Earlier in this book, we saw the way
that consciousness has nonlocal impact on health and well-
being. According to Sheldrake, each holonic level from the
cell, to the group, to the whole culture has a morphic field.
The morphic fields that surround living and social systems
seem to have memory or resonance that holds things in
place. The wonderful thing is that when the right chord is
struck, the morphic fields can communicate social successes
very rapidly and shift the ways things are more quickly than
we could have imagined.

Even in adversarial situations, groups using Applied
Meditation can carve new grooves through which energy
moves. Assume there is an important and controversial
issue at a city council meeting coming up that some members of your group will be attending. In advance, you can
have an Energy Circle during which people can intuit
where the spots of flexibility lie. Patterns will emerge,
revealing a good approach—one that is likely to be exactly
that which will sway council members. Then everyone can
energize that strategy.

During the Energy Circle, imagine bands of energy moving between those group members who are going to the

meeting—picture bands of energy that move to and from each of their hearts and minds. Assume that these bands carry information, weaving a web that supports everyone. Set the intention that these bands will be present when you are at the council meeting.

This Circle will have set the stage so that when the meeting is happening, channels of communication will already be in place. Group members attending will be fully attuned to one another during the council meeting and will find that they have an uncanny way of knowing what one another will say before saying it. Running energy like this creates power.

The combination of establishing clear intention before a meeting and the psychic rapport that you have established through meditating together makes a potent combination. I think of it as moving intention up a holonic notch. Now people are acting in a Circle as a whole, and not as separate individuals. Individual contributions synergize, and the collective mind that is created is brilliant. The group becomes one coordinated body in a great, choreographed dance. Not that someone else is choreographing the dance, but that the group is so finely tuned to one other that they are unified— this phenomenon is what athletes sometimes call being in the "zone" together, or "in flow."

Research has shown that with intention we can be so connected that it is as if we are in one body. There are many studies in which people have been paired, then placed in a different room, and one assigned to send a message while the other was supposed to receive it. Often the receiver's brain showed the same EEG pattern as the sender during the exact moments that they were occurring in the sender.[4]

Those of you attending the meeting can increase your effectiveness by setting another intention: Imagine bands of energy during the meeting moving from the hearts and minds of those who sit on the city council to each of your inner consciousnesses. Then imagine that those energy bands move from your inner consciousness to your conscious mind and back to the council members—doing this will enable you to connect directly to their hearts and minds. Envision the energy continuing to cycle through this way throughout the meeting. Intend compassion and clarity to be the currents that are moving in these bands.

This will help each of you to become attuned to the truths of all sides of the issue, and then to express yourself as effectively as possible. Like the technique of running energy, it may feel like an inconsequential story you create in your imagination, but it will have miraculous results.

I always envision these bands of connection when I am speaking publicly or doing facilitation work. During my presentation, I may find new examples to illustrate my thinking that haven't occurred to me before. Oftentimes, afterward someone tells me that what I had said was exactly what had happened to them.

Recently, I was leading a colleague though a meditation to help her get ready for challenges she was facing. I suggested that she sing to the cells in her body and that her song be carried into her body by her breath. I elaborated further, suggesting that she imagine ribbons of color accompanying her song. (Inner consciousness never seems to be bothered by mixed metaphors!) I had never used this particular imagery before. After the meditation, she told me that whenever she needed to calm herself down she sang to herself and imagined ribbons of color! Clearly, I was attuned to her inner consciousness.

I once was at a conference; we were in a late-night conversation about our work. One woman, using the common metaphor from Alcoholics Anonymous, said that there was an elephant in the room. Literally the moment she said it, someone we did not know walked into the room carrying a big stuffed elephant in her arms! Occurrences like this make the work we do feel enchanted. This same gathering was fraught with power struggles over the future of the organization. Merle Wolford, a Cherokee elder who was new to the scene, was advising me. Before I had described to her what was happening, she told me that she had a vision of two male elk fighting—vying to be the head of the herd. That evening I relayed this story to a friend, and as we turned to leave we saw that a car that had just pulled into the parking lot right next to us had huge elk antlers wired onto its radiator! Soon after that, we were invited to come hear an all-woman band that evening, "The Elktones."

The inside and outside worlds constantly mirror and dance with one another. Indigenous people of all the continents understand that there is no separation between the everyday and the sacred. When one works with spirit, synchronous unfoldings become common. They remind us that we are part of a wondrous whole, telling us if we are on the right path and moving in harmony with spirit. Our rational minds dismiss these events out of hand, but our hearts find them reassuring.

The challenge is to sense the energy currents and work with them. When meditating on actions we want to take together, an energy field is created which brings us into deep resonance with one another. In this field we hear the quiet whispers of spirit—even in harrowing circumstances.

In 1999, when the WTO was coming to Seattle, there was a groundswell of local and international organizing. My friend Ruby Phillips and I wrote a meditation to empower people to stand strong in a field of shared intention. We then trained people to lead this in meetings throughout the city. The flier that introduced the meditation said:

> We are poised at an important moment; the possibility of changing history is upon us. The WTO times will be intense. The danger of provocateur-inspired violence and police/media reactions are high. How do we effectively

express our outrage at the fact that the planet and all of her critics (including humanity) are careening down a path of destruction? Much is at stake—we do not want martial law and we do not want to provide an opportunity for the media to discredit us. With shared intent, we hold strong and offer a powerful presence and message to the media, the public, and those we oppose .... Tapping into and maintaining the strength of our collective intention makes us infinitely more effective (and safer).

The meditation was simple. It invited people to remember what was at stake, why they were there, and the fact that there were thousands who stood with them. At the end of it, people created their own symbol to represent our shared intention for standing strong in peace. The evening after the first day in the streets, when we successfully kept the WTO from convening, about a thousand of us met in a warehouse that was one of the main organizing sites. People shared stories of how they held strong even when being sprayed with tear gas and pepper spray or when horses were coming toward them. It was inspiring to hear all the stories! Many used the meditation and had practiced working with their symbols. They told us it was of great help to them in the high-tension moments when they were confronted by abusive police.

Throughout the evening we kept hearing reports that tear gas wielding police were coming closer to where we were. People were exhilarated, exhausted, fearful, and awed at the amazing success of the day. And there was a lot of controversy over actions for the next day. The mayor of Seattle had announced that downtown Seattle would now be a "no protest zone," stripping people of their first amendment rights. One thousand people had to come to a consensus about how we would all act in response to the announcement—would we ignore it and risk arrest or give in to an unjust and unconstitutional rule?

In the midst of the turmoil that night, I led a meditation using a bullhorn to be heard. If that many people can meditate under circumstances such as these, we can meditate anywhere!

In the discussion following, we empowered one another to go back on the streets in the face of martial law being declared and even more police being brought in. The WTO meetings ended in failure due both to the protests on the outside and the fact that the less developed nations stood together to resist inside. Some of the delegates said that they had been given strength to stand up by seeing the protesters outside. There is an Ethiopian proverb: "When spider webs unite they can tie up the lion."

Nearly eight years later, the City of Seattle settled a class action suit brought by the protesters, and the court found that there had been Fourth Amendment violations to the arrestees. The City paid $1,000,000 and agreed to train its officers better at all levels of the police department.[5]

I envision a time when working with reflection, imagination, and mindfulness are all publicly shared activities—bringing wholeness back to our world. Together, we can fine-tune our consciousness to one another, to the issue, and to anyone else involved. The energies we tune into in the imaginary world are elusive and hard to catch, but when we engage together, we weave our dreams together, creating strong webs of intention and unified action.

Power Is Present: Overcoming Habits of History

These are extraordinary times—full of great danger and great possibility. We need extraordinary ways to address the challenges we face. Imagine that we move up a few holonic notches and work from there. We can change how we carry history and anticipate our future. On a personal level, working with Applied Meditation, one can go back into one's past and rearrange the scenes that were wounding. Doing this changes the emotional charge. It begins the process of freeing us from repeating our history. On a societal level, I believe that when we as a people begin to engage in efforts of reconciliation, we do not change the past itself, but we shift the hold it has on us. This frees us to find new ways of being.

Our power lives in present time; we hold the past and the future inside us in this same moment. In meditation, we widen our Circle in ways that stretch the imagination. We can call on our deceased grandmother or a grandchild yet to be born—the possibilities are immense. Traditional cultures communicate with their ancestors to find wise ways to approach the challenges they face, and they take future generations into account when making important decisions. The trickster, the fool, the healer or the shaman cross boundaries and shake things up so that energy can settle into different patterns. Through their mischief, truth is revealed. When working with the Active and Receptive Imaginations becomes a collectivized activity, there is no telling what genius we might create!

In Circle, we expand our sense of ourselves. As Joanna Macy said:

> Act your Age. Since every particle in your body goes back to the first flaring forth of space and time, really as old as the universe. When you are lobbying at your congressperson's office, or visiting your local utility, or testifying at a hearing on nuclear waste, or standing up to protect an old grove of redwoods, you are doing that not out of some personal whim, but in the full authority of your fifteen billion years.

> Dare to vision. Out of this darkness a new world can arise, not to be constructed by our minds so much as to emerge from our dreams. Even though we cannot see clearly how it's going to turn out, we are still called to let the future into

our imagination. We will never be able to build what we have not first cherished in our hearts.[6]

There is an image that has haunted me for a long time. Every summer there is an exclusive, invitation-only, all-male gathering in a place north of San Francisco called Bohemian Grove. Bush (father and son), Cheney, Clinton, Rockefeller, and Kissinger have been among the hundreds of bank, corporate, and government heads who gather in the Redwoods. These meetings have been taking place for over a hundred years. It is said that the Manhattan Project, which brought the world the atomic bomb, was conceived there.[7]

Each year they hold a ritual called "The Cremation of Care," during which the participants burn care in effigy. What is the effect of this on the morphic field? Does this fortify callousness? What possibilities are there to rearrange the energy—to breathe space into it and to make compassion be what rises up rather than care going up in smoke?

What if we could change the fields of energy that dictate our cultural habits and dreams? This is all intangible, but that is the nature of working with spirit—it is profound and ineffable. If we take into account that traumatic events enter at the theta level of consciousness and grip memory, then the task of changing our culture is formidable—some may say unrealistic. If we are to be "realistic," we have already lost.

In World War II Berlin, families of mixed heritage—Jewish men and Gentile women—were allowed to stay together during the early part of the war. Then the Nazi bureaucracy decided to round up the men for deportation to concentration camps. Seven thousand were captured one night and brought to a central prison. Spontaneously, the next day, a thousand women gathered on street of Rosenstrasse at the police station and started chanting, "We want our men back! We want our men back!" They would not stop for three days. The Nazi police and Gestapo could not make them stop even at gunpoint. Eventually, the commanders realized they had to let the men go—all of them, or else a revolution might start that would sweep Germany.[8]

We often do not know the impact of our daily work for change. Sometimes changes seem to spring out of nowhere, the years of suffering, endurance, and hard work below the surface. Then suddenly, waves of change crest and echo across national boundaries and shift the ways of the world. In Poland, while there had been labor struggles for good working conditions and fairness during the early 1970s, they had been crushed. In 1979, there sprang up a small organization of twenty people—*Solidasnosk*, or Solidarity. It had the unique idea of democracy by workers, neither socialist nor anti-socialist. Within a few short weeks, its number swelled from twenty to twenty thousand, and by the next year it had grown to nine million. This movement became a foundation of change that eventually swept through the whole of Eastern Europe and the Soviet Union.

None of the actors in the above stories were concerned with being realistic. Perhaps we need to go beyond the "realistic" to loosen up the existing order. The challenge on a grand scale is how to go about changing the way we respond to the habits of history. Sheldrake tells us, cultural morphic fields are inherently conservative.[9] I think of these habits as well-worn ruts in the road. With mindfulness we do not need to fall into the same old ruts. The question is, how do we recognize them—and further, how do we create a vision of what we want instead? Remember, without a vision the problem itself dictates our behavior by default.

Fish do not see the water they swim in. Looking inside at our own consciousness by itself will not show us the particular cultural habits that need to be transformed. One of the participants in an early workshop of mine was a well-meaning bank executive. We did a meditation where everyone created an inner sanctuary and invited spirit guides to join them. Afterward, the executive described his guides as a man who took care of the grounds and a woman who took care of his sanctuary. His perception of his guides in subservient roles was normal to him. Psychic perception is not mediated through eyes, ears, or touch, but through the thought forms already residing in the mind. This is the clothing the energy uses to make itself visible.

Memories provide the vocabulary of one's imagination. As I said about working with the Active Imagination, if you have no flour in the pantry, it places severe limitations on the bread you bake. This is equally true for receiving insight with the Receptive Imagination. I have yet to meet a man who discovered sexism by looking within.

Each one of us tends to take our own beliefs for granted. Groups, organizations, communities, and nations all have sets of unexamined assumptions that hold injustice in place. We each bring different memories and different perspectives to the mix. So if we want to carve new cultural grooves we have to work and play with diverse groups of people. We need Circles to include both the CEO and the young mom who works at McDonald's. When we tell our stories, combine our experiences, and meditate together, we can weave new fields.

This is not easy; we need to come together in ways mindful that we each bring different histories. While we may share basic common needs, we may have different visions of how to meet those needs. When we approach Circles in openness our unexamined assumptions become apparent.

This can only work if we protect the integrity of the Circle. In a Circle, *everyone* contributes. Most of us have little experience of this kind of reciprocal relationship. People in positions of power are usually the least informed about issues of oppression. CEOs are used to being listened to, not listening. Their experience is that people treat them as though their words are the most important. The worker at

McDonald's has the opposite experience; she is used to being told to listen. Her experience tells her that to speak up is to risk getting in trouble. These habits are deeply ingrained, and we tend to duplicate them. The dynamic of who dominates time is not an issue of personality but social power. We need to set up ways of being together in a Circle that consciously shift the cultural currents and draw out each of our contributions.

The challenge is: how do we create ways of being in Circle that enable us to be whole and share our experience fully without provoking guilt, shame, or blame, and without feelings of anger, arrogance, and inferiority? This is a tall order, but I know that it can be done.

Weaving Trust: Leveling the Playing Field

Most of us have some aspect of who we are that has been looked down upon by mainstream culture. It may be our sexual orientation, religious affiliation, race, gender, class, disability, or other aspects. If we bring this part of our experience forward, we risk being trivialized, pathologized, and locked out. Surviving contemporary norms usually means assimilating, that is leaving behind important parts of ourselves.[10]

In order to reclaim our humanity, many of us have come together over the last few decades in groups, caucuses, and conferences of shared identity. We came together to share our stories and hear how others have been there too. In this work, we came to trust our own experience. In these separate spaces, we did not need to leave a part of who we are at the door. We got to be whole without having to explain ourselves. Many came to understand that these same aspects of themselves that have marked difference from the mainstream are, in actuality, gifts that enlarge humanity and illuminate ways society might come together in wholeness.

Now, the challenge is to call upon these gifts to create a new cultural force where we can be authentic, weaving different perspectives doing things in different ways. Fully out as human beings, we can be effective while having fun, share our anger and despair, knowing we are not alone. Calling on the wisdom of the ancestors, we are open to the vision of those who are younger. We are responsible to each, while holding each other with compassion. We are clear about our values, while embracing other perspectives.

We need to resist the pressure to regress into hiding parts of ourselves, to resist the all-too-familiar habits of "passing." When we make our particular differences invisible, it only puts the dominant norms back in control. *We are called to step up because it is the very aspects of our experience that we have had to leave behind that are the ones that will get all of us through.*

Bill's and my organization, Tools for Change, has been doing alliance building trainings for many years. Repeatedly, certain dynamics show up that obstruct the creation of truly multicultural contexts. The more assimilated we are, the more we tend to think of difference as the problem, as though difference is what is causing a fracture. When someone raises an experience that they had as a member of their social group, it is often met with: "We are all human, let's not focus on our differences." This makes people have to split themselves in order to be accepted into the fold. They have to cut off a key aspect of their experience if they want to get along. Social inequities crisscross through all of our relations; by acknowledging them without assigning guilt or blame, we invite our different stories into the room.

Privilege means being given more options by birth or social status. Imagine that you are swimming downstream. You feel that swimming is easy and you are a good swimmer. When you come across someone swimming upstream; they are having a difficult time making any headway. You might give them tips about how they could improve their stroke to make swimming easier. You are unaware that there are currents easing your efforts and unaware that these same currents cause problems for your fellow swimmer. You do not understand why they were not happy to receive your good advice. *Privilege is usually invisible to those who have it, and oppression is pervasive for those who do not.* As a result, those with privilege, however well intentioned, operate out of stereotypes and assumptions that further entrench inequity. At the same time, those who are oppressed can assume that the others are operating out of premeditated power plays, "It's obvious, how could they not know?"

Another result of privilege is that the more you have it, the more you are in the habit of seeing yourself as an individual devoid of social context; consequently you take everything personally. What often happens is that if one in a position of oppression points out the misinformation of a stereotype, they are usually met with a defense of good intentions. Since image is paramount in mainstream competitive culture, people often take feedback as a personal affront.

When defensiveness takes center stage, we never actually get to look at the impact of the attitudes and behaviors on the situation and the wider society. Motive becomes the topic of conversation, and consequences never enter the discussion. This, in turn, makes it likely that the person who raised the issue will feel frustrated and may get angry. A rupture occurs, and learning never takes place. We fail to make trust or justice. It is no wonder that many of us prefer to be in homogeneous settings.

Circling

Some of my most profound times have been sitting with people in Circles for Change, which Bill, myself, and other collaborators have held in cities across the U.S. The first circle we held in Seattle was as diverse as fifteen people could be in race/culture, age, gender, sexual identity, class, and ability. The diversity made for a curiosity in the room that was palpable— deep listening was our norm. Our horizons were stretched time and again.

We took great joy in discovering one another. Every week we shared commitment of time together, establishing sacred space, meditation, positive orientation, food, and exercises that opened the imagination. We had an altar with flowers, pictures of our ancestors, and other sacred objects. We marked our opening and closing with the lighting and blowing out of a candle. Doing this small ritual sets boundaries, invites reverence, and begins to build a positive energy field. Reverence makes space for mindfulness and gratitude.

Another vital aspect was bringing all voices into the room. After our opening, and frequently at other times, we would speak in round format. This sets a pattern that makes it easier for everyone to contribute fully. We were able to relax and just be with one another in our fullness. We knew that everyone mattered, and that if anything came up that was troubling, we would work through it. We would not leave anyone behind or banter accusations or defenses back and forth—we knew we would speak from the heart.

These were times of truth telling. We all had a glimpse into one another's souls—it was truly a sacred space we created together. It is in contexts like this one that we can unravel the cultural habits that bind us, can weave visions that inspire everyone—visions that have not left out whole communities of life on this planet.

We wove our voices together and built a strong field. The experience confirmed to me again how crucial diversity is. The relationships that we built over the months of our formal meetings have endured. We continue to share in each others' lives and help each other as we can.

Because there was an overt acknowledgement of issues of oppression, it went without saying that if they arose, we would talk about them. We developed trust quickly. It helped that there was not an atmosphere of "who is right and who is wrong." We were not looking for problems, but felt secure that if any came up we would sort out what was happening. In many groups, people either avoid the issues or will not let them go.

When we are in a Circle, we each need to be mindful and notice when we are withdrawing—that is if we are feeling or thinking something but not sharing it. We fracture the field when there is something we are holding back. We have learned our survival lessons well; sometimes we have to continue to remain silent. But if we have to censor ourselves when in a Circle, the Circle becomes weaker. If you find yourself thinking or feeling something that you are unable to share, ask yourself what understanding you would need everyone to have if you were to feel safe enough to share this part of your experience. Doing so will illuminate what will pave the way for you to express your full experience. To maintain well-being of the Circle, it is a good idea to regularly meditate on both what you might have held back, as well as appreciating the great moments you have experienced together. Share this with each other and you will further strengthen your Circle.

When there is tension in the room, like breathing through pain, lean in, breathe together, meditate together, and tell your truths. Mistakes are inevitable; what is important is to learn from them. Together, we can reflect on what is taking place between people, thinking relationally, not in terms of personality. When we separate impact from motive, we can discover what will bring healing and empowerment for all concerned. With generosity of spirit and a shared commitment to each other, we can sort it out. Practicing in this way enables us to become adept at recognizing the ruts in the road before we fall into them.

I believe that we need to pay at least as much, if not more, attention to the questions we ask as to the conclusions to which we come. The times call for good questions, not quick fixes. In our country, we have been conditioned not to speak up or question unless we already know the answer. The prevailing cultural currents keep us in patterns of looking for right and wrong, having the correct answers, and never sharing our dilemmas or vulnerabilities. When we fall prey to these patterns, we get stuck in ruts. Starting a conversation with a conclusion only takes us where we have been before. But questions take us to uncharted territory. They invite us to listen to what is emergent and what is in the field at this very moment. Questions carry us into new experience. They awaken curiosity and wonder, and they move us into greater states of openness.

People who meditate frequently are able to shift in and out of meditative states with ease. As a group starts to work together in this way, it will be able to call on intuition in thirty seconds. Cultivating an ease in moving in and out of deeper consciousness will greatly widen the parameters of discussion. When we enter into conversation through the door of calm connectedness, through an appreciation of the web of which we are part, then the quality of exchange illuminates our connections. The space between us lights up with insight and collaborative creativity. We can build on one another's ideas rather than getting caught in the trap of convincing and debating each other. When we have differing views, there is an understanding that multiple perspectives coexist, and it is not about deciding which one is best. We weave together our perspectives and something different for everyone emerges.

Circle work is about making reflection a collective activity. Look at history; look at who controls resources and who might be allies. Look at issues of consequence, envision the future, and listen to spirit. Use the questions embedded in the meditations at the end of this chapter as an invitation into inquiry.

We each have a particular piece of the puzzle. When we bring in our own ancestors and visions, we have the ingredients for strong web weaving. No matter how homogeneous your Circle appears, find the ways that you are diverse—this is what broadens your views. Circles are about opening up and bringing out the nuances of difference. Difference is about discovering the multiple ways of experiencing the world. It is difference that fortifies the web of community.

By doing projects together, you come to know one another in deeper ways. Empower your Circle and offer needed service in the world. Circles change the dream; they are training grounds to change the way we do things in the public sphere.

Respiriting Public Life

In Tools for Change, we believe it is essential to reclaim public life—make it whole. Make it accountable to our ancestors and to future generations and fill it with the stories of our lives—stories that are not individual but are part of the great patterns of history. We are not separate; our histories and our fates are entwined. Untangling our frightful past builds trust and enables us to look power squarely in the eye so we can build a world that honors us all. Securing the future is not a question of who wins.

When we trust each other, we move from feeling that we are up against one another, into knowing that we are all in it together. (What deck your quarters were on made no difference on the Titanic.) *Only in trust can we move up a holonic level and work with greater power.* The challenge is to find ways to be together that foster a spirit of affirmation and welcome—ones that celebrate life, that are authentic, ones in which people listen to one another deeply.

It is vital that we make reflection a publicly shared activity in all our endeavors. Rational consciousness promotes competitive approaches, whereas spirit creates a field of connectivity. For gatherings of any kind, a meeting, a hearing, or whatever it is, begin and end with spirit. It does not take long. Ask people to breathe together and remember what is sacred to them. Invite them to bring to awareness their shared intention. Any group can take a minute to do this, no matter how rushed or diverse. This deepens the shared resonance. Now, take it further—invite people to imagine their heart and mind connections forming a web that moves from person to person, creating a vibrant fabric that supports their shared work. You can invite people to create a symbol for that intention that will inspire them throughout.

After this avoid the usual round of introductions where people share their name and what they do for work. Instead, ask them to name their grandmother and tell a story about her, or ask for the name of a child for whom they want the world to be safe. This opens the context for story, heart, and the weaving of the powers of our pasts and futures.

Soon after the tragic events of 9/11, Vicki Robin called some friends together to help organize what she was calling Conversation Cafés.[11] She felt that it was essential to create ways of having meaningful conversations in public places. In thinking about how to make them inclusive and heartfelt, I suggested that we use a simple circular format. We start with a circle in which everyone speaks, asking people to wait before they respond to one another. This makes room for everyone to share what is on their mind and does not leave control of the topic to the first person who speaks. Follow this with another round in which people are invited to respond to each other. This simple process works to allow everyone's voice to come forth. Conversation Cafés have sprung up all over this country and in many others. People are hungry to meet and have meaningful conversation about the issues we all face. Meeting in a Circle and listening with our hearts, we discover one another and find fresh approaches.

To help shed light on seemingly intractable tensions in the Middle East, Tools for Change and Richmond Fisher, a Seattle-based attorney, organized a public day of reflection and dialogue. We wanted to have conversations that would be as intimate as what happens in our kitchens, so the facilitators brought their own small tables, complete with tablecloths and flowers. We supplied water, bread, candles, and stones to serve as talking pieces to pass around the circles. Lastly we provided some gummy bears for levity.

Conversation about the Middle East is one of the most difficult topics, usually turning polarized and vitriolic within a short time. This day, people were able to hear each other's confusion, fear, rage, and hopelessness without getting hooked or entrenched in their own positions. It was for many a transformative moment as they started to be able to think differently about the possibilities for peace. The work of building relationships based in trust is the precursor to any successful political dialog and, in a larger sense, transformation.

We need to make new ways of coming together, ways that do not silence us, that honor everyone's humanity. When we set a different stage, we do not get the same old show.

> If individuals and organizations operate from a generative orientation, from possibility rather than resignation, we can create the future into which we are living, as opposed to merely reacting to it when we get there .... Create an openness to listen to that implicate order.[12]

Without vision we recreate the world as it is, we perpetuate the status quo, living in the dream of individualism, materialism and alienation. Vincent Harding, African-American theologian, tells us:

Above all, where there is no vision, we lose the sense of our great power to transcend history and create a new future for ourselves with others ... Therefore, the quest is not a luxury; life itself demands it of us![13]

We can change the dream by awakening to our interconnections and stepping up to these times. Oren Lyons, Faithkeeper of the Turtle Clan, Onondaga Nation, Haudenosaunee, Iroquois Confederacy, spoke to the United Nations in 1992:

It seems to me that we are living in a time of prophecy, a time of definitions and decisions. We are the generation with the responsibilities and the option to choose the Path of Life for the future of our children, or, the life and path which defies the Laws of Regeneration. Even though you and I are in different boats, you in your boat and we in our canoe, we share the same River of Life—what befalls me, befalls you. And downstream—in this River of Life, our children will pay for our selfishness, for our greed, and for our lack of vision. Given this opportunity, we can raise ourselves. We must join hands with the rest of Creation.[14]

A Vision

I share this vision not because I expect it to be yours, but because vision ignites the imagination. You may want to read the next section slowly, giving yourself time to imagine what I am suggesting. Take a breath between sentences. Notice what visions arise for you and give them life. There is nothing that has ever been created that was not first imagined.

If we can imagine it, we can create it. What if trust were to society what oil is to machinery? Imagine a world that runs on trust. Imagine a world where we have learned how to be honest with ourselves and with each other—where the only safe way of being is to be honest. Imagine a world where intuition, spirituality, and emotions are all as valued as the intellect. Imagine a place where our stories weave wonder into the world and where care becomes the currency of exchange.

Imagine a society that lives in harmony with the cycles of nature, where human life is sustained on renewable energy as is nature itself, where the earth is cherished, and whatever is taken out is returned. Imagine knowing that there would always be a place for you and your family and a place for everyone's family. Imagine being able to assume that there will always be a place for your descendants, for all descendants, for humanity—a place on earth. Imagine how it feels to always belong in a diversified community, for it is the diversity in nature that gives the web of life its strength. Imagine a time when everyone cherishes diversity in people, knowing diversity gives community cohesion. Imagine being able to relax into our connectedness—into a web of mutually supportive relations with each other and with nature.

Imagine a world where what is valued most is not power but nurturance, where the aim is to care and be cared for, where the expression of love is commonplace. The dawn of each day is a blessing, reverence is in the air. We live as though life itself is an act of worship. Imagine a time when generosity is assumed. Creativity and laughter is everywhere.

Imagine a world where it is understood that enough is good and that more than enough is not, where there is a deep understanding of the difference between wants and needs. Imagine a world where greed, opportunism, coercion, and manipulation are all social crimes. Imagine a world where there is collective support in the overcoming of individual limitations, where mistakes are not hidden but welcomed as opportunities to learn. Imagine a place where there is no reason to withhold information, where honesty is a given.

Imagine a world where power without accountability was history. Imagine a world where bureaucracy, like the dinosaur, is extinct. Imagine a world on a human scale where work has regained its dignity and you are part of the decisions that make a difference. Imagine a time when curiosity, inquiry, and vulnerability are held sacred. Imagine a society that reveres patience rather than efficiency. Within patience there is respect, a deep trust—a knowledge that in its own time the rosebud will bloom.

Imagine everyone taking pleasure in making their communities beautiful. Imagine the whole of humanity honoring the same sense of responsibility for maintaining the earth. Imagine a world where trust and honesty—not power and deception—are the oil that make society thrive. If we can imagine it, we can create it.

People make history. We can choose respect, trust, and mutual aid. We can choose life. We can choose to heal the earth. We can choose to heal humanity. We can breathe life into this vision.

In relationship, spirit comes alive. May vision weaving be what we all do with our families, friends, and communities. May we bring vision into the center of public life, discovering what we are *for*.

The Earth and all who live upon her are sacred. Vision and conviction are the fuel and fiber of action. Together we heal present time. May we all live into the changes we want to make. As we embody our visions in the present moment, it makes them manifest. Together we heal future time. Together we heal.

MEDITATIONS

Induction

Many of the meditations in this chapter are very long. Feel free to use only parts of them at a time. They are also rich with questions conducive to collective inquiry.

Focusing on your breathing, breathing calmly, deeply ... Bring to awareness your physical relaxation symbol ... Let your body relax into the earth. Ground yourself ... Release any energies you no longer need, as your energy replenishes the earth, the earth replenishes you ... Imagine that the earth breathes ... Imagine breathing with the earth ... Relax into the trust of life's breath ... ...

Bring to awareness your symbol for mental relaxation ... Breathe in the sky. Feel the expansiveness of the sky relax your mind ... Let the sky open your mind. Sense that your mind is as vast as the sky. In the quiet of your mind you are fully receptive and creative ... Feel yourself as spacious inside as the skies ... Awareness is vast ... ...

Bring to awareness your symbol for emotional relaxation. Breathe out any "shoulds." Let them drop into the ground by their sheer weight ... Feel your heart breathe a sigh of relief ... Let go of all the "shoulds" ... Offer yourself some loving kindness ... Feel as though your heart relaxes into its natural state of loving compassion ... of connectedness ... Feel yourself relax into the web of life which holds us all ... held by life in each breathe you take ... ...

Bring to awareness your symbol for your creative self-restoring center ... Here vision is born; here creativity is born ... Here we listen to the whispers of spirit ... Here we can acknowledge our reverence for life itself ... Out of this receptive knowingness we gain the courage to work for a life-affirming world.

Feel the universal life force energy that flows through everything, flowing through you with each breath you take ... Life breathes ... Feel yourself part of the natural world ... Let yourself be strengthened by an appreciation of interdependence ... Acknowledge your gratitude to be part of the wondrous universe ... Interbeing ... ...

Feel kinship with people ... Imagine specific people whom you may not know but you may see them in the routine of your week, people you may imagine have a very different life than your own ... Imagine these people ... Feel kinship in your shared humanity ... As you breathe out, send them some loving kindness ... ...

Let yourself breathe in the power of the goodness of people, of humanity, of life ... As you open to the world inside, the world outside opens ... as naturally as breathing in and out ... Follow your breath out through the trees, and back into creatures ... and back to the plants again ... Breath weaves life ... Interbeing. We are woven together in life ...

If you like, you can send ribbons of good energy to those in your family and community ... to anyone or any being to whom you would like to offer some loving energy ... However you imagine this, you can breathe power into the webs of energy that form community ... ...

Finishing what you are doing ...

I am going to suggest several affirmations. If you wish to affirm them to yourself, repeat them to yourself after me; feeling their power, evoking their power, attuning yourself to their power ... Aligning your energies to the words as you repeat them to yourself ...

I believe in life ...

I honor the sanctity of the natural world upon which life depends ...

I experience myself as part of the whole of life, supported and doing my part to keep the web of life strong ...

I live in the spirit of interbeing ...

I am glad to honor the earth with good care ...

I open to truth ...

My personal power is born out of collective life ...

We gain strength from our connection to the peoples of the world ...

I am curious and always glad to discover different perspectives ...

Only what is good for everyone is good for me ...

I take only my fair share ...

I am trustworthy ...

I speak and listen from the heart ...

I honor the dignity of all people ...

I am enriched by cultural diversity ...

I observe the impact of all actions on our collective well-being and contribute to re-balancing where needed ...

I have integrity. I am honest with myself and others, I am true to principle ...

I am visionary and courageous ...

I always put my convictions into practice ...

I strive to create a fair, just, and sustainable world in all that I do and say ...

As naturally as breathing in and out, I both offer support and receive it ...

I am resilient; I maintain balance amidst change ...

I learn from the past, I welcome the future ...

I trust the future and work to bring about a future in which all life thrives ...

Take a moment and breathe in gratitude as you inhale ... and breathe out compassion as you exhale ... Gratitude to be alive; compassion for all life ... all life on the planet ... ...

Know that in focusing on affirmations, you evoke patterns of energy that manifest both within and around you ... You align your energies with them and you will discover yourself acting out of them.

If you like, you can invite any spirits from the past or future, nature beings, or friends who you would like to join you in this meditation; do this now ... Invite them to join you in your inner work ... ... Sense their presence ... Welcome them ...

Circling Together through Time and Space

An induction is not necessary for this, though use it if you like. Use your induction symbols on your own and if you have a symbol for collectivity use that as well. Work with only those paragraphs that are relevant. Leave long silences, especially at the end. Help people stay focused by repeating lines. If there are common areas of inquiry or intention-setting, have everyone imagine the context, then name the specific questions and intentions. Leave ample room between each of your remarks. Refrain from any explanations or asking "why" questions. (The questions should awaken the imagination not beta mind.) Circle members can also chime in and raise a question or intention. Punctuate remarks with long silences to give people the time they need to work with the energies. Feel free to insert relevant passages from other meditations to augment your collective reflection.

After the meditation, go around the Circle and have members share what they experienced. Hold off responding to one another until everyone who wants to has taken a turn. After the round, you may elect to go right back into meditation to reflect on how the different insights and visions weave together. Keep going in and out of meditation and sharing in round format to deepen your collective reflection, insight, and intention as long as you like.

Focus on your breath ... Feel breath roll in and out of your body ... Breathing ... As you inhale, bring to awareness your intention to be here ... Breath carries life. Breath weaves life. Let your breath bring you into this moment ... Here ... As you exhale, let go of distractions ... Extend your awareness to include all of us here ... Breathing ... We share this moment ... Feel us all breathing together ... Imagine as though when we exhale an energy field begins to come alive and hold us all ... Breathe life into our collectivity ... Tune to our hearts, they are beating inside each of us ... ...

Feel the presence we create as we share this moment ... Sense that our breath and heartbeats move into resonance with each other's ... As though there is a field of energy that holds us up ... or for you, it may feel like a web ... Energy that embraces us all ... it is of us, it is more than us ... Feel our Circle Spirit breathing alive here, now ... Sense the quality of energy present ... Feel resonance ... sense the tone ... Witness the energy take shape ... ...

We each bring our past here ... Imagine that we braid our pasts together to make for a strong circle ... a strong web ... Each with our particular histories ... each with our particular ancestors ... Sense the mix that makes for the whole ... Imagine that we invite the spirits of the past who we would like to join our Circle ... Imagine that we invite them to be with us now ... Welcome them ... Offer them your imagination to make their presence known ... What story do they bring? Imagine ... What sensibilities do they offer? Imagine ... Commune with them, converse with them ... Feel our Circle strengthened by their presence ... ...

All of the past is carried in our Circle, awesome ... The molecules that form the substance of our bodies have existed since the very beginning of time ... Imagine that as we breathe, as we inhale, we draw on the strengths from all time from time way, way back ... Time empowers us here, now. Feel it in our bones ... As we breathe, we draw on the great powers that have witnessed all of history ... here in the room; in the quiet here ... Wisdom ... Endurance ... Deep ... Awesome ... ...

If you like, you can extend your awareness to stretch out into a possible future ... Those who live in future time know this moment as history. They can tell you about it ... They know the unfoldings ... If you like, you can invite a spirit from a future time to join us in our Circle ... If you have invited a spirit, or maybe a few, to join us, welcome them now ... Know that spirit speaks through imagination ... What story has it brought? ... ...

There may be spirits in nature or other dimensions who would be happy to join us, who have gifts to offer us ... Listen. Open your imagination and listen deeply ... Notice the inclinations of your consciousness ... Listen ... Imagine ... Trust your knowing ... ...

Take time to commune with spirits, together spirits weave strong fields of energy. Fields that hold us all up ... fields that reveal the emergent realities that carry us into ever greater states of peace, and well-being ... ...

These energies enable us to open and listen to the whispers of spirit, of our collective spirit ... brilliant ... In the quiet, feel spirit ... However you experience this ...

Notice if anything is whispering? Listen ... Occasionally it shouts ... Listen ... Is there something that you need to be fully present in the Circle?

Note what the Circle is needing as we breathe with spirit together ... Is there anything that would help our Circle bloom into greater being? ... Trust your experience.

Tune to each person in the Circle ... Share presence with them ... Offer them loving kindness, as though you could breathe it out from your heart and offer it ... You may want to imagine ribbons of color carrying wonderful energy from your heart ... ...

The room fills with heart-weaving as we all breathe loving kindness ... ...

If there is a particular situation coming up to which you would like to send energy and aim clear intention, do this now ... ...

As you do, listen deeply, the situation may speak to you ... or the people ... or spirits in the situation may speak to you ... Listen ... Commune with them; converse with them ... ...

Feel energy weaving, webbing, building strong fields of intention, fields that welcome us when we get there.

Maybe you want to weave strands of love and insight between your hearts and minds ... Imagine it. Imagine it in detail ... ...

Set the intention that the energy continues moving between you, especially when it is needed ... You might want to invite any spirits to help hold the intention by lending their presence ... ...

Notice what the Circle wants to do or say ...

Notice if there is anything that you would like to say or ask of the Circle ... ...

Notice what offering can be made to honor the Circle ...

Imagine what offering might be made to honor the spirits ...

Imagine how you might carry out what you have discovered in the meditation ... What you want to express in Circle ...

Thank the spirits ... Thank the Circle ...

Hope Ripplings

Though you can use this on your own, this meditation is especially designed for groups. Use it in combination with the Circling Together through Time and Space. After working with it, do a round of sharing, then meditate again and imagine how everyone's hopeful moments empower everyone else's. Weave your hopes together into great visions that lift everyone into greater power for making change.

In the end, you may want to read parts of "A Vision" on 313 in the text. Feel free to embellish on it.

Take a moment, and scan through your experience. Notice what has given you hope ... What has inspired you in your past ... or touched your heart? ... It could be small things—a fresh breeze, a child learning, someone offering kindness, birds singing ... It could be great acts of courage ... Could be visionary or simple ... Scan your experience and notice signs of hope ... ... Small or large, profound or tiny, no matter, find the moments that touched you ... ...

Choose one and recreate the scene ... Remember the details ... Let the scene touch your heart all over again ... Make your heart sing ... breathe ... open. Feel it make you smile all over again ... Sense the quality of energy informing the scene ... As though there is an aura surrounding it ... It may transform into color, music, sense the good qualities in the air ... Now, however you imagine it, breathe this quality in ... Feel it inside you ... as you breathe, it gives you an energy boost ... and you breathe life into the energy too ... Now, imagine that as you exhale, this good energy moves out and everyone that it touches is inspired by it too ... It is infectious ...

What would happen in the streets? ... Follow the breeze—see what it transforms as it travels over the land, through town and city ... Imagine it ripples out and touches hearts and minds everywhere ... Zero in on a few different spots and see the transformation take place ... What happens? ... ...

Everywhere it touches, people breathe more life into it ... and it gains momentum ... It is also boosted by the ripples others have started ... they join ... Great acts happen ... Ripples become waves ... We are all lifted ... Waves of hope, of healing, life-affirming ...

These waves turn the tide ... Imagine what shifts take place. Zero in on a particular scene, maybe at school, or in the street, or at work ... or another place, notice how change takes place ... How do people relate to each other differently? ... Pretend this is the case ... The whole field glows ...

Creating Shared Intent for Perilous Times

When a boat is in dangerous waters, one centered person with strong intention can prevent it from capsizing.
—Thich Nhat Hanh

This meditation prepares people to be able to remain centered and unified in the midst of chaotic and potentially violent circumstances. Drawing on peoples' own sense of the sacred, the meditation weaves their spirits into a web of power so they can hold strong and offer a powerful presence, increasing both their effectiveness and safety. By using symbols, it empowers people to access their previous meditation experience in the midst of stressful circumstances. If people practice this meditation as a group a few times, and participants also occasionally take a moment in the midst of their daily activity to focus on their symbols, it increases the likelihood that they will spontaneously call upon their symbols when confronted with danger.

This meditation is also very useful for opening a meeting or a controversial discussion because it amplifies group cohesion. The first and last few paragraphs make a shortened version that can be completed in less than five minutes—or in less than one minute once people have created symbols. No induction, ending, or count out is needed with this meditation.

Bring your awareness to your body. Notice your body breathing ... Feel breath rolling through your body ... Feel the rise and fall of your breath ... Relaxed and full ...

Breath carries life. All that is alive breathes. Appreciate the simple miracle of breath ... Breath renews life ... As you breathe, feel your breath renew you now ... every cell of your body bathed by breath.

Feel your feet ... Feel the Earth ... Feel yourself supported by the Earth. Feel the stability of the Earth ...

(Optional) Grow roots down into the ground ... Draw strength from the Earth.

What you breathe out, the plants breathe in ... Breath weaves life together. Breath carries life ... Imagine as though the Earth itself is breathing with you ... As though the Earth and sky breathe, as though all that is, is alive ...

Remember the sacred ... ...

Life is sacred ... Remember the beauty and uniqueness of human beings living in different places on the Earth ... All people on the Earth are sacred ... Remember the life of the forests ... Remember the life of the seas ... Feel the power of the forests ... the animals ... the seas ... and deep in the Earth ... life everywhere ... ...

Now notice that all of us here are breathing ... Remember that we are all here to take a stand for life, for all living beings on the Earth. We are here together; together we are powerful ... Breathe the power of life ... Imagine that our breathing finds harmonic rhythms ... Notice how the quality of energy here is changing as we focus on our common purpose ... Bathe in this energy ...

Breathing our unity, breathing our common purpose ... breathing the power of our shared intention ... breathing with the Earth, breathing with each other, breathing the sacred ...

Imagine that we weave bands of energy between us ... Weaving our power together ... attuned to one another ... All supported in the web ... weaving webs of life ...

Now create a symbol or a gesture that represents this energy—whatever feels right to you. (Or bring to mind your symbol/gesture, if you already have one.) ... Know that when you call it to mind, you invoke our shared intent. Know that every time you invoke it, its power increases. Tell yourself this now ... ...

As you breathe out, send this power to where it is needed ... to work well with one another, to stand with all life ... Imagine bathing the situation with this energy ... ...

Tell yourself you will remember to call upon this energy. Tell yourself this now ... Expect it to be true. Envision the success of our shared intent ... Expect it to be true ... ...

(Optional) Imagine a chaotic situation ... Project yourself into it ... Call up your symbol. Evoke our shared intention ... Feel your feet; feel the Earth ... Breathe ... Breath creates space ... Draw upon the energy around you and imagine channeling it into our shared intention ... Feel everyone stand their ground ... You might want to imagine roots stretching deep into the Earth, breathing with the Earth, drawing strength from the Earth ... weathering the storm.

(Optional) Take some time to focus on the issues that we will be addressing in this meeting, and imagine that we remain focused and come up with our best collaborative thinking. (Name the issues, pausing between each.)

Begin to move your attention to an outer focus ... Bring the power of this shared intention with you ... Slowly, coming back to an outer focus of attention ...

When you are ready, open your eyes ...

Tree Wisdom: Patience, Endurance, Courage

This meditation can easily be adapted to taking an imaginal journey through an actual tree. If you would like to use it this way, skip the first two paragraphs and begin with the one that starts "Imagine the tree ... " When you greet it, imagine it as a being with intelligence and share your intention to take an imaginal journey through it. Ask it if this is okay and trust your inclinations; then if it feels right, continue on through the script. Provide long pauses in which to converse with the tree. (Use all of the text through "Appreciate the tree for the gifts it offers.") At the end send it some positive energy and bid it good-bye.

Imagine a tranquil, serene place ... a deeply peaceful place ... Peaceful energy that seems to be primordial ... Serenity that transcends space and time as though tranquility were in this place always ... ... Peaceful energy, that's all around you, breathe it in ... Peace ... tranquility ... Breathe it into your whole being ... ...

Somewhere nearby, there is a special tree, a tree that is very old ...

Imagine the tree ... Greet it. Let yourself be in front of this tree, see it different sides, imagine the bark, imagine the branches stretching up into the sky, the roots stretching down into the ground ... the smells ... This tree fully occupies its place, as though it's merged with this place ... It offers life to this place, this place supports its life ... As though the tree merges with this place ... Commune with the tree ... Imagine talking with it if you like ... ...

As you inhale imagine drawing in the sensations of this tree ... almost as though you merge with the tree, as the tree merges with the landscape ... Be in communion with the tree, however you experience this ... as though your body were the tree and you had roots that stretch deep into the earth and branches that reach up into the sky ... Breezes blow through and your roots hold the soil, enabling you to stand ... to
stand firm, with the wind and all the weather, through all the seasons ... Your roots bring up rich nutrients and water from the earth feeding your body as you stretch towards the sky ... Bask in the sun ... cleansed by the rain ... Life goes on around you. There are the birds, four-legged creatures, and people too. Sense the life of the tree here ... ...

This tree has its own way of living in time. Sense how this tree occupies time ... ... Sense the movement of day into night ... Sense the flow of the seasons ... ...

Imagine yourself being this tree, enduring through time ... enduring through storms, discover the world as this tree knows it ... Basking in the calmness in which this tree lives, growing out of the calm quietness ... ... As you commune with the tree if you like you can converse with it. The imaginal world gifts you with the experience of the tree.

Appreciate the tree for the gifts it offers ...

Imagine this great tree has taught you a different way of being in your life ... Imagine the sense of rootedness; rooted in your life ... ... Feel the tree reaching into the sky; feel yourself do this in your life ... ... Feel calm emanating from the whole of your being ... ... Sense the endurance that resides in you ... ... Feel patience, completely present in present time ... Patience ... primordial patience that enables you to blend with the currents of the moment ... Feel yourself taking your life moment by moment, a step at a time, grounded and open. Standing firm, yet reaching to the sky ... Embrace these qualities in your life ... ...

Patience gives you a well of strength. While you live in the present, the peaceful present, the present moment has expanded, making room for all that is so ... You can hear the whispers of the universe ... ... You merge with your life as the tree merges with the landscape ... Being patient, being peaceful, you can focus your awareness wherever you choose, discovering wisdom in the present moment ...

Just as the tree endures thousands of storms, know that you have all the endurance you need as you move through life. You stand strong in the storms that may come your way. Imagine this ... ...

As you breathe, experience that patience brings endurance ... ... and endurance brings courage ... Courage enables you to act on what you know to be true. Feel this ... Courage enables to breathe life into your convictions ... ... just as the tree's roots bring up water, sustenance from the depths of the earth and the tree grows strong and reaches for the sky. As you inhale, imagine drawing up courage from the depths of collective knowingness ... Draw up courage from the depths of humanity's wisdom ... from deep time, for the earth holds all of the past to nourish new life ... Imagine this ... Feel yourself growing strong ... empowered to reach into the world ... expressing your convictions ... Rooted in courage, give yourself permission to be bold ... ... Know that you can endure storms ... Know the world welcomes your truth ... Imagine filling your whole self with courage to speak your truth from your heart ... ...

Create a situation where in the past you may have remained silent ... Imagine the details ... Feeling the scene, now, breathe in courage ... Feel it give you the nerve to speak your piece ... Draw courage from the ground of being ... Imagine expressing what is in your heart ... Imagine courage coming right up into your feet, and up your backbone ... Let confidence emanate out of you ... Express yourself ... Breathe life into your convictions ... Imagine speaking up ... ...

Create a symbol for all that you are experiencing ... Know that you are fully capable of always giving life to your convictions. Know that others support you in doing so ... We gain strength from one another. Together we have patience, endurance, and courage to heal the world by giving life to our convictions.

Exploring Consequence

The questions in this meditation also loan themselves to collective investigation in group settings.

Life regenerates itself; life pulsates through you and around you all the time. Life is the wisest of teachers, when we listen to the spirit of life we learn … We come to know what is needed to heal our own body, our community, our society, and even the earth itself … Let life be your teacher, you can tap into deep knowing. Listen deeply and discover what is so. Sense the intelligence of the life. Trust nature, trust your own nature. As you open and breathe, what's true is always apparent.

Bring into the light of awareness any concern you would like to gain clarity about … It could be a project, a development in the community, a decision, a person who has come into your life, an event in the world … whatever you would like to explore. Choose one particular concern that you would like to gain clarity about … …

Like a film, play back scenes when this concern was present … Play them back in detail … Remember … the atmosphere … the quality of energy present …

Now notice each of the people involved … Intuitively sense each person … How open and flexible they each are … their intentions … their motivations … what are people aiming for? … their connections to others … Tune in to one person at a time, sense these things … … Notice what values weave through the scene … Witness … …

Who does each person trust? … What are they paying attention to? … Is the natural world present in peoples' hearts and minds? … One at a time, witness this … …

Are people aspiring toward similar visions? ... What's the quality of exchange between the different people involved? ... What is being woven? ... How do people feel about one another? ... Is everyone respected? ... Who is not there? ... Anyone excluded? ...

Is the atmosphere open? ... How does the energy move—is it fluid or brittle? ... Is respect for life itself present? ... Is there reciprocity between people? ... What resources are being used? ... What is being created? ...

Are people present for one another? ... Are people acting out of the same information? ... Is information shared freely? ... Where do they come from? ... ... Is power concentrated anywhere? ...

Notice what ripples out from what is taking place. What happens? ... ... What are the consequences? ... ... Who benefits? ... ... Is there damage anywhere? ... ...

With knowingness, sense the impact of what is taking place ... Take a particular action and trace it through time, from the choices that gave it life ... to what happens along its path ... Where does it end up? ... ...

If you like, explore different actions. Take them one at a time ... Witness where they come from and where they're going ... ...

Notice the different perspectives present, see it through other peoples' eyes ... ... Notice how people align ... How does what might take place impact different people? ... Different places? ... How does it impact the natural world? ... What resources are used? ... What gifts are offered? ... Is there reciprocity? ... Witness what is the case. Allow all of this to be revealed in your awareness ... Let the spirit of life be your teacher ... ...

What kind of responses will the situation evoke? ... What responses are called for? ... Does the course of action anywhere need to be adjusted? ...

Imagine reciprocal relations being woven wherever they may be needed ... How might things happen differently? ... ...

Notice who else might support any shifts needed to serve life itself ... How can whatever constricts the flow of life-giving energy be changed? ... How can transformation take place? ... Imagine being able to work together ...

Notice how you can act on all the insights you have discovered ... What needs to be communicated to whom? ... Imagine how and when you will act on what you now know ... .

Acknowledge life as your teacher ... With the intelligence of life you can always see deeply into any situation and intuit consequences ... You can come to know what is so and what is needed ...

Liberating Ourselves

Now create a place of power, a very special place for you to come and replenish yourself ... Create it now, with your imagination, a place where you feel your personal power, and the power of your culture ... It may be a place you have once been or a place you have often been, or maybe your place of power is solely a creation of your imagination—wherever it is, imagine being there ... Create it, feel it, be there ... Experience this place charged with power, power that springs from the source of life itself ... Power that arises out of great feats of endurance and creativity ... Imagine this is the home of spirit ... Feel the magnetic core of your being vibrating with the spirit of this space ...

If you like, you can commune with your ancestors here. Welcome ancestors who would like to accompany you in your inner work ... Or there may be other allies who you would like to invite to join you in this meditation ... Welcome them ... You may want to do some kind of ceremony with each other to honor your connections ... ...

The sounds of these words will carry you deeper and deeper, into the power of life itself ... Feel yourself moving down into the depths of beingness itself ... As you breathe, each exhalation gently releases you into a deeper place ... Feel yourself going deeper and deeper into yourself, into your source of knowingness ... where you are attuned with the great strengths you have inherited, powers that are your birthright ... Feel them in your breath ... Feel them in your bones ... It feels good to simply be present with yourself ... to reside in the presence of who you are ... Affirm yourself ... Affirm your culture ...

Your experience is clear ... Your knowingness is always right there, responsive to whatever is happening right then ... fully responsive in the moment, alert to what is so ... Feel your dynamism ... your integrity, knowing yourself, claiming yourself ... knowing you are okay, you are beautiful, fully possessing the space that is yours ... Feel that, claim your space, yourself ...

Riding the waves of change, feel your ability to reshape reality ... Experience the power you have ... You can respond however you wish, the choice is yours ... Feel that, acknowledge your clarity, acknowledge that your first response is right, for you know what is so for you ... You are the only one who knows what is so for you ... ...

Feel your full intelligence, beauty, power ... Give yourself permission to be fully you, to embody your fullest potential ... Breathe, fill up your entire self with your power ... Love your self ... Your body, love your body ... Your mind, love your mind ... Your emotional and spiritual self, your soul, love your whole self ... ...

Love your expression of life itself ... Expressing what it means to be human in your own particular way, trusting your intelligence, claiming your power, claiming your space whatever you do, wherever you go ...

Feel yourself moving through the world, fully possessing yourself, claiming your space, interchanging with whomever you see, with integrity, with power from within ... power that resides deep inside always ... Power that springs from those who have gone before … carry forth now … This is your time now. Feel power offered by allies that accompany you … Always responding the way you choose, putting forward what is true for you … … Acknowledge your confidence; you are a powerful being. You determine your choices …

You have fully claimed your personal power … so much so that the energy that emanates from you is so vibrant that it simply wouldn't occur to anyone to tell you what to think or what you can or cannot do … You know that you determine your choice. You define your situation … …

If anything comes into your awareness that sabotages your power, that cuts short your choices, that insults your integrity, if anything comes in that keeps you from fully possessing your space … Breathe out any tension and witness the scene … … You are fully responsive and you know what needs to be done to hold your space, to keep your power … Your allies will help … Transform the constricting energy and create an atmosphere of mutual respect …

Notice how the aspects of you that others may have dismissed are what offer power. These parts know how to get through … They are survivors … They're needed by everyone now … What you left at the door are ways of being that will shed light and illuminate a path that returns us all to wholeness … They know a different way … how things can be done differently … Experience how this is the case … …

If any scenes come to awareness in which you have been diminished in some way, rewrite the scenes … … If it is in your current life, as you imagine talking to the people, if that still does not change the scene, then with agility and knowingness, notice how to maneuver around it ... or through it ... ... Transform the negativity and redefine the situation maintaining your integrity, your boundaries, your choices ... You choose it, you define it ... Offer the situations the wisdom you and your allies have ... ...

Make room for your power, for you to become even more fully who you are ... If you have any anger, current or maybe ancient, breathe it out ... ... Let it soak down into the ground ... Offer yourself compassion ... Heal the bruised child that may reside inside you ... ... Sense the scars softening from all the dehumanizing experiences you never asked for ... ... Be kind to yourself ... Quiet your frenzy toward perfection, you are already more than good enough ... Love yourself ... Transform the energies of the past, re-create your life ... ...

(Optional) Replay your past, remember those times when you have been degraded, remember those experiences you never asked for ... times you have been dismissed, your feelings disregarded, your humanity ignored ... Remember the times when your abilities were doubted ... times when assumptions were made and taken as facts, sometimes spoken, sometimes not ... times you have been taunted ... Remember those times you never asked for ... Breath them out, clear them all out ... ... Re-create your life, heal yourself, love yourself ... ... Release them, breathe them out ... Transform the energy, let it all soak into the ground ... Re-create your life, heal yourself, love yourself ... ...

Fill yourself with gentleness, with kindness, with love for yourself and your people ... ...

If there are any voices inside you that tell you who you ought to be, what you should and shouldn't do, ground it, let it all soak down into the ground, healed by the earth ... Breathe it out ... ...

In doing so you empower yourself, you heal yourself with the fullness of life itself ... Now imagine healing yourself with the great powers that come from having weathered hard times, wisdom from history ... Breathe in this power ... Massage the scars ... Be sure that nowhere inside do you see yourself through their eyes ... Heal yourself and feel your horizons expand ... Feel yourself become more fully who you are ... Stretch the limits ... Break the limits ... Be true to your power ... ...

If there were any scenes you couldn't recreate, project a protective shield, like a mirror, a shiny silver mirror ... and bounce back all the dehumanizing energy. Bounce back their definitions of who you are and let those who want to keep you down see how hollow their stereotypes really are ... Bounce back all their projections, all their limited expectations, so they can see what is so ... Bring compassion into the scene ... ...

Know that with your knowingness, with your agility, you can move around these people with ease and maintain your own boundaries, maintain your own integrity. You always have the spirit of your allies with you ... Acknowledge all those who have supported you to be who you truly are ... Feel the love that you have for them ...

Feel the strength of our differences woven together ... Create a time in your mind's eye when we live in a culture of mutual respect ... a time that celebrates diversity ... a time when we no longer need our guards ... a time when power springs from within and we celebrate one another ... ...

Breathe in this energy ... Let this vision spread a sense of relaxed security through yourself ... ... Breathe it out, imagine it moves through the world and transforms all that it touches ... ...

If we can envision it we can create it. Know that this is so. Create a symbol for all that you are experiencing ... Tell yourself that you will remember to bring it to awareness whenever you need it ... In so doing you call on the great power to stand strong and transform the scene into one in which respect vibrates through everyone ... Imagine it.

Breaking the Constraints of "Normal"

Scan your life now; notice who you interact with, who is in your world ... ... Notice this at work, in the community ... Witness who is in your life now ... Broaden your view ... Does everyone have the same options you do? ... Notice who is there but not contributing in the different contexts of your life or who is being ignored even if they do ... ... Notice who is not there ... ...

Those who are different in some way offer a fresh look at the world ... "Normal" is seen in a new light ... The definition of what's possible expands—the world opens up and comes alive.

Recollect times when you discovered a way of being in the world you did not even know was possible ... You met someone who was different in some way, who had different ways of being, who had different ways of seeing ... or maybe you read or watched something that revealed people who had different approaches ... At first you might have thought they were less capable, only to find out they were more resourceful ... Your horizons expanded.

Remember ... ... You discovered life on the other side of the lines of possibility ... Limits were broken, horizons extended; the world became a richer more vibrant place ... You had to take a second look and reevaluate just what was so, just what was possible. Your world grew bigger ... opened up further— more room to be alive!

Remember when you had to redefine just what normal was. Recollect those times you discovered a different way of being in the world. Stereotypes shattered. Limits dissolved ... The world opened up ... Recall when this happened ... ...

Make note of any particular ways of being that narrow your world. Imagine shedding the norms that homogenize ... Ideas that say, "look the same, or if that can't be, at least act the same" ... ideas that assume some people are incapable ... Breathe out the ideas that make normal a very narrow place to live ... Breathe out the stereotypes ... Welcome difference ... It frees us all ...

There still may be ways you narrow your experience ... Who takes you outside your comfort zone? ... ... Who falls outside the bounds of what you think is okay? ... maybe someone who looks different? ... or acts different? ... who somehow is not how you think they're supposed to be ... ...

Look at your daily life and notice who you diminish in your own mind in some way ... ... Are there people you see regularly who you do not take notice of? ... people you do not bother to pay attention to, thinking they have little to contribute anyway ... ... Are there people you make sure to avoid? ... people who are labeled? Maybe you were taught they were not okay in some way ... You know better now ... Let go; breathe out these narrow thoughts ...

Open to the world of difference. Let yourself be enriched by it ... Replace prejudice and ignorance with curiosity and openness to discover the depth and breadth of humanity ... Be humble; there is no such thing as normal ... ... People have contributions that open the world up ... Feel a welcoming spirit begin to stir in your heart ... Feel your mind opening with curiosity ... Feel yourself glad to have the opportunity to get to know people ...

Who in particular do you run across in daily life that takes you outside your comfort zone ... ... Imagine opening to a particular person you have distanced yourself from ... ... Appreciate the opportunity for your horizons to expand ... Feel yourself opening your heart and mind when you are with this person. Imagine it ... ... Your horizons expand ... Imagine

how you might be the next time you see this
person ... ... Give yourself permission to move outside your
comfort zone ... to expand your comfort zone ... ... Imagine
breaking bread together. Imagine laughing ...

Group Care

Bring to mind the group, organization, or community you are
part of. Imagine a place you often meet ... Imagine everyone
gathering in this place. Re-create the details of the scene ... each
of the people, what they're wearing, where they're sitting, the
atmosphere of the scene ... ...

Feel the spirit that unites you, the convictions that you share ...
What you all believe in ... what you aspire to ... the visions that
you share ... Feel all of this flowing between you ... Give
yourself a moment to bring to the forefront of awareness the
importance of what you are doing and who you are doing it
for ... Know the spirit that unites you ... ...

Alone you cannot do it; together you can; together you can
make a difference; you need one another ... Feel the spirit of
your work ... Tune in deeply, experience the heartbeat of your
work ... the positive core that gives each of you strength ... ...

Acknowledge the qualities that each person brings ... Tune in
to one person at a time and appreciate the gifts this person
brings ... ... Imagine what will inspire each person to step into
their potential even more ... ...

Imagine everyone supporting everyone's greatest potential ... Imagine it specifically ... Imagine that there are bands of energy weaving between everyone's hearts and minds ... weaving a web that lifts your work up ... ...

Joined together you are a powerful force ... Building on one another, learning from one another ... Feel the dynamism ... Experience the vast intelligence of the collective heart/mind you create with each of your qualities joined together ... ...

Imagine that the collectivity is supported and supporting the larger community ... Trust the collective mind ... Know that together you can come up with the best course of action, together you are extremely resourceful. Let yourself reside in the collective heart/mind of which you are a part ... Trust it ... As everyone opens to trusting the whole, great power is generated ... Imagine working in concert, in harmony, dynamic and powerful ... ... Imagine being able to depend on one another ... to rely on your collectivity. Feel how it is to work in unison, all of you joined together in effective work, each person appreciated, each person adding to the whole ... Great power is unleashed ... ...

Imagine the collective intelligence being so fluid, so cohesive, that it can effectively respond to whatever new situations arise ... Feel the agility of the group ... responsive and open while staying on course ... People have different capabilities ...

All the different perspectives dance together ... If you all thought the same you would become dense, brittle, dogmatic—unable to fully grasp the situation, unable to rise to the occasion. Take time to rejoice in your differences ... ... they bring learning and ignite creativity ... Concentrating your energies, together you can always come up with the best course of action. Feel the spirit of your collectivity ... Trust it ... Relax into it ... ...

Feel the circulation of your group, fluid, open ... Breathe ... Feel the spirit of the group breathe ... Notice if there are any areas in the body of the group that are needing attention ... Listen to the group spirit ... ... Reflect, discover, notice: ... Where the energy is hot or cold, where it is fluid or dense ... How does the energy flow? ... Does it stand still anywhere? Is it too concentrated in one place and lacking in another? ... What is the quality of exchange between people? ... Is there anything that is silenced? ... ...

Are each person's talents fully exercised? ... Is everyone equally respected? ... Everyone affirmed? ... Is anyone being deferential? ... anyone being presumptuous? ... Is anyone becoming isolated? ... What would invite everyone to thrive? ... ...

Is support shared? ... Does everyone do the work of caring? ... Is there forgiveness and celebration shared? ... Is each person reliable? ... ... honest and sincere? ... What are people's intentions? ... Are people supported in the rest of their lives? ... How can the ties to the larger community be strengthened? ... ...

Any places that you noticed could be improved, imagine what could be done ...

Remember the positive core, breathe life into it ... Let it breathe life into the places of lack ... Imagine this ... ...

Trust the strength of your collectivity, of which you are all a part ... Imagine being cared for and supported by the collective resources ... Is there anything you need to ask for personally? ... Imagine expressing your concern ...

Take time to appreciate each of the people in your group ... Feel the life of your group always growing, always changing doing good work ... Learning and meeting the needs of the times ... Celebrate it. Trust the future.

Caring Acts Heal the Future

At the end of this meditation, before returning to waking consciousness, you may want to read parts of "A Vision" on page 313 in the text. Feel free to embellish on it.

Become aware of the web of life ... Life regenerates itself ... Life reproduces itself. Experience the resilience of life itself ... All forms of life give life to life of another form. All life belongs to the great web of life ...

Focus in on your own life now, the home that gives you shelter ... the clothing that gives you warmth ... the foods that give you sustenance ... Acknowledge the earth for providing for your life ... Acknowledge the work of others who produced your shelter, your clothing, your food—all the people involved from gathering, to transporting, to creating, to exchanging, all the people involved in every aspect of providing for your life ... the web of people producing for each other ... the work you do to pay for these things, what your work provides for others ... Each act is part of the whole ... ...

Notice the constant exchange of energy among people and between people and the earth ... ... Notice where there is balance, a give and take ... Where there is as much giving as receiving ... Just as your body gets sick, when it expends more energy than it receives or receives more than it expends, so too, with society ... so too, with the earth ...

Scan your home life, your work life, your community life, and notice how balanced the exchanges of energy are ... ... Sense how every act of everyone relates to the whole ... which actions give it strength and which deplete it ... ...

Witness your own personal lifestyle ... Notice how your actions affect others ... Notice how your actions affect the web of life ... ... As you discover the imbalances, as there are likely to be many in the way our society is now organized, send them healing energy ... and notice what can be done to increase balance ... ... Feel your concern ...

Scan your community and notice how others care ... Imagine awakening the depth of caring we all share ... Sense our caring, awakening all the numb spots ... Notice what this caring, healing, shared energy wants you to do ... ...

Let yourself be empowered by the care we share ... As we care for life, life makes us strong. Imagine that together we care for one another, no one is left out; instead all sharing the caring for each in our lives, for life itself ... ...

Feel the strength of life itself makes us equal to the challenge of the times ... Feel ourselves rising to the occasion, uplifted by life, by one another, to secure the future of life itself ... to secure the future of our children ... to secure the future of our children's children ... to secure the future of the earth.

Sense yourself expanding beyond your individual concerns ... Feel your separateness dissolve as you join with others in caring, in healing, in securing life itself ... ...

Rooted in the collective strength we share ... strength flowing through us like sap through trees ... Imagine being able to transform yourself and inspire others to transform themselves so that all that is done is done in accord with the balance of life ...

For the imbalances that you discovered earlier, imagine what is to be done to regain balance ... If you come across cynicism, complaining, powerlessness, envy, greed or any other energies that block the flow, that constrict life in yourself or in others, transform the energy, send it compassion, life-giving, healing energy ... ... Imagine openness being created ... The openness being filled with generosity and care ... ...

Imagine everyone having the confidence to care for the earth and each other ... We can secure the future of life ... Feel everyone returned to the wholeness of life itself ... A time when fences and bars have fallen away, a time when generosity and care flows between everyone ... everyone returned to the wholeness of life itself.

Count Out

Thank any spirits that have accompanied you through this meditation ...

Go over all that you have experienced in this meditation ... insights you have gained ... any choices you have made ... Imagine yourself acting on them in your life ... Commitment, conviction, and action are the carriers of transformation. Appreciate your own self for the work you have done ... ...

Know that the very fact that you can imagine all these things makes them real—makes them possible. The energy already exists. Remember who in your life you can cultivate these energies with. In relationship spirit comes alive.

Remember all the people everywhere who share care ... Imagine a time when all life, all the plants, all the creatures, all the people are held sacred ... Reverence is in the air ... Care is shared ... powerful relations are built which support all of life ... Feel yourself supported. Feel yourself supporting the web.

Take a moment and channel loving kindness to anyone or any situation which could use some support at this time ... ...

In a moment I'm going to count from one to five; at the count of five, you will open your eyes remembering all that you have experienced ... feeling refreshed, revitalized, and relaxed ...

bringing with you the great powers you have tapped ... Ready and able to act on them.

ONE—becoming more aware of the room around you ...

TWO—coming up slowly now ...

THREE—at the count of five, you will open your eyes feeling relaxed, revitalized, and refreshed, remembering all that you have experienced ...

FOUR—coming up now, bringing with you your vision ...

FIVE!—eyes open, feeling refreshed, revitalized, and relaxed, remembering all that you have experienced, feeling a sense of well-being. Ready and able to express the visions you have invoked.

Afterword

Recently, when meditating on transforming the feelings of urgency that often plague me so that I could be in a more trusting place, I had a vision: it began with a group touring the Museum of Natural History in New York City. It became apparent that the world had been at a deep peace for a long time. The huge dinosaur that was previously in the rotunda had been replaced by a gigantic armored tank. All the displays of the objects that used to be from the "primitive times" were now displays of the instruments of war.

Then the next part of the vision was outside. The "artifacts" that used to be on display were now back in the hands of the people from whose cultures they had been taken. They were being used for the purposes for which they were made: to hold the world in sacred ways. Our group wanted to know how to live in balance. There was a man from a traditional culture who was helping modern people learn the ancient ways of knowledge. There was some clamor in the group to find out what this man had to offer. He turned and said, "What is your hurry? There is eternity."

Notes

Chapter One: Reawakening Inner Consciousness

1　"Stress is epidemic in the western world. Over two-thirds of office visits to physicians are for stress related illness. Stress is a major contributing factor, either directly or indirectly, to coronary artery disease, cancer, respiratory disorders, accidental injuries, cirrhosis of the liver, and suicide, the six leading causes of death in the United States." From www.stressfree.com/stress.html.

2　Silva Mind Control is the original inspiration for many of the trainings that spawned the Human Potential Movement, including EST, Mind Dynamics, and Life Spring. See www.silvamethod.com for information about their work.

3　David Bohm, Wholeness and the Implicate Order (New York: Routledge & Kegan Paul, 1980). Also see Michael Talbot, The Holographic Universe (New York: HarperCollins, 1996).

4　The healing power of mindfulness has been the subject of much study in the last twenty years. See the work of John Kabat-Zinn, which can be found at www.umassmed.edu/cfm/index.aspx. Also see John Kabat-Zin, *Full Catastrophe Living: Using the Wisdom of Your Body and Mind to Face Stress, Pain and Illness* (New York: Delacorte, 1990); Melissa Blacker, "Meditation," in Holistic Health and Healing, ed. Mary Anne Bright (Philadelphia: F.A. Davis, 2002); and Saki Santorelli, *Heal Thy Self: Lessons on Mindfulness in Medicine* (New York: Bell Tower, 1999).

5 I use beta, alpha, theta, and delta, and as a language to describe consciousness. The last twenty years of body/mind research have become increasingly sophisticated in mapping the relation of these frequencies to the functioning of the brain and its development as well as identifying how even higher frequency waves help in coordination of mental activity. See for example: M. Steriade, "Grouping of Brain Rhythms In Corticothalamic Systems," Neuroscience 137, no. 4 (2006); N. Axmacher, F. Mormann, G. Fernández, C.E. Elger, J. Fell, "Memory Formation by Neuronal Synchronization," *Brain Research Review* 52, no. 1 (August 30, 2006):170–82; and J.G.R. Jefferys, R.D. Traub, and M.A. Whittington, "Neuronal networks for induced '40 Hz' Rhythms," *Trends in Neurosciences* 19 (1996): 202–208. Additionally, see: www.brain washed.com/h30/dreamachine/bwstates.html.

6 The higher frequency gamma waves mentioned in the last note are associated with intense meditation, heightened states of ecstasy, and other mental activities. See Antoine Lutz, et al., "Long-term Meditators Self-Induce High-Amplitude Gamma Synchrony during Mental Practice," *PNAS* 101, no. 46 (2004): 16369–16373.

7 Charles Laughlin, John McManus, and Eugene d'Aquili, *Brain, Symbol, and Experience* (New York: Columbia University Press, 1990); and Eugene d'Aquili and Andrew Newberg, *The Mystical Mind:*

Probing the Biology of Mystical Experience (Minneapolis: Augsburg Fortress, 1999).

8   Felicia Huppert and Nick Baylis, "Well-Being: Towards an Integration of Psychology, Neurobiology, and Social Science," Philosophical Transactions of the Royal Society B: *Biological Sciences* 359, no. 1449 (2004): 1447–1451; and Jeffrey M. Schwartz and Sharon Begley, *The Mind and the Brain: Neuroplasticity and the Power of Mental Force* (New York: Harper Collins, 2002).

9   Paul Ekman, Richard J. Davidson, Matthieu Ricard, and B. Alan Wallace, "Buddhist and Psychological Perspectives on Emotions and Well-Being," *Current Directions in Psychological Science* 14 (2005): 59–63; Richard J. Davidson and John Kabat-Zinn, "Alterations In Brain and Immune Function Produced by Mindfulness Meditation," *Psychosomatic Medicine* 65 (2003): 564–570.

10 Imagery International is an association of professionals who do work with imagery. If you would like to find professionals in your area, see www.imagery international.org. If you would like to know more about the individual sessions I do with people go to www.toolsforchange.org.

11 Belleruth Naparstek, *Invisible Heroes: Survivors of Trauma and How They Heal* (New York: Bantum, 2004). This book is comprehensive work on using imagery for healing PTSD. It includes stories, research, physiology, and exercises for working with PTSD.

12 http://rescomp.stanford.edu/~cheshire/Einstein Quotes.html

13 Jerry Mander, *Four Arguments for the Elimination of Television* (New York: Morrow Quill Paperbacks, 1978).

14 ibid.

Chapter Two: Bringing Meditation Into Your Life

1   Lynne McTaggart, *The Intention Experiment: Using Your Thoughts to Change Your Life and Your World* (New Jersey: Free Press, 2007). See www.theintention experiment.com.

Chapter Three: Creating a Language to Speak to Your Deeper Self

1   James McClenon, *Wondrous Healing* (DeKalb: Northern Illinois University Press, 2002).

Chapter Five: It's All Energy

1   Fritjof Capra, *The Turning Point* (New York: Simon & Schuster, 1982). This book describes, in easily understandable terms, the findings and political implications of physics, and the limitations of the classic scientific paradigm. Carolyn Merchant, *The Death of Nature* (San Francisco: Harper & Row, 1980), is a comprehensive book detailing the history of science. Additionally: Susan Griffin, *Women and Nature* (New York: Harper & Row, 1978), and Starhawk, *Dreaming the Dark, Appendix A* (Boston: Beacon Press 1977).

2   See Vine Deloria Jr., *Spirit and Reason: A Vine Deloria Reader* (Golden: Fulcrum Books, 2000); John Mohawk, *Utopian Legacies: A History of Conquest and Oppression in the Western World* (Santa Fe: Clearlight Press, 1999); and Haunani-Kay Trask, *From a Native Daughter* (Honolulu: University of Hawaii Press, 1999). These indigenous authors show how this world view has had a devastating impact on the earth and her people, especially native people.

3   Capra, *The Turning Point.*

4   Gary Zukav, *The Dancing Wu Li Masters* (New York: William Morrow, 1980).

5   Capra, *The Turning Point.*

6   McTaggart, *The Intention Experiment.*

7   Edgar D. Mitchell and Dwight Williams, *The Way of the Explorer* (London: G. Putnam, 1996) and *Psychic Exploration* (New York: Putnam, 1974)

8   Larry Dossey, M.D., *Reinventing Medicine: Beyond Mind-Body to a New Era of Healing* (New York: HarperCollins, 1999).

9   Edgar D. Mitchell, *Psychic Exploration* (New York: Putnam, 1974).

10 See Brenda J. Dunne and Robert G. Jahn, "Consciousness and Anomalous Physical Phenomena," Princeton University, Princeton Engineering Anomalies Research Group, 1995; Robert Jahn and Brenda Dunne, *The Margins of Reality* (New York: Harcourt Brace, 1987); Dean Radin and Roger Nelson, "Evidence for Consciousness Related Anomalies and Random Physical Systems," *Foundations of Physics* (1989); and Jessica Utts, "An Assessment of the Evidence for Psychic Functioning," http://anson.ucdavis.edu/~utts/air2.html.

11 Associated Press, September 12, 2002.

12 Benjamin B. Wolman, ed., *Handbook of Parapsychology* (Van Nostrand Reinhold, 1986). For a write-up of an experiment that reveals how different expectations on the part of the scientist affects results, see Richard Wiseman and Marilyn Schultz, "Experimenter Effects and Remote Detection of Staring," *Journal of Parapsychology* 61 (1997).

13 Russell Targ and Jane Katra, *Miracles of Mind: Exploring Non-Local Consciousness and Spiritual Healing* (Novato: New World, 1999). See www.fire docs.com/remoteviewing or www.remoteviewers.com/index.htm.

14 Jim Schnabel, *Remote Viewers: The Secret History of America's Psychic Spies* (New York: Dell Books, 1997).

15 Dean Radin, *The Conscious Universe* (New York: Harper Collins, 1997) and *Entangled Minds: Extrasensory Experience a Quantum Reality* (New York: Simon and Shuster, 2006) The arena of parapsychology is vast, the actual demonstrated impacts of mind on the material world are subtle, and the theoretical basis for describing and understanding them is still in its infancy, but a number of studies have revealed the intimate relationship of mind and matter through PSI, precognition, and telekinesis. Those who research these areas even at major institutions are still dismissed by mainstream science.

16 C. G. Jung, "Synchronicity: An Acausal Connecting Principle" in Collected Works Vol. 8 (Princeton: Princeton University Press, 1970), 843–845.

17 Arthur Koestler, *The Roots of Coincidence* (New York: Random House, 1972). In a remarkable book, Elizabeth Lloyd Mayer describes a workshop offered at an American Psychotherapeutic Association meeting. More than sixty therapists, neurosurgeons, and other healers talked about what really happens in their healing work. Stories of synchronous events, precognitive dreams, and other anomalous events abounded. Most of the participants had never publicly talked about it for fear of ruining their reputation. She reflected on their dilemma, "They have all betrayed their own quintessential empiricism—knowing based in their own deeply valued sense-experience."
See Elizabeth Lloyd Mayer, *Extraordinary Knowing: Science, Skepticism, and the Inexplicable Powers of the Human Mind* (New York: Bantam Press, 2007); and Stanislaw Groff, *When the Impossible Happens: Adventures in Non-Ordinary Reality* (San Francisco:

Sounds True, 2006); and David E. Young, Jean-Guy Goulet, *Being Changed by Cross-Cultural Encounters: The Anthropology of Extraordinary Experience* (Toronto: Broadview Press, 1994).

18 Joanna Macy, *World As Lover, World As Self* (Berkeley: Parallax Press, 1991). Also see Macy's *Mutual Causality in Buddhism and General Systems Theory: The Dharma of Natural Systems* (New York: State University of New York Press, 1991) and *Coming Back to Life: Practices to Reconnect Our Lives, Our World* (Gabriola Island: New Society Publishers, 1998) for a nuanced and inspiring exploration of co-arising.

19 Vine Deloria Jr., *The World We Used to Live In: Remembering the Powers of the Medicine Man* (Golden: Fulcrum Publishing, 2006). Also see the series *Profiles of Healing: An Encyclopedia of Indigenous Cultural Healing*, especially *Walking Thunder: Dine Medicine Woman*; for an academic exploration, see James McClenon, *Wondrous Healing* (DeKalb: Northern Illinois University Press, 2002).

20 http://www.kirael.com/the-hopi-prophecy-land-of-no-time-2.html

21 Quoted in Arthur Koestler, *Roots of Coincidence*.

22 Lynn McTaggart, *The Intention Experiment*.

23 Erik Peper interview in Mander, *Four Arguments*.

24 Mander, *Four Arguments*.

25 Susan R. Johnson, M.D., "Strangers in Our Homes: TV and Our Children's Minds" (Zaytuna Institute, 1999); and Keith Bruzell, "The Human Brain and the Influences of Television Viewing" (Wyllaned Institute, 1997).

26 Mihaly Csikszentmihalyi and Robert Kubey, "Television Addiction" *Scientific American* (February 2002).

362 ◆ Practical Meditation for Busy Souls

27 Federal Communications Commission Fact Sheet (July 1, 1999). See www.fcc.gov/Bureaus/Mass_Media/Factsheets/factvchip.html.

28 Media Use in America, a study by Mediascope. See also Jean Kilbourne, *Can't Buy My Love: How Advertising Changes the Way We Think and Feel* (New York: Touchstone, 2000). The paperback version of the book is titled Deadly Persuasion.

29 Federal Communications Commission Fact Sheet (July 1, 1999). See www.fcc.gov/Bureaus/Mass_Media/Factsheets/factvchip.html.

30 Letty Cottin Pogrebin, *Grow Up Free: Raising Your Child in the 80's* (New York: William Morrow, 1978).

31 Federal Communications Commission Fact Sheet (July 1, 1999). See www.fcc.gov/Bureaus/Mass_Media/Factsheets/factvchip.html.

32 Pogrebin, *Grow Up Free.*

33 Jean Kilbourne, "The Naked Truth: Advertising's Images of Women" speech given at the Woldenberg Art Center (November 13, 1996).

34 William Braud, *Distant Mental Influence* (Charlottesville: Hampton Roads Publishing Company, Inc., 2003).

35 ibid.

Chapter Six: Tapping Universal Energies

1 The Berkeley Psychic Institute may be reached at http:/www.berkeleypsychic.org

2 If you would like to investigate how science has studied prayer, see Larry Dossey, M.D., *Healing Words* (San Francisco: HarperCollins, 1993), *Prayer Is Good Medicine* (San Francisco: HarperCollins, 1996), and *Reinventing Medicine: Beyond Mind-Body to a New Era of Healing* (New York: HarperCollins, 1999).

Chapter Seven: We are all Healers

1   Herbert Benson, M.D., *Timeless Healing: The Power and Biology of Belief* (New York: Scribner, 1996). See www.mbmi.org. Benson has made significant contributions to the field of body/mind medicine in his work with what he calls the "relaxation response" and "remembered wellness," a term he uses instead of "the placebo effect."

2   Janice K. Kiecolt-Glase, Ph.D. and Ronald Glase, Ph.D., "Mind and Immunity," *Mind Body Medicine: How to Use Your Mind for Better Health*, eds. Daniel Goleman, Ph.D. and Joel Gurin (Consumer Reports Books, 1993).

3   National Institute for Health Care Management, *Changing Patterns of Pharmaceutical Innovation* (Washington, DC, May 2002).

4   For example, a major medical school in the Northwest attempted to patent a genetic test in 1999 that was designed to detect sensitivity to a pesticide. This would enable an employer to screen out farm workers who were sensitive to it and allow them to use a highly toxic chemical with fewer safeguards. See also Troy Duster, *Back Door to Eugenics* (Routledge, 1990).

5   David Baltimore, a Nobel Prize-winning biologist, claims: "Instead of guessing about how we differ one from another, we will understand and be able to tailor our life experiences to our inheritance. We will also be able, to some extent, to control that inheritance." Ralph Brave, "Governing the Genome," *The Nation* (December 21, 2001).

6   See Ralph Metzner, "The Split between Spirit and Nature in Western Consciousness," *Noetic Sciences Review* 25, (Spring 1993); also see the eloquent writing of Morris Berman, *Reenchanting the World and*

Coming to our Senses (Ithaca: Ithaca Cornell University Press, 1981).

7 Capra, *Turning Point*.

8 Ivan Illich, *Medical Nemesis* (New York: Bantam, 1976). The depressing reality is that this is as true in the twenty-first century as it was twenty five years ago.

9 Barbara Starfield, M.D., M.P.H., "Is U.S. Health Really the Best in the World?," *The Journal of the American Medical Association* 284: 483–485 (July 26, 2000).

10 John Wennberg, M.D., of Dartmouth Medical School, quoted by Gina Kolata, "More May Not Mean Better in Health Care, Studies Find," *New York Times* (July 21, 2002).

11 Andre Gorz, *Ecology as Politics*, (Detroit: South End Press, 1980).

12 Irving Kirsch, Thomas J. Moore, Alan Scoboria, and Sarah S. Nicholls, "The Emperor's New Drugs: An Analysis of Antidepressant Medication Data Submitted to the U.S. Food and Drug Administration," *Prevention & Treatment*, Volume 5, Article 23, July 15, 2002.

13 Harris Dienstfrey, "Mind and Mindlessness in Mind-Body," *Consciousness and Healing: Integral Approaches to Mind-Body Medicine*, eds. Marilyn Schlitz, Tina Amorok, and Marc S. Micozzi (Oxford: Churchill Livingstone, 2004).

14 Bruce Lipton, Ph.D., *The Biology of Belief: Unleashing the Power of Consciousness, Matter, and Miracles* (Santa Rosa: Mountain of Love/Elite Books, 2005). Lipton is a cellular biologist who details what takes place at a cellular level in the exchange of information. See: http://www.brucelipton.com.

15 Gorz, *Ecology as Politics*.

16 Lipton, *Biology of Belief.*

17 Schlitz, Amorok and Micozzi, *Consciousness and Healing*. See also: Daniel Benor, M.D., *Healing Research, Volumes I–IV* (Southfield: Vision Publications, 2001); Dossey, *Reinventing Medicine* and http://www.thehealingmind.org; Naparstek, *Invisible Heroes*; and http://www.healthjourneys.com /research _resources.asp.

18 Larry Dossey, "What Does Illness Mean" in *Consciousness and Healing: Integral Approaches to Mind-Body Medicine*, eds. Marilyn Schlitz, Tina Amorok, and Marc S. Micozzi (Oxford: Churchill Livingstone, 2004).

19 Caryle Hirshberg, "Living with Cancer: From Victim to Victor, the Integration of Mind, Body, and Spirit" in *Consciousness and Healing: Integral Approaches to Mind-Body Medicine*, eds. Marilyn Schlitz, Tina Amorok, and Marc S. Micozzi (Oxford: Churchill Livingstone, 2004).

20 O. Carl Simonton, M.D., Stephanie Mathews-Simonton, and James L. Creighton, *Getting Well Again* (New York: Bantam, 1978). Over the past fifteen years, their work has continued to deepen and has helped people around the world. See their website www.simontoncenter.com. See also the work of Martin L. Rossman, *Guided Imagery for Self Healing*, revised edition (Novato: New World Library, 2000).

21 For those of us who are secular, it is important to note that the efficacy of prayer and healing is well-documented. Again, please see the works of Larry Dossey, M.D. for a compilation, review, and summary of research on the impact of prayer and what he calls the "nonlocal" mind: *Reinventing Medicine, Healing Words*, and *Prayer Is Good Medicine*.

22 Gorz, *Ecology as Politics*.

23 See "Robins Story" on www.hepcmeditations.org.

Chapter Eight: Making Your Life Work for You

1 Jane Roberts, *The Nature of Personal Reality* (Englewood Cliffs: Prentice-Hall, 1974). All of Jane Roberts's books are good, but this one is required reading for anyone who wants to understand the dynamic relationship between consciousness and reality or experience and beliefs.

Chapter Nine: Spirit Lives in Relationship

1 Joanna Macy and Molly Young Brown, *Coming Back to Life: Practices to Reconnect Our Lives, Our World* (Gabriola Island: New Society Publishers, 1998) Also see http://www.joannamacy.net/html/living.html.

2 ibid.

3 Rupert Sheldrake, *A New Science of Life: The Hypothesis of Morphic Resonance* (Rochester: Park Street Press, 1995); and Rupert Sheldrake, *Dogs that Know When Their Owners are Coming Home, and Other Unexplained Powers of Animals* (New York: Three Rivers Press, 1999). See also: www.sheldrake.org.

4 http://aacap.org/page.ww?section=Facts+for+Families &name=Teen+Suicide,www.sprc.org/stateinformation /PDF/statedatasheets/sprc_national_data.pdf, and http:// webappa.cdc.gov/sasweb/ncipc/mortrate10_sy.html.
   Also see: James W. Prescott, Ph.D., "The Increasing Psychiatric Disability of Children and Youth in America: Why?" at www.primal-page.com/prescott.htm.

5 Donna E. Shalala, "Message from the Secretary of Health and Human Services," www.mentalhealth.org/ youthviolence/surgeongeneral/SG_Site/home.asp, and http://www.cdc.gov/ncipc/dvp/YV_DataSheet.pdf.

6 "The National Nursing Home Summary," (2007) at www.cdc.gov/nchs/fastats/nursingh.htm.

7 For a great video showing how people cooperated during the crisis in Argentina see *Hope in Hard Times*, available at www.movingimages.org.

8 Dean Ornish, M.D., *Love & Survival: 8 Pathways to Intimacy and Health* (HarperPerennial, 1999).

9 Mab Segrest, *My Mama's Dead Squirrel: Lesbian Essays on Southern Culture* (Ann Arbor: Firebrand Books, 1990).

10 Thich Nhat Hanh, *Anger: Wisdom for Cooling the Flames* (New York: Riverhead Books, 2001). This book, and his many others, are all great offerings toward bringing peace to the heart and to the world. See www.plumvillage.org.

11 Barbara Holmes, *Race and the Cosmos: An Invitation to View the World Differently* (Harrisburg: Trinity Press, 2002).

Chapter Ten: The World in Which We Live

1 Rainforest Action Network, www.ran.org/info_center/factsheets/04a.html. Also see The Nature Conservancy, http://www.nature.org/rainforests/explore/facts.html.

2 www.ran.org/fileadmin/materials/education/fact sheets/RAN_RainforestFood.pdf.

3 www.ran.org/info_center/factsheets/04b.html and www.nature.org/rainforests/explore/facts.html.

4 Lester Brown, "Soil Erosion: A Food and Environmental Threat" from www.unfpa.org/parliamentarians/documents/IPCIpaperBrown.doc, and *Plan B 2.0: Rescuing a Planet Under Stress and a Civilization in Trouble* (New York: W.W. Norton & Company, 2006). Also see David Pimentel, Environment, Development, and Sustainability (8:119—137, 2006)

5   See www.coral.org and "World View of Global Warming," at http://www.worldviewofglobalwarming.org/pages/rising-seas.html.

6   See: www.iucn.org/themes/ssc/red_list_2004/Extinction_media_brief_2004.pdf and http://www.commondreams.org/archive/2007/04/30/862/.

7   *On Biocultural Diversity: Linking Language, Knowledge, and the Environment*, ed. Luisa Maffi (Washington DC: Smithsonian Institute Press, 2001). For more on the relation of biological and cultural literacy see www.terralingua.org.

8   http://www.globalissues.org/TradeRelated/Facts.asp.

9   Kevin Danaher, "The Global Paradigm Shift," in *A Time for Choices: Deep Dialogues for Deep Democracy*, ed. Michael Toms (Gabriola Island: New Society Publishers, 2002).

10 Chellis Glendinning, *Off the Map* (Gabriola Island: New Society Publishers, 2002).

11 U.S. Census in 2000, as cited in: Gordon Hurd, "Safety Net Sinking," *ColorLines* (Summer 2002).

12 United for a Fair Economy at http://www.faireconomy.org/press/2005/EE2005_pr.html. Also see: http://www.energybulletin.net/

13 Chuck Collins and Felice Yeskel, *Drifting Toward Economic Apartheid in America* (New York: The New Press, 2000).

14 The DCDC Global Strategic Trends Programme, 2007–2036 Development Concepts and Doctrine Centre (London: DCDC, 2007); see also Dean Allen Pfieffer's article on the Pentagon report on climate change at www.energybulletin.net/1349.html and "Climate Change, Peak Oil, and Nuclear War" by Bill Henderson, 24 February, 2007 at www.countercurrents.org.

15 See http://www.energybulletin.net and http://www. lifeaftertheoilcrash.net.
These websites provides access to the vast literature and debates on peak oil. See also: Richard Heinman, *The Party's Over: Oil, War, and the Fate of Industrial Societies* (Gabriola Island: New Society Publishers, 2005)

16 The evidence is overwhelming and now a part of mainstream conversation. For a good perspective on the issues see: George Monbriot, *Heat! How to Stop the Planet Burning* (New York: Penguin, 2007); and Clive Doucet, *Urban Meltdown: Cities, Climate Change, and Politics as Usual* (Gabriola Island: New Society Publishers, 2007).

17 Dale Allen Pfeiffer, *The End of the Oil Age* (self published: DAP, 2004); see www.mountainsentinel.com.

18 John Perkins, *Confessions of an Economic Hitman* (New York: Plume Books, 2006) and Steve Hiatt, ed., *A Game as Old as Empire* (San Francisco: Berrett Koehler, 2007).

19 Richard J. Barnet and Ronald E. Muller, *Global Reach* (New York: Simon & Schuster, 1974).

20 John Stockwell, www.thirdworldtraveler.com/Stockwell /JStockwell_quotations.html.

21 *San Francisco Chronicle* (April 21, 1984). See also Philip Agee, *Inside the Company: CIA Diary* (New York: Doubleday, 1975). He also resigned from the CIA.

22 Thomas Friedman, *The Lexus and the Olive Tree* (New York: Anchor Books, 2000).

23 Eve Goldberg and Linda Evans, *The Prison Industrial Complex and the Global Economy* (Berkeley: Prison Activist Resource Center, 2001) and www.ojp.usdoj .gov/bjs/prisons.htm.

24 www.plumvillage.com.

25 ibid., and World Watch Institute, www.wri.org.

26 As quoted by Deloria Jr., *Spirit and Reason*. See also: National Priorities Project: http://nationalpriorities. org/index.php?option=com_wrapper&Itemid=1822

27 Holmes, *Race and the Cosmos*.

28 Thich Nhat Hanh, *Interbeing: Fourteen Guidelines for Engaged Buddhism*, third edition (Berkley: Parallax Press, 1998).

29 We want to draw a connection between our work and that of the Pachamama Alliance, (www.pachamama. org) and the Dream Change Alliance (www.dream change.org). These organizations are dedicated to reawakening from the dream of "Western Civilization" and changing it to a life affirming one of interconnec- tion.

30 Joanna Macy, www.joannamacy.net.

31 See www.ecn.org/communitas/en/en126.html.

32 Joanna Macy, www.joannamacy.net.

33 See City Repair at http://www.cityrepair.org/ and Detroit Summer at http://detroitsummer.blogspot. com.

34 Alan Weisman, *Gaviotas: A Village to Reinvent the World* (White River: Chelsea Green, 1998); For updates on Gaviotas see http://www.friendsofgaviotas.org/ about.htm, and http://www.urbanecology.org.au/ articles/gaviotas.html.

35 See Detroit Summer at http://detroitsummer.blog spot.com; for other examples see: www.justfood.org (in New York), http://www.greensgrow.org (in Philadelphia), http://www.growingpower.org (in Milwaukee), and http://www.sygw.org/ (in Seattle).

36 Marina Sitrin, ed., *Horizontalism: Voices of Popular Power in Argentina* (New York: AK Press, 2006); also see *Hope in Hard Times*, available at www.moving images.org.

37 www.justfood.org.

38 See www.indymedia.org and New Dimensions, which broadcasts inspiring radio programs with a holistic perspective worldwide at www.newdimension.org.

39 http://www.wiserearth.org is dedicated to illuminating the powerful emergent movement of some 90,000 or more non-profits and NGOs around the globe that are helping us move to a sustainable and just world; also see: Starhawk, *Webs of Power* (Gabriola Island: New Society Publishers, 2002).

40 See http://icci.nativeweb.org/boletin/19/english.html #macas.

41 See www.restorativejustice.org, www.avpusa.org, www.justiceworks.info, and www.zenpeacemakers.org.

42 Jim Merkel, "Prison without Walls: Kerala's Open Prison Draws on Strengths of Community Life," *In Context*, No. 38:48 ff (1994).

43 Joanna Macy, www.joannamacy.net.

Chapter Eleven: Reclaiming Wholeness in Our World Secures the Future

1 Quoted by Christina Baldwin, *Calling the Circle* (New York: Bantam, 1998).

2 Harrison Owen, *The Power of Spirit* (San Francisco: Berrett-Koehler, 2000).

3 See the work of Christina Baldwin at www.peerspirit.com; Jack Zimmerman, *The Council Way* (White River: Bramble Co., 1997).

4 Again, see: Radin, *Entangled Minds*; McTaggart, *Intention Experiment*; and Braud, *Distant Mental Influence*. Also see The Global Consciousness Project at http://noosphere.princeton.edu.

5 *Seattle Post-Intelligencer,* April 2, 2007.

6   Joanna Macy, "Personal Guidelines for the Great Turning," at www.joannamacy.net/html/great.html# personal.

7   See the following websites for more information on Bohemian Grove; www.sonic.net/~kerry/bohemian/ bibliography.html, www.sonomacountyfreepress. com/bohos/bohoindx.html, and http://www.jones report.com/articles/210607_bg.html

8   Nathan Stoltzfus, *Resistance of the Heart: Intermarriage and the Rosenstrasse Protest in Nazi Germany* (Piscataway: Rutgers University Press, 1997). Also see: Margo Adair and Shea Howell, "Breaking Old Patterns, Weaving New Ties," a pamphlet available at www.toolsforchange.org.

9   Rupert Sheldrake, "Extended Mind, Power, and Prayer: Morphic Resonance and the Collective Unconscious Part III," *Psychological Perspectives* (Spring 1998): 67–78.

10 For a full discussion of building trusting and enduring alliances across social divides, see the two pamphlets I coauthored with Sharon Howell: "Breaking Old Patterns and Weaving New Ties" and "The Subjective Side of Politics," both available at www.toolsfor change.org.

11 See http://www.conversationcafe.org. There are Conversation Cafes in many places; if there isn't one in your area, the website has all you need to start one.

12 Joseph Jaworski, *Synchronicity: The Inner Path of Leadership* (San Francisco: Berrett-Koehler, 1999).

13 Vincent Harding, *There is a River, the Black Struggle for Freedom in America* (New York: Harcourt Brace & Company, 1981).

14 See www.sixnations.org. See also Oren Lyons, et al., ed., *Exiled in the Land of the Free: Democracy, Indian Nations, and the U.S. Constitution* (Clear Light, 1992).

Acknowledgments

We continue to hold deep gratitude for our communities in Seattle and San Francisco, which are weaving new ways of being to help the planet survive.

Many midwives have supported this book. Our heartfelt thanks goes to Susan Nelson who tenaciously researched both the state of the world and mass media; she is a testament to the reality that it is possible to maintain a good sense of humor in the midst of opening to the devastation. Susan also helped think through Chapter Ten and pitched in with proofreading. Deep appreciation to Autumn Riddle with whom we tossed chapters back and forth through virtual space, piling up versions in our computers, each better than the last. Autumn combed out the rough drafts, occasionally adding key insights rooted in her own years of Applied Meditation and Buddhist meditation practices. We also hold much gratitude for Nina Laboy, who, after reading a section, would always offer encouraging feedback, telling us confidently that most of the work was already done. Though in hindsight there was always more than either one of us thought, without her cheering us on, we are not at all sure the work would have gotten done. Thanks goes to Sharon Howell, with whom Margo loves to collaborate because she always offers new insights. Sharon brought the state of the world and the signs of hope into focus. It makes our hearts sing when we think of the participants in our Energy Circles and trainings who shared their struggles and visions. Their stories are an unending source of learning and inspiration for us.

We would also like to express our gratitude to Vivi Curutchet for her perpetual support. Deep bows to Viki Sontag and Ruby Phillips. Each is a model of living in a manner that deeply integrates political action and spiritual practice. To all the participants in our Circles for Change, thanks for widening our horizons and touching our hearts. Thank you all.

The writings of Larry Dossey, MD, Joanna Macy, Lynne McTaggart, and Rupert Sheldrake all accompanied us through the many months of writing and had a deep impact on our thinking. Thank you each for the great contributions your work has made. You might think it hokey, but all the flowers in our garden kept Margo company and Bill sane. Over the many months, there must have been hundreds that accompanied us. Margo thanks Bill for planting them and we thank the soil for nourishing them.

Thanks to Stefan Dasho, for having composed the music accompanying the tapes and CDs. Additionally, a great big thank you goes to Greg Scott for engineering the sound for the CD. We would also like to appreciate Barbara Moulton for help in the sticky business of contract negotiation. Lastly great big thanks goes to Sourcebooks for seeking us out. A special appreciation goes to Deb Werksman at Sourcebooks who is a pleasure to work with.

Permissions

Resources

Tools for Change

Co-directed by Margo Adair and William Aal, Tools for Change is dedicated to inspiring a cultural transformation in which history, heart, spirit, values, and vision are all at the center of public life. Their approach weaves together Applied Meditation, sharing stories and heart-felt dialog which inspires generosity of spirit and collective genius.

They offer public trainings and a full range of organizational services including facilitation, mediation, and leadership development. Of special interest is their unique approach to facilitation for meetings and events in multi-cultural contexts. Come to www.toolsforchange.org for resources on Applied Meditation and alliance building, downloadable meditations, community building, and schedule of events.

Individuals May Wish to Contact us for

- *Custom Recorded Meditations* tailored to specific individual or group needs: Margo or Bill will work with you in person or on the phone. Then they record a meditation that weaves together, in your language, your best memories, talents, sensibilities, and visions. These tailored meditations are a great resource for any major life transition (marriage, retirement), chronic health issues, surgery or life threatening illness, creative projects, exams, or group planning.

- *Applied Meditation Trainings:* Basic—explore imagination, intuition, and mindfulness; Advanced—hone your practice; Leadership—design and lead meditations for individual problem solving and group settings.
- *Applied Meditation Practice Circle:* Get together on a regular basis to meditate. We offer information to help start and sustain a Circle.

Circles for Change are designed to facilitate people discovering and living into their aspirations. They offer a way for people bring the power of spirit into daily life and support one another to develop the clarity and courage needed to effectively take action on their values. *Tools for Change* provides support materials to start your own Circle.

Resources Available from *Tools for Change*:

- *Self Care for Hepatitis C:* Applied Meditation for a Healthy Liver, an audio CD and instruction booklet, co-produced by Margo Adair and Robin Roth. We support special healing circles for people with Hepatitis C. Contact www.hepcsmeditations.org for more information.
- *Applied Meditation Recordings.* The 45 meditations in this series are designed to help you work with this book. Most of these meditations will also be available in CD and Mp3 formats. See www.toolsforchange.org for details.

Additional Publications:

- *The Subjective Side of Politics* (co-authored with Sharon Howell) explores the impact of social and historical power relations on our assumptions, and how we might create just and fair relations.

- ***Breaking Old Patterns: Weaving New Ties*** (co-authored with Sharon Howell) provides tools to establish inclusive environments.
- ***From Leadership to Empowerment:*** transforming our image of the lone leader to emergent collective leadership.

For more information:
www.toolsforchange.org
tools@toolsforchange.org
2408 E Valley, Seattle, WA 98112
(1-800-998-6657)

About the Authors

Margo Adair has been in the forefront of exploring the connections between consciousness, politics, and spirituality. Developer of Applied Meditation, she has woven together political, psychological, and spiritual perspectives for personal, interpersonal, and planetary healing. This approach to working with consciousness integrates intuition, intention, and mindfulness. It has been used by therapists and healing practitioners around the world. Her work on trusting one's own awareness, creativity, and intuition has influenced the development of movements for change over the last thirty years.

She travels extensively, offering workshops and consulting. She makes her home in Seattle where she maintains a private practice.

William Aal is deeply involved in social and environmental justice work with a particular focus on agricultural sustainability and social healing. He joined forces with Margo fifteen years ago. They founded Tools for Change Institute to support bringing the power of spirit into multicultural settings. He is especially versed in opening the imagination, awakening peoples' best thinking, and inspiring group transformation. As a former manager in the non-profit and information technology worlds, he focuses on working with group reflection unleashing collective genius in organizational settings.